D0481671

PRAISE FOR *RANDOMISTAS*

'*Randomistas* is a tour de force – an engaging, passionate, how-to account of randomised experiments. After reading Leigh's book, you'll be baffled at the many businesses and governments yet to catch on. Fortunately, Leigh also offers a simple guide that anyone can follow. If the next generation of policymakers follows his advice – and let's hope they do – this book will literally change the world.'
DAVID HALPERN, head of the UK's Behavioural Insights Team, author of *Inside the Nudge Unit*

'*Randomistas* takes the reader on a great journey about how data and experiments can make the world a better place, one policy at a time.'
DEAN KARLAN, professor of economics at Yale

'The subject of this book could hardly be more vital: are we humble enough to admit we may be wrong, and do we care enough to learn? *Randomistas* is rigorous, impassioned and tremendous fun. Everyone should read it.'
TIM HARFORD, author of *The Undercover Economist* and *Fifty Things That Made the Modern Economy*

'Packed with tantalising tales, *Randomistas* is essential reading for anyone interested in debunking myths and uncovering hidden truths.'
STEVEN LEVITT, co-author of *Freakonomics*

RANDOMISTAS

How radical researchers are changing our world

ANDREW LEIGH

YALE UNIVERSITY PRESS
NEW HAVEN AND LONDON

For information about this and other Yale University Press publications, please contact:
U.S. Office: sales.press@yale.edu   yalebooks.com
Europe Office: sales@yaleup.co.uk   yalebooks.co.uk

Set in Minion Pro by Marilyn de Castro
Printed in Great Britain by TJ International Ltd, Padstow, Cornwall

Library of Congress Control Number: 2018932125

ISBN 978-0-300-23612-5

A catalogue record for this book is available from the British Library.

10 9 8 7 6 5 4 3 2 1

CONTENTS

1

SCURVY, SCARED STRAIGHT AND *SLIDING DOORS*

As Commodore George Anson's six warships rounded the tip of South America, he knew his plans were unravelling. Commissioned by the British government to capture Spanish colonies in Panama and Peru, Anson had been at sea for half a year. The seas were rough and a Spanish squadron was chasing him, but the greatest threat to the men on board was a disease: scurvy.

Anson's expedition left England in 1740 with 1854 men. Four years later, just 188 of them returned. Of the eight ships that set out, only one made it back. Writer Stephen Bown describes the voyage as the worst medical disaster ever to take place at sea. Six months in, men were dying daily. At first, the corpses were sewn into their hammocks and thrown overboard. But after a time the living sailors became too weak to deal with the dead, and they were left below deck, where they had drawn their last breaths.

Sailing an eighteenth-century warship required many men. Anticipating that some would die of scurvy, captains often took along extra personnel. But Anson's losses exceeded expectations. With few men having the strength to work, some of the warships crashed into rocks off South America. One ship, the *Wager*, was ripped apart on the jagged rocks of southern Chile. Some of the sailors drowned because they were too weak to swim ashore.

Scurvy affects the body's connective tissues. At first, victims feel tired and uncoordinated. They bruise easily and their legs begin to swell. Then their gums become inflamed, their breath grows foul and their skin becomes blotchy. Sailors were shocked to see old battle wounds beginning to bleed and bones that had healed separating again. An anonymous surgeon wrote of his own afflictions with the disease: 'It rotted all my gums, which gave out a black and putrid blood. My thighs and lower legs were black and gangrenous, and I was forced to use my knife each day to cut into my flesh in order to release this black and foul blood ... And the unfortunate thing was that I could not eat, desiring more to swallow than to chew.'[1] In the final stages, patients' gums swell up so much they cannot eat. Internal bleeding leads to death.

During the age of sail, more than 2 million sailors died from scurvy, more than from skirmishes, storms and shipwrecks combined.[2] In 1499 Portuguese explorer Vasco da Gama lost over half his crew to scurvy. In 1520 his countryman Ferdinand Magellan lost two-thirds of his crew to the disease.[3] In the Seven Years' War (1756–63), Britain raised 185,899 sailors; only 1512 died in action, while 133,708 died of scurvy.[4] Put another way, a British sailor in the Seven Years' War had less than a 1 per cent chance of being killed in action, but a 72 per cent chance of dying from scurvy.

Everyone had their own theory on how to fight the disease, with doctors variously proposing wine, ginger and salts. But because none of the remedies was carefully tested, scurvy continued to run rampant. In the absence of evidence, whether a doctor's crackpot solution was adopted depended on his status and confidence. Sailors continued to die in their thousands.

Then, in 1747, a 31-year-old ship's surgeon by the name of James Lind ran a remarkable experiment. Several months into the voyage of the HMS *Salisbury*, most of the crew were affected by scurvy. Lind decided to try different treatments on twelve sailors with advanced scurvy, 'as similar as I could have them'. He took other people's theories and found a way to test them. Lind's randomised trial tested six treatments, with each being given to a pair of sailors. The first group got a litre of cider, the second 4 millilitres of sulphuric acid ('elixir of vitriol') and the third 80 millilitres of vinegar. If those last two treatments weren't bad enough, the fourth group were made to drink 250 millilitres of seawater, while the fifth group got a mixture of nutmeg, garlic, mustard-seed, horseradish, balsam of Peru and gum myrrh. The sixth group received two oranges and one lemon. Apart from the treatments, all the patients were fed the same diet and kept in the same part of the ship.[5]

It didn't take long for the experiment to show results. Lind reported that 'the most sudden and visible good effects were perceived from the use of oranges and lemons', to the extent that one of the patients who had been given citrus fruit was ready to return to duty in less than a week. By contrast, the patients given acid, vinegar and seawater did not improve. Given that sulphuric acid was the British Navy's main treatment for scurvy, this was an important finding.

The results were clear, but, as any researcher knows, a convincing result doesn't immediately lead policymakers to change their minds. It took Lind six years to write up the results, in a book titled *A Treatise of the Scurvy*. The 456-page work was dedicated to Commodore George Anson, whose expedition had lost nine-tenths of its men. Unfortunately, although Lind's experimental results were spot-on, his theoretical explanations for why citrus worked were hocus-pocus.[6] The treatise was largely ignored in the years after its publication.

For the next few decades, scurvy remained the single greatest risk to long sea voyages. The longest sea voyage that the British government was contemplating was the one to Australia. Scurvy showed its symptoms within a couple of months, and the voyage to Australia took six to twelve months.

By luck, both the exploratory voyage of James Cook in 1768–71 and the First Fleet of Arthur Phillip in 1787–88 stumbled upon ways to keep scurvy at bay. Cook gave his men sauerkraut, malt and lemon juice, and called in to port every two or three months for fresh food. He wrongly thought the main preventatives were sauerkraut and malt, but nonetheless managed to return to London without losing a single sailor to scurvy.[7] Like Cook, Phillip's expedition mistakenly thought sauerkraut and malt could ward off scurvy.[8] But the passengers on the First Fleet were saved from its worst ravages by frequent stops along the way. The convicts ate fresh food at Portsmouth before leaving Britain, and then en route at Tenerife, Rio de Janeiro and the Cape of Good Hope. Even so, the disease threatened the voyage. On 26 January 1788, after raising the English flag at Port Jackson, Phillip wrote in his diary that 'the scurvy began to rage with a virulence which kept the hospital tents generally supplied with patients'.[9]

Cook and Phillip were lucky, but scurvy returned with a vengeance on the Second Fleet (1789–90), which had a death rate of nearly one in three.

Then, in the 1790s, a disciple of Lind, surgeon Gilbert Blane, was able to persuade senior naval officials that oranges and lemons could prevent scurvy.[10] In 1795 – almost fifty years after Lind's findings – lemon juice was issued on demand; by 1799 it became part of the standard provisions.[11] In the early 1800s British naval sailors were consuming 200,000 litres of lemon juice annually.[12]

The British may have been slow to adopt Lind's findings, but they were faster at curing scurvy than their main naval opponents. An end to scurvy was a key reason why the British, under the command of Admiral Lord Nelson, were able to maintain a sea blockade of France and ultimately win the 1805 Battle of Trafalgar against a larger force of scurvy-ridden French and Spanish ships. Unlike Commodore Anson six decades earlier, Lord Nelson didn't have to fight while scurvy ravaged his crew.

In the age of sail, over 160,000 convicts and many more free settlers made their way to Australia. Had James Lind not found a way of preventing scurvy, many of those settlers – ancestors of present-day Australians – would have died at sea. In fact, it is possible that if the scurvy randomised trial had been conducted by another colonial superpower, Australia's national language might be French, Dutch or Portuguese.

*

You might think some things are so obvious we don't need randomised trials to prove them.

- If you have bad back pain, an X-ray will help pinpoint the problem.

- To discourage early pregnancy, ask teenage girls to care for a baby doll that's programmed to demand attention at all hours.

- After-school programs are a great way to help troubled youths.

- Microcredit can solve world poverty.

- If you want people in developing countries to sleep under a bed net to prevent insect-borne disease, don't just give it to them – ask them to pay for it, so that they value it.

Each of these statements sounds completely reasonable, doesn't it? Unfortunately, all five claims are completely wrong. For non-specific back pain, X-rays don't help. Girls who cared for an infant simulator for a week were twice as likely to become teenage mothers.[13] Many after-school programs have no measurable impact. Rigorous micro-credit studies have found it makes only a small impact. Free distribution of bed nets massively increases take-up.

Sometimes randomised trials do confirm conventional wisdom – but their real value is when they surprise us. Talk to people who run a lot of experiments, and you'll discover a sense of scepticism about how far gut feel can take us. In a world as complicated as ours, one of the things I admire about those who run randomised trials is that they're modest about their understanding of the world. Many embody the philosophy of Albert Einstein, who once said, 'The more I learn, the more I realise how much I don't know.' The recognition that we can use our failures to do better next time has been dubbed a 'growth mindset'.[14] It contrasts with a 'fixed mindset', in which we fear setbacks because we regard our talents and abilities as static. People who have a growth mindset know that we can become smarter over time, so long as we take the effort to learn what works and what does not.

Like James Lind, these 'randomistas' – as Nobel laureate Angus Deaton once dubbed them[15] – have an independent streak. As former Netscape head Jim Barksdale liked to joke to his staff, 'If we have data, let's look at data. If all we have are opinions, let's go with mine.' Randomistas know that the alternative to using rigorous evidence is often to follow the HiPPO – the Highest Paid Person's Opinion. In Africa, the hippo is the most dangerous large animal on the continent; HiPPOs can be just as deadly. Randomised trials can save lives, whereas privileging hunches over facts can be lethal.

Today, randomised trials are being run for all kinds of unexpected purposes. Researchers in the Netherlands randomly assigned primary school students to a sports program run by one of the nation's top soccer teams, to see if it helped them perform better in maths and reading (it didn't).[16] In Washington DC, researchers randomly offered a *Washington Post* subscription to households to see how it affected their political views (it made them more likely to vote Democrat).[17] A French experiment found that winning a spot in a boarding school boosted test scores for disadvantaged students.[18] A team of economists used a randomised trial in India to test whether better cooking stoves would improve health by reducing indoor air pollution (the effect was temporary, lasting only a year or so).[19] In Ethiopia, a randomised trial tested whether getting a job in a sweatshop improved people's lives (most quit within a few months).[20] In Oregon, trials have compared whether delinquent youths do better in foster care or group care (foster care seems to be better, particularly for girls).[21]

Randomised trials are in your life, whether you like it or not. In most advanced countries, governments won't pay for pharmaceuticals unless they've undergone a randomised evaluation. Increasingly, the world's smartest aid agencies are looking for the same level of evidence before they allocate funds to a project. Did you use the internet today? Congratulations, you've most likely participated in several randomised trials. Netflix, Amazon and Google are constantly using experiments to hone their sites.

Randomised trials have the power to surprise us. In 1978 a documentary film set in a New Jersey jail hit American screens. Narrated by a young Danny Glover, *Scared Straight* brought a group of juvenile offenders face to face with hardened criminals. The youngsters were supposed to be 'scared' onto the straight and narrow by the tough-talking prisoners, who described life behind bars. In one scene, the young people were ordered to take their shoes off so they could feel what it was like to have their possessions taken away. One of the convicts then growled, 'You know if you get up and touch one of them shoes, I'm gonna break my leg off in your ass.'

Scared Straight not only won an Oscar, it also inspired policy-makers across America to set up Scared Straight programs. Mostly, these policymakers relied on anecdotes as their evidence. Sometimes they pointed to low-quality evaluations, which compared participants with youths who refused to take part. These studies concluded that Scared Straight cut crime by up to half.[22]

If policymakers had listened to more careful assessments, they might have been a little more sceptical. As early as 1978, criminologist James Finckenauer conducted the first randomised evaluation of the Scared Straight program.[23] 'The evidence showed that the kids who went on the program were at greater risk of offending than those who didn't.'[24] As researchers like to say, 'data is not the plural of anecdote'.

Many ignored Finckenauer's randomised study, but over time further rigorous evaluations were carried out and reached the same conclusion. In 2002 the non-profit Campbell Collaboration put out a systematic review of the evidence.[25] It reported that Scared Straight didn't cut crime; it increased it by as much as one-quarter. Furthermore, some of the young participants reported that inmates stole from them and sexually propositioned them.

Like the Terminator, Scared Straight has been hard to kill. In 2011, A&E aired a television program called *Beyond Scared Straight*, which continued to perpetuate the myth that Scared Straight works.

Humans love a good story. But statistics help us tell the difference between fact and fairytale. Scared Straight makes a cracking tale, but at its heart is a myth. However, since stories are often more appealing to us than dry evidence, it took decades for governments to finally scrap it.

*

Another example of randomised trials upending accepted wisdom is in job training for disadvantaged youth. In the mid-1980s the US government commissioned a major randomised trial of job training programs. The experiment found that young people who participated in the programs earned less over the subsequent three years than those who didn't get the training.[26] Other randomised trials found that while job training did no harm, it didn't do much good either.[27]

These were depressing findings, but they prompted researchers to look into other ways to help disadvantaged youth. A Chicago 'Parent Academy', which pays parents for attending workshops with early childhood experts, boosts performance for white and Hispanic students (though not for black students).[28] Mentoring programs for disadvantaged high schoolers help reduce absenteeism (though do less for academic outcomes).[29] Upbeat text messages sent to adult education students lower dropout rates by one-third.[30]

To evaluate a policy is simply to ask, 'Does it work?' The catch is, we need to know what would have happened if the program hadn't been put in place. As if we are entering the world of sci-fi (cue minor chords), we need to know something that never happened.

In the film *Sliding Doors*, we follow the life of Gwyneth Paltrow's character, Helen, according to whether or not she manages to catch a train. In one plotline, she catches the train, finds her boyfriend in bed with another woman, dumps him and starts her own public relations company. In another, Helen just misses the train, gets robbed in the street and juggles two badly paid jobs – oblivious to her boyfriend's infidelity. What makes *Sliding Doors* a fun movie is that we get to see both pathways – like rereading a Choose Your Own Adventure book. We get to see what economists call the 'counterfactual' – the road not taken.

We can't truly see the counterfactual in real life, but sometimes it's pretty darn obvious. If you want to know how good winning the school raffle feels, just compare the facial expression of the winner with the faces of everyone else. If you want to know what a hailstorm does to a car, compare vehicles in a suburb hit by a storm with those in a part of town the storm missed.

But sometimes counterfactuals aren't as obvious. Suppose you decide to treat a bad headache by taking a painkiller and going to bed. If you wake up in the morning feeling better, you'd be unwise to give the tablet all the credit. Perhaps the headache would have gone away by itself. Or maybe the *act* of taking a pill was enough – the placebo effect. The problem gets more difficult when you realise that we sometimes seek help when we're at a low point. Most sick people recover by themselves – so if you want to find out the effect of going to the doctor, it would be ridiculous to assume that the counterfactual is having a runny nose for the rest of your life. Similarly, most people who lose a job ultimately find another, so if you want to find out the impact of job training, it would be a mistake to assume that the participants would otherwise have remained jobless forever.[31]

Researchers have spent years thinking about how best to come up with credible comparison groups, but the benchmark to which they keep returning is the randomised trial. There's simply no better way to determine the counterfactual than to randomly allocate participants into two groups: one that gets the treatment, and another that does not.

In practice, participants can be allocated to random groups by drawing slips of paper from a hat, tossing a coin or using a random number generator. Suppose that we asked everyone in the world to toss a coin. We would end up with nearly 4 billion people in the heads group, and nearly 4 billion in the tails group. Both groups would be comparable in terms of things we can easily measure. For example, each group would have similar numbers of men, millionaires and migrants. The groups would also be alike in ways that are impossible to measure. Each group would contain similar numbers of people with undiagnosed brain cancer, and similar numbers of people who will win tomorrow's lottery. Now imagine we asked the heads group to get an extra hour's sleep that evening, and then surveyed people the next night, asking them to rate how happy they were with their lives on a scale from 1 to 10. If we found that the heads group were happier than the tails group, it would be reasonable to conclude that a little more snooze helps lose the blues.

The beauty of a randomised trial is that it gets around problems that might plague an observational analysis. Suppose I told you that surveys typically find that people who slumber longer are happier. You might reasonably respond that this is because happiness causes sleep – good-tempered people tend to hit the pillow early. Or you might argue that both happiness and sleep are products of something else – like being in a stable relationship. Either way, an observational study falls prey to the old critique: correlation doesn't imply causation.

Misleading correlations are all around us.[32] Ice-cream sales are correlated with shark attacks, but that doesn't mean you should boycott Mr Whippy. Shoe size is correlated with exam performance, but buying adult shoes for kindergarteners isn't going to help. Countries with higher chocolate consumption win more Nobel prizes, but chomping Cadbury won't make you a genius.[33]

By contrast, a randomised trial uses the power of chance to assign the groups. That's why farmers use randomised trials to assess the quality of seeds and fertilisers, and why medical researchers use them to test new drugs. In most cases, randomised trials provide evidence that's both stronger and simpler. The results are not only more likely to stand up to scrutiny, but also easier to explain to your uncle. As one social researcher recalls from learning about random assignment: 'I was struck by the power of this novel technique to cut through the clouds of confusing correlations that make the inference of causality so hazardous ... I have never lost my sense of wonder at this amazing fact.'[34] There are some limits to randomised trials – which I'll explore in Chapter 11 – but in most cases we're doing too few randomised trials, not too many.

When Angus Deaton used the term 'randomistas', he didn't mean it as a compliment. In his own field of development economics, he felt that randomised trials were being used to answer questions to which they were poorly suited. As the saying goes, to the person with a hammer, everything looks like a nail. In development economics, Deaton felt his colleagues were whacking too many problems with randomised trials.[35]

It's certainly true that not every intervention can – or should – be randomised. A famous article in the *British Medical Journal* searched the literature for randomised trials of parachute effectiveness.[36] Finding none, the researchers concluded (tongue-in-cheek): 'the apparent protective effect of parachutes may be merely an example of the "healthy cohort" effect ... The widespread use of the parachute may just be another example of doctors' obsession with disease prevention.' Using similar critiques to those levelled at non-randomised studies in other fields, the article pointed out the absurdity of expecting everything to be randomly trialled.

The parachute study has been widely quoted by critics of randomised evaluations. But it turns out that experiments on parachute efficacy and safety are widespread. The US military use crash dummies to test the impact of high-altitude and low-altitude jumps, and soldiers have conducted randomised parachute experiments to improve equipment and techniques.[37] One randomised study, conducted at Fort Benning in Georgia, sought to reduce sprained ankles, the most common parachuting injury. The experiment found that wearing an ankle brace reduced the risk of ankle sprains among paratroopers by a factor of six.[38]

The same goes for other instances where it would be wrong to take away the treatment entirely. It would be absurd to withhold pain medication in surgery, but anaesthetists frequently conduct randomised trials to see which painkiller works best. In fiscal policy, no reasonable government would ignore an impending recession, but it might quite reasonably roll out household payments on a random schedule, which would then teach us how much of the money got spent.[39] The control group in a randomised trial doesn't have to get zilch. In many cases, it may get an alternative treatment, or the same treatment a bit later. Sometimes randomised trials are best used to tweak an existing treatment. At other times, they can be used to tackle the biggest questions, like how to avert disaster.

The claim that randomised trials are unethical isn't the only criticism levelled at them. Detractors also argue that randomised trials are too narrow, too expensive and too slow. Again, these are fundamental challenges, but they aren't fatal. Admittedly, specific studies can be narrow, but that's a reminder to be careful in interpreting the results. For instance, if a drug works for women, we shouldn't assume it will work for men.[40] In the case of scale, it's true that some studies can cost millions and take decades. But there has been a proliferation of fast, cheap randomised trials. Businesses are increasingly using trials to tweak processes, while government agencies are employing administrative data to conduct low-cost experiments.

*

Steels Creek resident John O'Neill said that as the fire came towards him, it 'sounded like ten or twenty steam trains'. The sky turned red, black and purple. He screamed at his children to get inside the house, and they lay on the floor, wet cloths on their faces to keep the smoke at bay. Embers hit the windows. It was, O'Neill said, 'like being inside a washing machine on spin cycle and full of fire'.[41]

O'Neill and his family lived through Black Saturday, the deadliest fires ever to hit Australia. In February 2009 Victoria experienced a blistering summer heatwave after a decade of drought. Temperatures were at record highs, and the winds were strong and dry. As one expert later noted, these conditions created an extraordinary inferno. The flames were up to 100 metres tall, and fire temperatures as high as 1200°C. Aluminium road signs melted. Eucalyptus oil from the gum trees ignited in the canopy, creating 'fireballs' – parcels of flammable gases that were blown up to 30 kilometres ahead of the fire front.

The fire produced its own atmospheric conditions, with the convection column creating an internal thunderstorm. Like an angry beast, it shot out lightning, creating new fires. As one firefighter put it, 'This thing was huge, absolutely huge ... just full of ember, ash, burning materials. This thing was absolutely alive.'[42] The total amount of energy released by the fire was equal to 1500 Hiroshima atomic bombs.

In the Murrindindi Scenic Reserve, a team of firefighters came across nineteen frightened campers, but were unable to evacuate them before the fire cut the exit road. They gathered the campers up and drove the fire truck into the nearby river. For the next ninety minutes, they sprayed water on the truck roof as the fire raged around.[43]

By the end of Black Saturday, 173 people had died and thousands of homes had been destroyed. Reviewing the disaster and its aftermath, a royal commission recommended that more research be done to understand the unpredictable behaviour of fires in extreme conditions.

In the Canberra suburb of Yarralumla, CSIRO researcher Andrew Sullivan is standing in front of a 25-metre-long wind tunnel. At one end is a fan the size of a jet engine, capable of sucking in as much air in a single second as the volume of a small swimming pool. At the other end is a glass-walled section. 'Here's where we light the fires,' he tells me. When he tells me it's called 'the Pyrotron', I'm reminded of a character from the X-Men.

Opened the year before the Black Saturday bushfires, the Pyrotron is where Sullivan and his team conduct experiments on fire behaviour. What makes some species of trees burn faster than others? How do spot fires combine to form a single fire front? How effective are powder suppressants compared to simply spraying water? If they didn't randomise their experiments, Sullivan points out, researchers could easily go astray. Like Scouts practising for their fire lighting badge, scientists who spend a day setting fires in the Pyrotron will probably get steadily better at the task. So if researchers were to gradually dial up the air flow with each successive experiment, they might end up thinking they were learning about air flow when in fact they were measuring the effect of a better prepared fire. By randomising the order of their experiments, scientists are more likely to unveil the truth.

Randomised fire experiments are also an important part of the response to climate change. Nearly one-quarter of global greenhouse-gas emissions come from fires, so reducing the carbon emitted from bushfires could be a cost-effective way of addressing climate change. Experiments in the Pyrotron by Sullivan and his fellow researchers found that low-intensity fires emit less carbon dioxide and carbon monoxide, suggesting that backburning operations could be a valuable way of cutting down greenhouse-gas emissions.[44]

Randomised fire experiments aren't just conducted inside the safety of the Pyrotron. One of Australia's greatest bushfire researchers, Alan McArthur, ignited and observed over 1200 experimental fires during the 1950s and '60s. Many of McArthur's fires were lit on the aptly named Black Mountain in Canberra – within sight of the Pyrotron. These experiments helped provide insights as to how quickly fires move through grasslands, eucalypt forests and pine plantations. For firefighters, McArthur's work showed the risk of fighting on hilly surfaces, because fires move more quickly uphill than on the flat.

For the general public, McArthur's legacy is in producing the first fire danger ratings systems, which converted weather data into an easy-to-understand five-point risk scale.[45] In bushfire-prone areas across Australia, these signs stand by the roadside today. After the Black Saturday fires, they were updated to add a sixth risk category: 'Catastrophic'. By carrying out randomised experiments, McArthur came up with a straightforward way to convert complex weather data into a simple fire risk index.

*

In 1769, sixteen years after the publication of Lind's randomised trial on scurvy, a surgeon by the name of William Stark decided to experiment on himself to see how different foods affected scurvy.[46] He began with a month on just bread and water, then began supplementing this with foods one at a time, including olive oil, milk, goose and beef. Two months in, he contracted scurvy. Stark continued to document his precise food intake and his own medical condition, as he added in more foods, including butter, figs and veal. Seven months into the experiment, he died, aged twenty-nine. At the time, Stark had been considering adding fresh fruit and green vegetables to his diet, but was still working through bacon and cheese.

Stark has been described as one of history's 'martyrs of nutrition'.[47] But if he had read Lind's treatise, he might have saved himself significant pain, not to mention an early death. Lind stands as a reminder not only of the value of carrying out high-quality evaluations, but also of the importance of making sure the results are acted upon.

2

FROM BLOODLETTING
TO PLACEBO SURGERY

Standing in a sparkling white operating theatre, I'm watching my first surgery. On the bed is a 71-year-old patient having her hip replaced. Around the room are nurses, an anaesthetist, a representative of the company that makes the artificial hip, and an observing doctor. In the centre, gently slicing open the woman's hip with a scalpel is Melbourne surgeon Peter Choong. Easy-listening music plays from the stereo. The atmosphere in the room couldn't be calmer. It's a familiar operation, and the team know each other well.

First incision made, Peter puts down his scalpel, and picks up a bipolar diathermy machine. Now he's burning the flesh instead of slicing it, a technique that reduces bleeding and speeds recovery. The room smells like a barbecue. Back to the scalpel, and a few minutes later Peter is in to the hip joint. To clean it out, he uses a device like a power drill. On the end is a metal sphere the size of a ping-pong ball, its rough surface designed to shave the hip socket until it's perfectly smooth. When he pulls it out, the ball is covered in bone and blood. Not for the first time, I'm glad I ate a light breakfast.

Modern surgery is a curious combination of brawn, technology and teamwork. One moment, Peter is swinging a hammer or lifting a knee joint. Next, he is fitting a prosthesis, watching a computer screen as crosshairs indicate precisely the angle of fit. The tension rises when the bone cement is mixed. As soon as the two compounds are combined, a nurse begins calling time: 'Thirty seconds ... one minute ... one minute 30.' At four minutes, it's inserted into the patient. At five minutes, the artificial joint is attached. Everyone in the room knows the cement will be hard at ten minutes. After that, the only way to change the angle of the prosthesis is to chip the hardened cement out from inside the bone.

In an operating theatre, the surgeon is in command. And yet for all his expertise, Peter is surprisingly willing to admit what he doesn't know. Is it better to perform hip surgery from the front (anterolateral) or the back (posterolateral)? Should we encourage obese patients to get a lap-banding operation before knee surgery? How early should we get patients out of bed after a joint replacement? For antiseptic, is it best to use iodine, or does the cheaper chlorhexidine perform equally well?

Over the coming years, Peter hopes to answer each of these questions. His main tool: the randomised trial. A few years ago he led a team that conducted a randomised trial to test whether total knee replacement was better done the conventional way, or with computer guidance to help line up the implant.[1] Across 115 patients, the study showed that computer assistance led to a more accurate placement of the artificial knee, and higher quality of life for patients. In other studies, he has randomised particular surgical techniques and strategies for pain management post-surgery.[2]

Most controversially, Peter Choong is a strong supporter of evaluating surgical operations against a control group who receive 'placebo surgery'. For control group patients, this typically means that the surgeon makes an incision and then sews them up again.

Placebo surgery – also known as 'sham surgery' – is used when researchers are uncertain whether or not an operation helps patients. In one famous study, surgeons tested whether keyhole knee surgery helped patients with osteoarthritis.[3] At the time, the operation was performed more than a million times a year around the world. But some surgeons had doubts about its effectiveness. So in the late 1990s a group of surgeons in Houston conducted an experiment in which some patients received keyhole surgery, while others simply received an incision on their knee. Only when the surgeon entered the operating suite did an assistant hand them an envelope saying whether the surgery would be real or sham. Because the patients were under a local anaesthetic, the surgeons made sure patients were kept in the operating theatre for the same length of time as in the real operation, and manipulated the knee as they would for a surgery. Two years later, patients who received sham surgery experienced the same levels of pain and knee function as patients who had real surgery.

Sham surgery dates back to 1959, when a group of Seattle doctors became sceptical of a technique used to treat chest pain by tying tiny knots in chest arteries.[4] They randomly performed the experiment on eight patients, and simply made incisions in the chests of another nine. The study found that the technique had no impact, and the surgery was phased out within a few years.

In recent years, sham surgery has shown no difference between a control group and osteoporosis patients who have bone cement injected into cracked vertebrae (a procedure known as vertebroplasty).[5] Sham surgery has even been performed by neurosurgeons, who found that injecting fetal cells into the brains of patients suffering from Parkinson's disease had no more effect than the placebo treatment, in which patients had a small hole, known as a burr hole, drilled into the side of their skulls.[6]

The most stunning sham surgery result came in 2013. After the finding that knee surgery didn't help older patients with osteo-arthritis, a team in Finland began to wonder about the knee surgery performed for a torn meniscus, the piece of cartilage that provides a cushion between the thighbone and shinbone. Their randomised experiment showed that among middle-aged patients, surgery for a torn meniscus was no more effective than sham surgery.[7] This operation, known as a meniscectomy, is performed millions of times a year, making it the most common orthopaedic procedure in countries such as Australia and the United States.[8] While some surgeons acknowledged the enormous significance of the finding, others were not so receptive.[9] An editorial in the journal *Arthroscopy* thundered that sham surgery randomised trials were 'ludicrous'. The editors went so far as to argue that because no 'right-minded patients' would participate in sham surgeries, the results would 'not be generalizable to mentally healthy patients'.[10]

Yet sham surgeries are growing in importance, as people realise that the placebo effect in surgery is probably bigger than in any other area of medicine. A recent survey of fifty-three sham surgery trials found that the treatment only outperformed the placebo 49 per cent of the time. But in 74 per cent of cases, patients appeared to respond to the placebo.[11] In other words, three out of four patients feel that a surgery has made them better, even though half of the evaluated surgeries don't work as intended. The results suggest that millions of people every year are undergoing surgeries that make them feel a bit better – yet they would feel just as good if they had undergone placebo surgery instead.

Such a huge placebo effect is probably explained by the fact that surgery is a more invasive procedure than other medical interventions, and by the particularly high status of surgeons. As the joke goes, people are waiting in the cafeteria line in heaven when a man in a white coat cuts in and takes all the food. 'Who's that?' one asks. 'It's just God,' another replies. 'He thinks he's a surgeon.'[12] Yet the results of sham surgery trials suggest that the profession is far from infallible. For nearly half of the procedures that have been evaluated in this way, the surgeon might as well have started by asking the patient: 'Would you prefer the full operation, or should we just cut you open, play a few easy-listening tracks and then sew you back up again?'

Ethical questions will continue to be one of the main issues confronting sham surgery. In the 1990s one surgical text stated baldly that 'sham operations are ethically unjustifiable.'[13] To confront this, researchers have gone to extraordinary lengths to ensure patients understand what is going on. In the Houston knee surgery trial, patients were required to write on their charts: 'On entering this study, I realize that I may receive only placebo surgery. I further realize that this means that I will not have surgery on my knee joint. This placebo surgery will not benefit my knee arthritis.' Surgeons explain to each patient that the reason for the randomised trial is that the world's leading experts truly do not know whether the surgery works, a situation known as 'clinical equipoise'. Because we are uncertain about the results of the treatment, it is possible that those who get the sham surgery may in fact be better off than those who get the real surgery.

Despite the advocacy of surgeons such as Peter Choong, sham surgery remains in its infancy. A study of orthopaedic surgeries in Sydney hospitals found that only about one-third of procedures were supported by a randomised trial.[14] Sydney surgeon Ian Harris points out that patients sometimes regard aggressive surgeons as heroic and conservative surgeons as cowardly. Yet 'if you look beyond the superficial you often find that the heroic surgeon will have bad results ... it is harder, and possibly more courageous, to treat patients without surgery'.[15] Harris notes that more aggressive surgeons are less likely to be criticised and less likely to be sued – and get paid a lot more.

Pittsburgh orthopaedic surgeon John Christoforetti tells of how the randomised evidence led him to advise a patient not to seek knee surgery for a meniscal tear. The man responded by going online and giving the surgeon a one-star rating and a rude comment. The patient firmly believed he needed the operation. 'Most of my colleagues,' Christoforetti says, 'will say: "Look, save yourself the headache, just do the surgery. None of us are going to be upset with you for doing the surgery. Your bank account's not going to be upset with you for doing the surgery. Just do the surgery."'[16] Sometimes it can be easier to ignore the evidence than to follow it.

*

In the Bible, the book of Daniel tells the story of an early medical experiment. King Nebuchadnezzar is trying to persuade Daniel and three other young men from Judah to eat the royal delicacies. When Daniel replies that they would prefer a vegetarian diet, he is told that they may end up malnourished. To settle the matter, the king agrees that for ten days the four young men will eat only vegetables, and will then be compared with youths who have eaten the royal delicacies. At the end of the experiment, Daniel and the other three are in healthier condition, so are allowed to remain vegetarian.

Daniel's experiment wasn't a random one, since he and his colleagues chose to be in the treatment group. But the Bible's 2200-year-old experiment was more rigorous than the kind of 'pilot study' sometimes we still see, which has no comparison group at all.

In the ensuing centuries, randomised medical trials steadily advanced. In the 1540s French surgeon Ambroise Paré was a battlefield surgeon charged with tending to soldiers who had been burned by gunpowder. For these men, the chances of survival were grim. A few years earlier, in the Battle of Milan, Paré had found three French soldiers in a stable with severe burns. As he recounted in his autobiography, a passing French soldier asked if there was any way of curing them.[17] When Paré said there was nothing that could be done, the soldier calmly pulled out his dagger and slit their throats. Paré told him he was a 'wicked man'. The soldier replied that if it had been him in such pain, he hoped someone would cut his neck rather than let him 'miserably languish'.

Now Paré was responsible for an even larger group of burned soldiers. A bag of gunpowder had been set alight, and many Frenchmen had been wounded. He began applying the remedy of the day – boiling oil mixed with treacle. But at a certain point, he ran out of hot oil and switched to an old Roman remedy: turpentine, oil of roses and egg white. The next morning, when he checked the two groups of soldiers, Paré found that those who had been treated with boiling oil were feverish, while those who had received the turpentine (which acted as a disinfectant) had slept well. 'I resolved with myself,' he wrote, 'never so cruelly to burn poor men wounded with gunshot.'

By the standards of today, Paré's experiment has its flaws. Suppose he had begun treating the most badly burned soldiers first, and then moved on to those with lighter injuries. In that case, we might expect those treated with oil to be in a worse condition, regardless of the effect of the remedy. Yet while Paré's study was imperfect, medicine continued to inch towards more careful analysis. Two centuries after Paré, Lind would conduct his scurvy experiment on a dozen patients who were 'as similar as I could have them'.

An important step on the road towards today's medical randomised trials was the notion that patients might be more inclined to recover – or at least to report that they were feeling better – after seeing a doctor. In 1799 British doctor John Haygarth became frustrated at the popularity of a quack treatment known as 'Perkins tractors'. The tractors were simply two metal rods, which were to be held against the body of the patient to 'draw off the noxious electric fluid' that was hurting the patient. In an experiment on five rheumatic patients, Haygarth showed that wooden rods performed just as well as Perkins tractors, giving rise to the idea of the placebo.[18]

The placebo, Haygarth pointed out, was one reason why famous doctors might produce better results than unknown ones. If authoritative doctors evoked a larger placebo effect, he reasoned, then their patients might be more likely to recover, even if their remedies were useless. And indeed, the air of authority was highly prized by doctors of the time, despite the poor quality of their remedies. One of the main treatments used by doctors was bloodletting, which involved opening a vein in the arm with a special knife, and served only to weaken patients.[19] It wasn't until the early 1800s that a randomised trial of bloodletting was conducted on sick soldiers. The result was a 29 per cent death rate among men in the treatment group and a 2 per cent death rate in the control group.[20] Medicine's bloody history is memorialised in the name of one of the discipline's top journals: *The Lancet*. Before there was evidence-based medicine, there was eminence-based medicine.[21]

In nineteenth-century Vienna, high-status doctors were literally costing lives.[22] At a time when many affluent women still gave birth at home, Vienna General Hospital largely served underprivileged women. The hospital had two maternity clinics: one in which babies were delivered by female midwives, and the other where babies were delivered by male doctors. Patients were admitted to the clinics on alternate days. And yet the clinics had very different health outcomes. In the clinic run by midwives, a mother's chance of death was less than 1 in 20. In the clinic run by doctors, maternal mortality was 1 in 10: more than twice as high. Patients knew this and would beg not to be admitted into the doctor-run clinic. Some would give birth on the street instead of in the doctors' clinic, because their chance of survival was higher.

To Ignaz Semmelweis, the doctor in charge of records, the results were puzzling. Because the two clinics admitted patients on alternate days, the health of the patients should have been similar. Indeed, it was almost as though the Vienna Hospital had set up a randomised trial to test the impact of the two clinics – and discovered the doctors were doing more harm than good. In trying to uncover reasons for this, Semmelweis first observed that midwives delivered babies while women lay on their sides, while doctors delivered babies while women lay on their backs. But when the doctors tried adopting side delivery, it didn't help. Then he noted that when a baby died, the priest walked through the ward with a bell; he theorised that this might be terrifying the other mothers. But removing the priest's bell also had no impact.

Then a friend of Semmelweis was poked by a student's scalpel while doing an autopsy, and died. Noticing that his friend's symptoms were similar to those of many of the mothers who died, Semmelweis theorised that doctors might be infecting mothers with 'cadaverous particles', causing death by puerperal fever. He insisted that doctors wash their hands with chlorine from then on, and the death rate plummeted. Only thanks to Semmelweis and an accidental ran-domised trial did it become safer to give birth attended by a Viennese doctor than on the streets.

And yet, like Lind's findings, Semmelweis's insistence on hand-washing was rejected by many medical experts of the time.[23] The germ theory of disease was yet to be developed. Many doctors were insulted by the suggestion that the hands of gentlemen like them-selves were unclean, and by the implication that they were responsible for infecting their patients. After Semmelweis left the Vienna General Hospital, chlorine handwashing was discontinued.

In the mid-1800s, large elements of medicine remained pro-foundly unscientific. Addressing the Massachusetts Medical Society in 1860, physician Oliver Wendell Holmes Sr said, 'I firmly believe that if the whole *materia medica* [body of medical knowledge], as now used, could be sunk to the bottom of the sea, it would be all the better for mankind, and all the worse for the fishes.'[24] As historian David Wootton noted in *Bad Medicine*, his 2006 book on the history of medical missteps: 'For 2,400 years patients have believed that doctors were doing good; for 2,300 years they were wrong.'[25]

*

Slowly medical researchers came to rely less on theory and more on empirical tests. At the end of the nineteenth century, diphtheria was the most dangerous infectious disease in the developed world, killing hundreds of thousands of people annually.[26] To test the impact of serum treatment, Danish doctor Johannes Fibiger devised a randomised trial.[27] Like the Vienna maternity hospitals, Fibiger assigned people to alternate treatments on alternate days. He found that patients given the serum were nearly four times less likely to die. The demand for Fibiger's treatment was so great that in 1902 the Danish government founded the State Serum Institute to produce and supply the vaccine to its citizens.

In the coming decades, randomised medical trials became more common. In the 1930s researchers suggested that the risk of investigators biasing their results could be significantly reduced if the person administering the drugs did not know which was the control and which was the treatment. Trials in which the identity of the treatments was hidden from both the patient and the administering doctor became known as 'double-blind' studies. In one telling, the term came from blindfold tests that the Old Gold cigarette company carried out to promote its products.[28]

In the 1940s a randomised trial showed that antibiotics did not cure the common cold.[29] A trial in 1954 randomly injected 600,000 US children with either polio vaccine or salt water.[30] The vaccine proved effective, and immunisation of all American children began the following year. The 1960s saw randomised trials used to test drugs for diabetes and blood pressure, and the contraceptive pill.[31] Strong advocates of evidence-based medicine, such as Alvan Feinstein and David Sackett, argued that the public should pay less attention to the prestige of an expert and more to the quality of their evidence.

One of the best-known advocates of evidence-based medicine was Scottish doctor Archie Cochrane, whose early training was as a medical officer in German prisoner-of-war camps during World War II. In one camp, Cochrane was the only doctor to 20,000 men. They were fed about 600 calories a day (one-third of what is generally considered a minimum daily intake). All had diarrhoea. Epidemics of typhoid and jaundice often swept the camp. When Cochrane asked the Nazi camp commanders for more doctors, he was told: 'Nein! Aerzte sind überflüssig.' ('No! Doctors are superfluous.')[32] Cochrane was furious.

But over time, Cochrane's anger softened. When he considered which British men lived and died, Cochrane came to understand that his medical expertise had little impact. He did his best, but was up against the limits of 1940s therapies. As Cochrane later acknowledged, what little aid doctors could provide was largely ineffective 'in comparison with the recuperative power of the human body'. This was particularly true when he cared for tuberculosis patients, tending to them in the clinic before officiating at their funerals ('I got quite expert in the Hindu, Moslem, and Greek Orthodox rites').

After the war, Cochrane wrote, 'I had never heard then of "randomised controlled trials", but I knew there was no real evidence that anything we had to offer had any effect on tuberculosis, and I was afraid that I shortened the lives of some of my friends by unnecessary intervention.'[33] Cochrane realised then that the Nazi officer who had denied him more doctors might have been 'wise or cruel', but 'was certainly right'.

Reading Cochrane's memoirs, it is hard not to be struck by his honesty, modesty and tenderness. He jokes that, 'It was bad enough being a POW, but having me as your doctor was a bit too much.'[34] At another point, he tells the story of the night when the Germans dumped a young Russian soldier into the ward late one night. The man's lungs were badly infected; he was moribund and screaming. Cochrane had no morphine, only aspirin, which did nothing to stop the Russian crying out. Cochrane did not speak Russian, nor did anyone else on the ward. Eventually, he did the only thing he could. 'I finally instinctively sat down on the bed and took him in my arms, and the screaming stopped almost at once. He died peacefully in my arms a few hours later. It was not the pleurisy that caused the screaming but loneliness. It was a wonderful education about the care of the dying.'[35]

In the final decades of his life, Cochrane challenged the medical profession to regularly compile all the relevant randomised controlled trials, organised by speciality. In 1993, four years after Cochrane's death, British researcher Iain Chalmers did just that. Known at the outset as the Cochrane Collaboration – and today simply as Cochrane – the organisation systematically reviews randomised trials to make them accessible for doctors, patients and policymakers. Today, Cochrane reviews are one of the first places that doctors will go when they encounter an unfamiliar medical problem. Chalmers also created the James Lind Alliance, an initiative that identifies the top ten unanswered questions for dozens of medical conditions: its aim is to guide future researchers towards filling in the gaps.

Thanks to the work of past medical randomistas, new drugs must now follow an established path from laboratory to market. Since the late 1930s, when an experimental drug killed more than a hundred Americans, most countries require initial safety testing to be done on animals. Typically, this involves two species, such as mice and dogs.[36] If a drug passes these tests, then it moves into the clinical trial phase. Phase I trials test safety in humans, based on less than a hundred people. Phase II trials test the drug's efficacy on a few hundred people. Phase III trials test effectiveness in a large group – from several hundred to several thousand – and compares it with other drugs. If a drug passes all these stages and hits the market, post-marketing trials monitor its impact in the general population and test for rare adverse effects.

What are the odds of success? A recent US study found that if you started with ten drugs, four would be knocked out by Phase I trials. Four more would flunk Phase II trials. Of the remaining two drugs, one would either fail Phase III trials or get rejected by the Food and Drug Administration.[37] In other words, only one in ten drugs that look promising in laboratory and animal tests ends up finding its way onto the market. For drugs used to treat cancer and heart disease, the odds of a drug making its way from lab to market are lower still.

In each case, those taking the new drug are compared against people taking a fake drug. The word 'placebo' comes from the Latin *placere*, meaning 'to please'. It reflects the fact that people can respond differently when they receive what they believe is an effective treatment. When medical researchers see a change in outcomes among people who have only taken sugar pills, they call it 'the placebo effect'.

Early research on the placebo effect turns out to have overstated the power of placebos, wrongly conflating the natural tendency of patients to recover with the impact of placebos. Modern researchers now doubt that the placebo effect actually helps our bodies heal faster. But it does seem to affect self-reported impacts, such as pain.[38] For alleviating discomfort, the placebo effect works in surprising ways. For example, placebo injections produce a larger effect than placebo pills.[39] Even the colour of a tablet changes the way in which patients perceive its effect. Thanks to randomised trials, we know that if you want to reduce depression, you should give the patient a yellow tablet.[40] For reducing pain, use a white pill. For lowering anxiety, offer a green one. Sedatives work best when delivered in blue pills, while stimulants are most effective as red pills. The makers of the movie *The Matrix* clearly knew this when they devised a moment for the hero to choose between a blue pill and a red pill. Blue would wipe his mind and make him happy; red would show him how truly terrifying the world is.

If we simply compare patients who take a pill with those who do not, then we might wrongly attribute the impact entirely to the active ingredients in the tablet. By contrast, a well-designed randomised trial strips out the placebo effect – for example, by comparing pain levels among patients who are given white sugar pills with pain levels among patients who are given identical-looking white aspirin tablets.

*

Patients with severe emphysema used to be treated with lung volume reduction surgery, until a randomised trial showed that it significantly increased the risk of death.[41] After minor strokes, neurosurgeons would once routinely perform an extracranial to intracranial bypass (connecting an artery outside the skull with one inside the skull). The surgery was supported by case studies, but a randomised trial showed that it produced worse outcomes.[42] For a patient whose bowel is caught up in scar tissue, experts used to favour laparoscopic surgery to 'unpick' the adhesions – until a randomised trial showed that this kind of surgery did not reduce pain or improve quality of life.[43] Beta-blockers, which had previously been thought to endanger patients with heart disease, have now been shown in randomised trials to lower the chance of death.[44]

Among postmenopausal women, early studies of those who chose to take hormone therapy suggested that the treatment might reduce the incidence of cardiovascular disease. By the turn of the twenty-first century, around 90 million hormone therapies were being prescribed for newly postmenopausal American women. Then randomised controlled trials showed that hormone therapy had only negative impacts: raising the risk of stroke and the risk of obstruction of a vein by a blood clot.[45] For doctors, changing the advice they gave to patients wasn't easy. As Chicago physician Adam Cifu describes his experience, 'I had to basically run back all those decisions with women. And, boy, that really sticks with you, when you have patients saying, "But I thought you said this was the right thing."'[46]

Medical ethics dictate that researchers should stop a trial if there is evidence of harm. Until the early 2000s, it was normal to treat severe head injuries with steroid injections. Then a trial in Glasgow began randomising patients to receive either a steroid injection or a placebo injection. Halfway through, researchers saw that the death rate among those who received the steroid was 21 per cent: considerably higher than the 18 per cent death rate among those who received a placebo.[47] The results were conclusive enough to stop the study and publish the results. Head injury patients no longer get steroid injections as a routine matter.

Randomised trials have also helped doctors do a better job of screening. For years, doctors have responded to patients with non-specific back pain by ordering CT scans, MRIs or even X-rays. In recent years, randomised trials have shown that the results of such tests don't help medical professionals treat pain.[48] In fact, patients with back pain who were randomly assigned to get an X-ray ended up with a higher level of self-reported pain and more frequent follow-up visits to the doctor.[49]

An even tougher area is cancer screening. If screening were error-free, it would be straightforward to roll it out. But it turns out that screening comes with costs as well as benefits. In a systematic review of randomised trials of breast cancer screening, Cochrane concluded that 'for every 2000 women invited for screening throughout 10 years, one will avoid dying of breast cancer and 10 healthy women, who would not have been diagnosed if there had not been screening, will be treated unnecessarily. Furthermore, more than 200 women will experience important psychological distress including anxiety and uncertainty for years because of false positive findings.'[50]

The European Randomized Study of Screening for Prostate Cancer, covering men in the Netherlands, Belgium, Sweden, Finland, Italy, Spain and Switzerland, is now able to compare mortality rates thirteen years after blood-test screening. With more than 160,000 men in the trial, the death rate is slightly lower for men who have been screened for prostate cancer (commonly known as 'PSA screening'). But the difference is small – one death averted for every 781 men who are screened – and the researchers are not yet confident that they have enough evidence to justify prostate cancer screening for every man aged over fifty.[51]

*

For my own part, randomised trials have helped shape how I look after my health. I used to take a daily multivitamin tablet, until I read a study that drew together all the available randomised trials of vitamins A, C and E, beta carotene and selenium.[52] The study found that for otherwise healthy people, there is no evidence that extra vitamins make you live longer. If anything, those who took vitamin supplements seemed to live shorter lives. Not wanting to send myself to an early grave, I stopped taking multivitamin tablets.

The same goes for fish oil. Based on a 2002 study, millions of people in advanced countries began popping pills made from mushed-up sardines and anchovies.[53] Yet a decade later, a much larger, systematic review of randomised studies found no evidence that omega-3 supplements prevented heart attacks.[54] So I dropped the fish oil tablet too.

As for the rest, I can't help thinking of Tim Minchin's beat poem 'Storm' every time I accidentally wander into the 'herbal remedies' section of the supermarket. In it, Tim imagines himself responding to an advocate of natural medicine:

'By definition', I begin
'Alternative medicine', I continue,
'Has either not been proved to work,
Or been proved not to work.
Do you know what they call "alternative medicine"
that's been proved to work? "Medicine".'

I love running, so I'm always on the lookout for randomised trials on exercise science. After reading randomised trials, I've opted to choose my running shoes based on comfort, moving away from the 'stability' models that I'd been wearing for many years.[55] After a marathon, I'll wear compression socks, since an Australian trial showed that they significantly boost recovery.[56] When training, I'll try to include some high-intensity bursts, based on a randomised trial that found that the cardiovascular benefits of sprint training are five times greater than for moderate exercise.[57]

Around home, when I have to remove a bandaid from one of my sons, I'll remind them that a randomised trial by James Cook University researchers found that the fast approach was less painful than the slow approach.[58] When I sip my morning brew, I take pleasure in the randomised evidence showing that coffee protects against DNA breaks.[59] And after reading the evidence on annual medical check-ups, I'm persuaded that they do not reduce my chance of falling ill, but do add to the cost of the health care system. For example, in the United States, annual physicals account for one-tenth of doctor visits, despite expert bodies recommending against them for people who aren't showing any symptoms of illness.[60]

*

Medical researchers were among the earliest pioneers of randomised trials. Indeed, I've chosen to start this book with health care precisely because it's so far ahead of many other fields. One of the reasons that modern medicine is saving more lives than ever before in human history is its willingness to test cures against placebos or the best available alternative. If it works, we use it; if not, it's back to the lab. In just one field – strokes and neurological disorders – there are around 50,000 Americans alive today thanks to recent randomised trials.[61] For every new treatment – AIDS drugs, the human papillomavirus vaccine, magnetic resonance imaging, genetic testing – medicine has discarded old ones – bloodletting, gastric freezing, routine circumcision and tonsillectomy.[62]

But there is still more that medicine can do to benefit from randomised trials.[63] As we have seen, surgical randomised trials remain comparatively rare, with hospitals conducting tens of thousands of medical procedures every year that are not supported by good evidence. Surgeon Ian Harris gives the example of spine fusion surgery for back pain: an operation now performed on 1 in 1000 Americans each year, even though randomised trials show no better results than for intensive rehabilitation.[64] Harris notes that 'the more you know, the harder it gets ... a conflict develops between what you understand to be true, based on scientific research ... and what everyone else is doing'.[65] Surgeon and author Atul Gawande argues that 'pointless medical care' costs hundreds of billions of dollars annually.[66] Each year, one in four Americans receives a medical test or treatment that has been proven through a randomised trial to be useless or harmful.[67] An Australian study identified over 150 medical practices that are commonly used despite being unsafe or ineffective.[68] The randomistas not only need to produce more evidence, they also need to do a better job at publicising what they know already.

3

DECREASING DISADVANTAGE, ONE COIN TOSS AT A TIME

T he first time Daniel's mum threw him out of home, he was thirteen.[1] He'd grown up around drugs, alcohol and dysfunction, and thought it was 'fun ... a big adventure'. Through his teenage years, he describes a cycle of his mother saying, 'Come back', 'Get out', 'Come back'. When Mum didn't want him at home, Daniel couch-surfed with friends or slept on the streets. Pretty soon, he says, 'I didn't worry too much about where I was, I would just get really drunk and lie down.' Daniel stumbled from alcohol to marijuana, pills and ice. He began stealing from strangers and family. Because of the methamphetamines, Daniel's teeth had holes in them, and his face was covered in scabs. He lost 25 kilograms.

When Daniel's brother offered a few words of advice, Daniel took a swing at him with a machete. The blade missed, and the incident finally made Daniel realise the extent to which his life had got out of control. He stopped the drinking and drugs, found a place to live and finally got a job.

Hard-core poverty almost always involves more than one source of stress. Daniel's case involved crime, drugs and unemployment, compounded by poor education, few friends and bad health. And yet he was lucky because he managed to get help at the age of twenty-one. What can we do to help people who have been homeless for decades?

In Melbourne, the Sacred Heart Mission has been working closely with long-term homeless people since 1982. A few years ago, the organisation proposed to trial a new intensive casework program, targeted at people who had been sleeping rough for at least a year. When they pitched the idea to their philanthropic partners, one donor urged that it be evaluated through a randomised trial.[2]

Guy Johnson, who worked in community housing and would eventually help conduct the research, was pretty sceptical at first.[3] People in the community sector, he told me, 'freak out at the word experimental', and prefer to select participants based on need, not chance. But Johnson came to regard randomisation not only as the most rigorous method for evaluating the program, but also the fairest way of deciding who got the service.

Discussing the prospect of such an experiment with homeless people, the research team were reminded that missing out is a regular part of these people's lives. Social service agencies sometimes 'cherry-pick' clients or reject those who have been difficult in the past. People with complex needs can miss out altogether. When staff at an agency know they are being externally evaluated, they can engage in 'soft targeting' to make their programs look better.

A randomised experiment is different. Anyone who satisfies the basic entry criteria has the same probability of getting into the program. This means that everyone starts with an equal chance.

Participants may not be happy when they find themselves in the control group: one person's response was a simple 'fuck you'. But the people conducting the study found that most homeless people understood the importance of having a credible comparison group. 'Rather than being cruel and unjust,' wrote researchers Guy Johnson, Sue Grigg and Yi-Ping Tseng, 'we felt that randomisation was the most fair, equitable and transparent means of allocating places in, and evaluating the impact of, social welfare programs.'[4]

The 'Journey to Social Inclusion' experiment was Australia's first randomised trial of a homelessness program. The intervention lasted for three years.[5] For the forty or so people in the treatment group, it provided intensive support from a social worker, who was responsible for only four clients. This caseworker might help them find housing, improve their health, reconnect with family and access job training. Another forty people in the control group did not receive any extra support. Both groups were paid $30 to answer surveys every six months.

What might we expect from the program? If you're like me, you'd have hoped that three years of intensive support would see all participants healthy, clean and employed. But by and large, that's not what the program found. Those who were randomly selected into the program were indeed more likely to have housing, and less likely to be in physical pain. But Journey to Social Inclusion had no impact on reducing drug use or improving mental health. In fact, those who received intensive support were more likely to be charged with a crime (perhaps because having stable housing made it easier for the police to find them). At the end of three years, just two people in the treatment group had a job – the same number as in the control group.[6]

While it's disappointing that the program didn't bring most participants back into mainstream society, it's less surprising once you begin to learn about the people it seeks to assist. In many cases, they were abused in childhood (the mother of one participant used to put Valium in the child's breakfast cereal). Most had used drugs for decades, and they were used to sleeping rough. Few had completed school or possessed the skills to hold down a regular job. If they had children of their own, more often than not they had been taken away by child protection services.

The Journey to Social Inclusion program is a reminder of how hard it is to turn around the living standards of the most disadvantaged. If you've been doing drugs for decades, your best hope is probably a stable methadone program. If you're in your late forties with no qualifications and no job history, a stable volunteering position is a more realistic prospect than a steady paycheck. If all your friends have criminal histories, it'll take more than a day a week with a social worker for you to build a stable social network. Change is possible, but it is more likely to be incremental than immediate. Hollywood loves to depict overnight transformations, but the more common trajectory for someone recovering from deep trauma looks more like two steps forward and one step back.

Unless we properly evaluate programs designed to help the long-term homeless, there's a risk that people of goodwill – social workers, public servants and philanthropists – will fall into the trap of thinking it's easy to change lives. There are plenty of evaluations of Australian homelessness programs that have produced better results than this one. But because none of those evaluations was as rigorously conducted as this one, there's a good chance they're overstating their achievements.

*

In Los Angeles, Maricela Quintanar said the biggest difference was the quiet. Gone was the party music, the sound of drug deals, the gunshots.[7] 'The only noise here is the cars,' she told a reporter.

It was 1997, and 28-year-old Maricela had moved with her family from a public housing project on the east side of the city to a privately rented apartment on the west side. Five years earlier, the videotaped beating of Rodney King had led to riots that left more than fifty people dead. Now, Maricela's family was part of an experiment to test one of the biggest questions in social science: how much do neighbourhoods matter?

For decades, scholars had argued over the causes of poverty, debating the effect of factors such as money, motivation and race. Many also believed that bad neighbourhoods kept poor people poor. If true, this had profound implications for poverty, suggesting that governments should worry not only about the adequacy of the social safety net, but also about geography.

To help answer this question, the US government had set up a randomised experiment known as the 'Moving to Opportunity' program. In five cities – Baltimore, Boston, Chicago, New York and Los Angeles – thousands of people living in high-poverty neighbourhoods signed up to be part of a program that gave them a chance of moving to a better area. They were then randomly assigned to one of three groups. One group was given a subsidised housing voucher and required to move to a low-poverty neighbourhood. Another group was given a housing voucher with no strings attached. A control group did not receive any voucher, and mostly stayed where they were, in public housing.

Maricela's family was randomly assigned housing in a low-poverty neighbourhood. With her husband and their two primary-school-aged children, she moved to Cheviot Hills on the opposite side of Los Angeles. On the west side, the children did better at school, but life was lonelier. In the early years after their move, the Quintanar family would return to their old east side neighbourhood each weekend to shop, meet friends and attend church.

Like fans awaiting a release by their favourite band, social scientists have hung on each wave of results of the Moving to Opportunity experiment.[8] At first, the results seemed disappointing. Adults who moved were no more likely to be employed. Children who moved did not seem to have better school results or fewer behavioural problems. A further wave of studies showed that girls who moved were less inclined to get into trouble, while boys engaged in more risky behaviours. For a family like the Quintanars, with a son and a daughter, this would not have been an overwhelming endorsement of the program.

The one way in which moving did seem to benefit families was in terms of health. Those who moved to low-poverty neighbourhoods were less likely to be obese, and tended to have better mental health. This should not have been surprising, given the level of danger in the communities from which families were moving. As one Baltimore boy told researchers, 'I don't like living around here 'cause people getting killed for nothing.'[9] A Chicago mother in the control group kept her young children indoors most of the time because 'bullets have no names'.[10]

Then, in 2015, researchers at Harvard matched up results from the experiment with taxation data, allowing them to look at the earnings of children who moved to a low-poverty neighbourhood before age thirteen.[11] The results were striking. Movers had earnings that were nearly one-third higher than those who'd stayed in a high-poverty neighbourhood, with the effect being roughly similar for men and women. Sustained over a lifetime, this suggests that a child who moves to a lower-poverty neighbourhood in their pre-teen years will earn $300,000 more over a lifetime. The societal gains massively outweighed the cost. Even the government came out ahead, with the participants paying more in additional taxes than the housing vouchers cost to provide.

In the United States, large-scale social experiments date back to the 1960s. As President Lyndon Johnson announced a 'war on poverty', policymakers considered whether providing a guaranteed income equal to the poverty line might discourage people from working. From 1968 to 1982, experiments across nine sites randomly assigned families into treatment and control groups, and then surveyed their work patterns. The experiments showed that providing a guaranteed income reduced time spent working, but the impact was smaller than many critics expected – around two to three weeks per year.[12] In coming years, the experiments helped shape reforms to the welfare system, including a massive expansion to wage subsidies in the 1990s under President Bill Clinton.[13] Promising that 'If you work, you shouldn't be poor', Clinton doubled the size of the Earned Income Tax Credit, pointing to the strong economic evidence that the program helped the poorest families. Today, the Earned Income Tax Credit is one of the nation's largest anti-poverty programs. Current estimates suggest that it keeps 5 million Americans above the poverty line.[14]

Another large-scale social experiment of that era was the RAND Health Insurance Experiment. Run from 1974 to 1982, researchers randomly assigned thousands of American families to health-care plans with varying levels of co-payment, ranging from 0 to 95 per cent. The study concluded that higher co-payments increased the chances that patients would discontinue treatment.[15] For patients who were both poor and sick, the co-payments led to worse health outcomes, with those who suffered from high blood pressure being 10 per cent more likely to die when their plan had a high co-payment.[16]

The RAND study remained the most important experimental evidence on health insurance until 2008, when an unusual situation arose in Oregon.[17] The state's government had decided to expand the number of low-income families covered by public health insurance by about 10,000. But for every available place, they had nearly nine people who wanted a spot. The government decided that the fairest way of allocating the new health-care places was to allocate them through a public lottery.

In effect, a lottery is a randomised trial. So by tracking the health of lottery winners and losers, researchers were able to study the impact of getting health insurance. They found that winning health insurance led to greater use of health services. And, just as with the RAND experiment, Oregon researchers found that being randomly selected to get health insurance meant that people reported better physical and mental health. In a typical year, a person with health insurance had sixteen more days in which they felt physically healthy, and twenty-five more days in which they felt mentally healthy.

Some lottery wins are more coveted than others. On 1 December 1969, CBS News suspended its regular programming to provide live coverage of the Vietnam draft lottery.[18] In a glass cylinder were 366 blue balls, each labelled with one day of the year. Every young man aged eighteen to twenty-six knew that the earlier his birthday was pulled out, the more likely he was to be conscripted to the military. September 14 was the first birthday drawn out, June 8 the last. The draft spawned street protests, and protest songs, from Creedence Clearwater Revival's 'Fortunate Son' to Pete Seeger's 'The Draft Dodger Rag'.

The immediate impact of being conscripted was a risk of being killed, and more than 17,000 American draftees lost their lives in Vietnam. What about those who survived? Jim, whose birthday was the second one drawn out, recalls that the military 'taught me how much I was capable of doing, and that nothing was impossible.'[19] But for others, the trauma of Vietnam left lifelong scars. As one returning veteran put it: 'A couple of years ago someone asked me if I still thought about Vietnam. I nearly laughed in their face. How do you stop thinking about it? Every day for the last thirty-eight years, I wake up with it, and go to bed with it.'[20]

In a series of studies, economists have analysed the Vietnam draft lottery as though it were a randomised trial. Among those of draft age, we should not expect the life outcomes of a man born on September 14 to be different from someone born on June 8. Any significant differences reflect the impact of military service.

For the United States, researchers found a significant negative impact on lifetime earnings, with most of the penalty coming in the 1970s and '80s.[21] Using the randomised experiment of the Vietnam draft, it turns out that veterans are also more likely to have moved interstate, and more likely to work for the government.[22] Some things are unaffected by service: veterans are just as likely to be married as non-veterans, and are just as healthy.[23] However, having a lower draft number (which made people more likely to be conscripted) did shape people in other ways. For example, in the early years after the war, those with lower draft numbers were more likely to be jailed for a violent crime.[24] Two decades after the Vietnam War ended, surveys found that having a low draft number made men more likely to support the Democratic Party, and more likely to hold anti-war beliefs.[25]

In Australia, the birthday conscription lotteries operated in a similar fashion, but the impact of being drafted to serve in Vietnam turned out to be quite different. Results from Australia's draft lotteries suggest that those who went to Vietnam were no more likely to commit a crime, but were significantly more likely to suffer from mental health problems.[26] The draft lottery evidence also suggests that Vietnam service had a much bigger negative impact on the earnings of Australian veterans than on that of American veterans.[27]

*

43

One of the big questions in social policy is how to help unemployed people find jobs. Unemployment means more than a lack of income – for many people it also represents a loss of self-esteem. As Scottish philosopher Thomas Carlyle once put it, 'A man willing to work, and unable to find work, is perhaps the saddest sight that fortune's inequality exhibits under this sun.'

Economists have long known some of the factors that seem to inoculate against joblessness. Strong literacy and numeracy skills, a post-school qualification, a sunny disposition and plenty of experience are all factors that make people less likely to become unemployed. Unfortunately, none of these is easy to achieve. So what might society do to help a struggling jobseeker who lacks these qualities?

Over recent decades, researchers have increasingly turned to randomised trials to test which programs might help unemployed people find jobs. As we've seen, this has often produced disappointing findings, such as the randomised evaluation of US job training which found that young people who participated in the programs earned less than those in the control group.[28] It's possible that the problem lies not with job training programs themselves, but with over-ambitious designers. After all, most of these programs lasted only weeks, and cost at most a few thousand dollars. Should we really have imagined that they would raise earnings – every year – by thousands of dollars?[29]

Ron Haskins, a social policy expert at the Brookings Institution, argues that rigorous evaluations of education and employment programs typically find that around 75 per cent 'have little or no effect'.[30] Still, there are some glimmers of light. Randomised trials in Denmark, Sweden and the United States point to the value of meetings with caseworkers in helping people transition from joblessness into work.[31] Part of the effect happens before the meeting, when the job-finding rate jumps by around 40 per cent. Just as we tend to brush our teeth

44

before seeing the dentist, a meeting with a caseworker appears to improve people's focus on finding a job.

Fortunately, there's also evidence that meetings themselves can help people find work, with job-finding rates increasing by 20 to 30 per cent afterwards. This perhaps reflects the fact that being an unemployed jobseeker can quickly become soul-destroying without someone to help guide you through the process. Because many unemployed workers have never been jobless before, caseworkers can provide advice on the best ways to search, how to write a résumé and how to get ready for an interview.[32]

Occasionally, inexpensive interventions have a significant payoff. In 2010 and 2011 the German government posted out a cheerful blue brochure to over 10,000 people who had recently lost their jobs.[33] *'Bleiben Sie aktiv!'* ('Stay active!'), the leaflet urged unemployed people. It discussed how the German economy had been recovering after the financial crisis, reminded people that unemployment can be bad for your physical and mental health, and suggested different ways they might look for a job. The leaflet boosted employment rates among those who received it. Each leaflet cost less than €1 to print and post, but boosted earnings among the target group by an average of €450. If you know another government intervention with a payoff ratio of 450 to 1, I want to hear about it.

Because job search is a kind of competition, we need to make sure that programs are having a population-wide impact. To see this, imagine that there's only one job available, and you were likely to get it over me. Now, suppose I am chosen for a program that improves my interview skills and I get the job instead. A randomised trial might show that the job search program worked because it gave me an edge. But if that came at your expense, then it's not clear that society is any better off. In this example, the program helped its participants but did nothing to bring down the overall unemployment rate.

We don't worry much about this issue when we're evaluating new medical treatments. After all, you and I aren't competing to be healthy. But in a situation where one person's gain might be another's loss, a randomised trial can give a misleadingly rosy view of the effectiveness of a program.

In 2007 the French government agreed to a novel way of answering this question.[34] Rather than just randomly assigning jobseekers, they ran a huge experiment across 235 different labour markets. Not only would jobseekers be randomly chosen for intensive help, but the experiment would vary the share of people in a given town or city who were in the experiment. In some places, the experiment would cover all the jobseekers, while in others it would cover just one-quarter of people looking for a job. Unfortunately, the trial showed a bigger effect when it was covering a smaller share of the population, suggesting that a good part of the 'gains' were simply due to displacement effects. This disappointing finding is a useful reminder of how tricky it can be to design policies that bring down the total unemployment rate.

In the face of rapid automation, some warn of a future labour market in which 'Humans Need Not Apply'. In such an environment, they argue, it might make more sense to provide unconditional cash payments than to insist jobseekers keep looking for work. In January 2017 Finland set about testing this approach by randomly selecting a small group of unemployed people. Those in the study receive a 'basic income' of €6720 per year, which continues to be paid even if they find a job.[35] The experiment, which covers 2000 people, will report its results in 2019. Advocates of a 'universal basic income' eagerly await the findings.

*

In recent decades, millions of young Americans have signed 'virginity pledges', promising to refrain from sex until they are married. The first such program – 'True Love Waits' – saw teenagers pledging 'to be sexually abstinent from this day until the day I enter a biblical marriage relationship'. However, randomised evaluations of abstinence-only programs found no evidence that they reduced the age at which young people first had sex, or the number of sexual partners they had.[36]

One possibility is that a virginity pledge is not taken particularly seriously. For example, one survey followed up five years after people had signed a virginity pledge, and found that four out of five youths denied that they had done so.[37] But it's also possible that abstinence-only programs are causing harm, by discouraging young people from planning for safe sex. After signing a virginity pledge, young people might feel it's a bit hypocritical to carry a condom or go on the pill. Some evidence suggests that abstinence-only programs lead to an increase in unsafe sex, pregnancy and exposure to sexually transmitted diseases.[38]

By contrast, other social policy programs have passed randomised trials with flying colours. Noticing the powerful impact of cigarette taxes in deterring young people from starting smoking, some researchers have experimented with financial incentives to encourage quitting.[39] One firm in the United States offered employees up to $750 if they could quit smoking for a year.[40] Those randomly chosen for the program were 10 percentage points more likely to quit. Because smokers have worse health and take more breaks during the day, they tend to be less productive than non-smokers.[41] One study suggested that the productivity gap between smokers and non-smokers exceeds $2000 a year.[42] This suggests that paying employees $750 to kick the habit is a great deal for the company – even ignoring the benefits to workers and their families.

Similarly strong results could be seen in a randomised trial in the Philippines, in which smokers were invited to deposit money into a savings account.[43] After six months they took a urine test for nicotine. Those who passed got their money back. Those who failed saw their savings donated to charity. The average deposit was significant – enough to buy cigarettes for half a year. Not surprisingly, participants wanted the money back, and this boosted their odds of quitting by 3 to 6 percentage points.

Mark Twain once said, 'Quitting smoking is easy. I've done it a thousand times.' The results from randomised trials suggest that perhaps Twain – who was often looking for ways to earn money – only needed the right financial incentive.[44]

We saw at the start of the chapter that programs for the long-term homeless don't necessarily move them into employment. But targeted assistance can achieve more modest goals. In New York, one experiment focused on people being released from psychiatric hospitals: strengthening their ties to friends and family, and providing emotional support.[45] Those randomly chosen to get support were five times less likely to be homeless. Timely assistance kept them off the streets.

Smart social policies can make a difference, but when it comes to building opportunity, plenty of people have argued that education is crucial. In a moment, I will delve into the world of educational experiments. But before that, let's take a pause from the research findings to look at some of the stories of randomistas who have shaped the field.

4

THE PIONEERS OF
RANDOMISATION

Charles Saunders Peirce had a rare nerve condition in which a slight touch of the face can trigger an agonising sensation as powerful as electric shock. According to his biographer, the pain caused him to be 'aloof, cold, depressed, extremely suspicious, impatient of the slightest crossing, and subject to violent outbursts of temper'.[1] To control it, he turned to drugs, including ether, morphine and cocaine. Peirce was largely home-schooled – by his father, a mathematics professor at Harvard. When Peirce himself arrived at Harvard, he often found himself bored in class, and graduated near the bottom of his year. Yet in 1885 Peirce published one of the first randomised experiments in the social sciences.[2] The goal was to test the accuracy of our sense of touch. In particular, the experiment aimed to assess how good we are at comparing physical weights. If I put a blindfold on you and put two different weights in your hands, I'll bet you could easily distinguish one object that weighs 50 per cent more than another. But could you tell the difference if the discrepancy in weights was just 10 per cent? Or 1 per cent?

Peirce's experiment was designed as follows. The test subject put one finger on a balance scale. From behind a screen, an experimenter added or removed small weights, based on random draws from a special pack of cards. The subject then said whether the weight had increased or decreased. At each sitting, the experiment was repeated fifty times. Peirce and his co-author, graduate student Joseph Jastrow, took turns to play the role of subject and experimenter. When the weight difference was 10 per cent, they found that the person being tested could correctly pick it nine times out of ten. But with a weight difference of just 1 per cent, the odds of success fell to two in three. Given that dumb luck would yield a success rate of one in two, this suggests that we don't have much ability to discern tiny differences.

Writing more than a century later, statistician Stephen Stigler argues that Peirce's study remains one of the best conducted experiments in psychology.[3] The researchers took care to ensure that the subject could not see how the weights were being varied, and used randomisation to prevent any subconscious biases from affecting the pattern of adding and subtracting weights. Future psychologists would learn from the weight study, and apply the same methods in their randomised experiments.

Peirce was a genius and a polymath. He would write out questions with his left hand and answer them with his right. His collected papers total over 100,000 pages, most of them unpublished. Peirce also made contributions in mathematics, astronomy, chemistry and meteorology. He is best known for his work as a philosopher, founding the philosophic tradition known as pragmatism.

But while he was working on his most famous paper, Peirce was embroiled in a scandal that led to him being fired by his university, Johns Hopkins. His wife having left him several years earlier, Peirce had begun living with another woman, Juliette. When the university's leadership found out about this 'immorality', they dismissed him.

Peirce hoped he might find a job at Harvard, where his father had enjoyed a prestigious academic career. But he had a powerful foe. While he was an undergraduate student, Peirce had vandalised a bench in one of his chemistry classes. He was fined a dollar at the time, but the episode would prove far costlier in the long term.[4] The chemistry instructor, Charles Eliot, became president of Harvard in 1869 and held the position for the next forty years. Eliot had formed a lifelong dislike of Peirce and vetoed him being employed at Harvard in any form. After his firing from Johns Hopkins, Peirce never again worked in academia. He spent the rest of his life trying to subsist on occasional jobs and the generosity of friends.

Peirce's randomised trial foreshadowed an entire discipline of experimental psychology. His protégé, Joseph Jastrow, became a professor of experimental and comparative psychology at the University of Wisconsin–Madison and published widely, using empirical techniques to help expose psychics as clever tricksters. Unlike Peirce, Jastrow was held in high regard by the profession; he served as president of the American Psychological Association and enjoyed fame through his regular psychology columns in popular magazines. Today, experimental psychology continues to blossom, its findings published in dozens of academic journals and eagerly reported in the media.[5] But Charles Peirce, the brilliant randomista who helped kickstart the field, would spend his final two decades unable to afford to heat his house, subsisting on bread donated by the local baker, and writing on the back of old manuscripts because he was too poor to buy paper.

Peirce is one of four pioneers of randomised trials whose lives I explore in this chapter. Working across psychology, agriculture, medicine and social policy, these men and women succeeded in persuading many sceptics of the value of controlled experiments. Their stories are a window into the unusual mix of talents required to be a successful randomista.

*

At an afternoon tea party in England in the 1920s, Ronald Fisher drew a cup of tea from the urn. Seeing Muriel Bristol standing next to him, he politely offered it to her. She declined, telling him that she preferred to put the milk in first. 'Nonsense,' smiled Fisher, 'it makes no difference.'[6]

At this point, many women might have just taken the cup. Fisher – a thin, short man with a beard and glasses – was hardly the most handsome man in England, but his reputation as a mathematician was growing rapidly. However, Bristol was not just any woman – she was an algae specialist at the research centre where they both worked. She held her ground. At this point, chemist William Roach, standing nearby, chimed in: 'Let's test her.' Could Bristol really tell how a cup of tea had been made?

Fisher quickly set out the experiment. With Roach as his assistant, they began pouring cups of tea, randomly varying whether the milk went into the cup first or last. Each time, Bristol took a sip, and confidently announced how the beverage had been prepared.

Eight cups of tea later, the tea party experiment had proven something new about each of the participants. In every instance, Muriel Bristol had correctly identified whether they were prepared by adding tea to milk, or milk to tea – showing that, for a connoisseur, it really does make a difference. Ronald Fisher, whom many now regard as the father of modern statistics, used the example to think about how many cups were necessary to distinguish luck from skill. William Roach might merely have been the assistant in the experiment, but evidently he performed with panache, for Bristol shortly afterwards accepted his marriage proposal.

Ronald Fisher was the youngest of five children. His mother, Kate, died when he was fourteen. For an academically inclined young man,

Fisher's nearsightedness might have been thought a serious impediment, but he turned it to his advantage – becoming adept at visualising problems in geometrical terms, rather than by working through pages of numerical proofs.

At twenty-two, Fisher graduated from Cambridge with first-class honours. He worked for a time as a high school maths teacher, then as a statistician in the City of London. When he was twenty-nine, he turned down a job at University College London for a much less certain proposition – casual employment at the Rothamsted Experimental Station in Hertfordshire. For Fisher, Rothamsted had one advantage: data. The centre had been running agricultural randomised trials for decades, and so provided the raw material for him to develop his statistical methods.

By the time of his fortieth birthday, Fisher had developed the statistical tests that are used today in almost every empirical paper published in the social sciences. Over his career, his research would also revolutionise biology – creating the 'modern synthesis' that used mathematics to integrate Mendelian genetics with Darwinian selection. And in farming, Fisher's experiments helped boost crop yields, saving millions from hunger and starvation.[7]

Yet Fisher had flaws aplenty. His early work on maximum likelihood techniques helped popularise the method, but his proofs were wrong. He was one of the most prominent eugenicists of his age – an advocate of the view that society should encourage the upper classes to have more children. In the aftermath of World War II, as a group of scientists worldwide sought to promote racial equality, Fisher disagreed, arguing that people of different races differed profoundly in their intellectual capacities. When early studies showed a link between smoking and lung cancer, Fisher questioned the credibility of their statistics.

Fisher's first published paper had been titled 'The evolution of Sexual Preference'. So it was either ironic or fitting that his own marriage eventually broke down. Perhaps exploiting his newfound freedom, he set up a mouse breeding program in his home – using the results for his own research papers. At the end of his life he took up a role as a senior research fellow at the Commonwealth Scientific and Industrial Research Organisation in Adelaide. He died there in 1962.

*

The first sign of tuberculosis is the cough. At first, most patients think they just have a cold. But as the weeks go on and the bacteria grows in the lungs, it becomes more painful. Many begin to cough up phlegm or blood. Tubercular patients lose their appetite, start to sweat at night and develop a fever. Sometimes the nails on their fingers and toes become enlarged. Unless a proper course of antimicrobial drugs is administered, active-stage tuberculosis will claim the lives of half of those infected.[8]

When World War I broke out, Austin Bradford Hill was finishing high school. Coming from a prominent British family, he was expected to follow his father into medicine. He was, in his own words, 'head of the school, captain of football, in the cricket XI, champion cross country runner, and a prig'.[9] Signing up as a naval pilot, Hill was sent to the Dardanelles, but contracted tuberculosis along the way, and was 'sent home to die'.

Hill was one of the lucky ones. Doctors administered the prevailing treatment: collapsing the infected lung. After a lung abscess and nine months in bed, he began a slow recovery. A career in medicine was now out of the question, but a family friend suggested that he could study economics by correspondence, so he signed up and completed his degree at the University of London in 1922. By now, Hill was well enough to travel, and the same family friend arranged for him to get a research grant to study the poor health of young people in rural Essex. Studies of occupational illness followed, documenting the medical condition of London bus drivers, cotton spinners and printers.

Hill loved medicine so much he read textbooks in his spare time. But his economics training gave him an entree into the burgeoning field of medical statistics. Hearing that a famous statistician was lecturing at University College London, Hill went along to listen. 'It was mathematical and entirely over my head,' he recalled, 'but I learned in the practical side of the course.' Within a few years, he would be combining research with teaching – but with a much less technical style. Hill's lectures were regarded as so crisp and clear that they were published in 1937 in *The Lancet*.

When it comes to medical statistics, 'common sense is not enough', Hill argued in his first published lecture. 'Mistakes which when pointed out look extremely foolish are quite frequently made by intelligent persons, and the same mistakes, or types of mistakes, crop up again and again.'[10] At the risk of seeming 'too simple', he proposed to set out the most frequent 'fallacies and misunderstandings', and show how to avoid them.

The lectures would ultimately become *Principles of Medical Statistics*, the most famous textbook in the field. But Hill was careful not to push his audience too far. 'I deliberately left out the words "randomisation" and "random sampling numbers" at that time, because I was trying to persuade the doctors to come into controlled trials in the very simplest form and I might have scared them off … I thought it would be better to get the doctors to walk first, before I tried to get them to run.'

In 1946 he saw his chance. Researchers at Rutgers University had been studying organisms that live in soil, and one of them, streptomycin, seemed to be effective against tuberculosis.[11] The US army tested the antibiotic on three patients. The first died, the second went blind, and the third recovered rapidly. This third patient's name was

Bob Dole – he would eventually become majority leader of the US Senate and the Republican presidential candidate in the 1996 election.

A success rate of one out of three was hardly conclusive, and Hill saw an opening to conduct a British trial of the new tuberculosis treatment. It had been three decades since he himself was 'left to die' from the disease, and tuberculosis still claimed the lives of 180,000 Britons annually.[12] Having spent the past ten years teaching doctors about the problems inherent in studies that just compared the treated with the untreated, Hill pushed hard for the streptomycin trial to be randomised. In the end, scarcity clinched it: 'We had no dollars and the amount we were allowed by the Treasury was enough only for, so to speak, a handful of patients. In that situation I said it would be unethical not to make a randomised controlled trial – the first of its kind.'

That bold claim – that it might be unethical *not* to conduct a randomised trial – was characteristic of Hill's self-confidence. Medical randomised trials were essentially unknown, and yet here he was telling the profession that a failure to conduct one would be immoral. Hill had no formal training in medicine, or in statistics, but he had spent years thinking through the issues as he taught his students and engaged with his research colleagues. The trial was a success, and streptomycin today remains one of the drugs that is used to treat tuberculosis.

In the past two centuries alone, tuberculosis has killed more than 1 billion people – more than the combined toll from all the wars and famines in that time.[13] Among the victims of 'the white plague' were Frédéric Chopin, Anton Chekhov, Franz Kafka, Emily Brontë, George Orwell and Eleanor Roosevelt. Today, tuberculosis still accounts for more than a million deaths worldwide each year. Strains of the disease that are resistant to streptomycin and other antibiotics are becoming increasingly prevalent. Austin Bradford Hill didn't eliminate the disease that nearly killed him. But he did help to transform medicine. As one colleague wrote of his contribution, Hill brought 'a quantitative approach to the prevention of diseases'.

*

After four decades of conducting randomised trials in social policy, Judith Gueron has dozens of maxims for researchers: 'Never say that something about the research is too complex to get into.' 'If pressed on an awkward issue about random assignment, do not give an evasive answer ... if site people [those implementing the experiment] forcefully ask if you really mean they will have to deny services to those in the control group, say "yes".' 'If someone is unreservedly enthusiastic about the study, he or she doesn't understand it.'[14] It's hard-won wisdom, emerging from more than thirty large-scale social policy trials, involving a total of 300,000 participants.[15]

In 1974 the Ford Foundation and six federal government agencies created the Manpower Demonstration Research Corporation, now known simply as MDRC. Its mission was to improve understanding about what worked in social policy by conducting random assignment studies. Judith Gueron, then aged thirty-three and having received her Harvard economics PhD just a few years earlier, became MDRC's first research director.

Raised in Manhattan, Gueron attributes her ambition and confidence to having a father who told her 'for as long as I can remember, that girls, and I in particular, could do anything'.[16] In her work at MDRC, she would need this self-belief. Not only were the fields of economics and policy evaluation heavily male-dominated, but experiments were a radical idea. At that time, academics didn't get tenure by doing randomised trials, but with complex mathematical models. MDRC was 'a lonely band of zealots'.[17]

Gueron's first major experiment tested whether long-term welfare recipients and people considered 'unemployable' could be supported into jobs. Random assignment had never before been attempted on a large multisite employment program of this scale. Gueron's team were warned it would be impossible, that 'asking program operators to turn people away would be like asking doctors to deny a patient a known cure'.[18]

To address the criticism that they were being cold-hearted towards a deserving group of people, MDRC came up with a clever solution: they would expand the size of the treatment group so that it used every last dollar of available funding. That meant their detractors could not credibly claim that having a control group denied worthy recipients from getting a supported job. Even if you scrapped the control group, the number of people who received the treatment would be unchanged.

Gueron recalls how the staff felt as the program was rolled out. They all hoped it would succeed, but had to keep reminding themselves that it probably would not. 'Fortunately for MDRC in these formative years, we had random assignment – with its inexorable comparison of experimental versus control outcomes – to keep us honest and help us avoid the pitfalls of advocacy research'.[19] To Gueron, MDRC was not just 'another do-gooder organisation'. Staff morale had to hinge on rigorous evaluation, not on whether the programs it scrutinised turned out to be effective.

When the results from the first evaluation rolled in, they showed that the supported work program helped women, but not men. And even for the women the impacts were small. When participants found employment, the government reduced their welfare benefits. Since the jobs didn't pay much, the net effect was only a slight fall in poverty rates. The program was effective, but no panacea. Yet to Gueron, what mattered most wasn't the results, but how they had judged the program. A naive evaluator might simply have looked at the raw outcomes, which showed that more men found jobs than women. Yet a randomised evaluation showed that this had nothing to do with the program: men in the control group were just as likely to get jobs as men in the treatment group. It took randomisation to reveal the truth. Gueron was 'hooked . . . on the beauty and power of an experiment'.[20]

Throughout the 1980s and '90s, Gueron worked with state and local agencies across the United States. These were controversial times for welfare policy. Ronald Reagan had told his campaign rallies the story of a 'Cadillac-driving welfare queen': an African-American woman who defrauded the welfare system.[21] Critics claimed that forcing welfare recipients into low-paid jobs was 'modern-day slavery'. Bill Clinton ran for president on a pledge to 'end welfare as we know it'. The debate over income support was fuelled by ideology on both sides.

And then there was MDRC. Read the newspapers of the era, and you come across prudent comments from Gueron: 'We should be cautious about what we've got here', 'We haven't found the pink pill', it's not a 'quick fix for poverty'.[22] Even when social programs paid for themselves, her praise was measured.

Getting started with a new randomised evaluation could be tough. In San Jose, Gueron wanted to evaluate a job-training program for young migrants from Mexico. The managers of the program told her that turning away people at random was inconsistent with their mission – the staff would never agree to it. So she met with the staff and explained why random assignment was uniquely reliable and believed. A positive finding, Gueron told the team, might convince the federal government to fund programs like theirs. 'They agonized about the pain of turning away needy young people, and they talked about whether this would be justified if, as a result, other youth gained new opportunities. Then they asked us to leave the room, talked more, and voted. Shortly thereafter, we were ushered back in and told that random assignment had won.'[23] The evaluation showed positive results, and prompted the federal government to fund an expansion across fifteen more sites.

Many of MDRC's evaluations showed that programs worked, but they rarely worked miracles.[24] Sometimes the successes were confined to particular groups of participants, or to certain welfare offices. The experiments often overturned the preconceptions of the social work community. In Louisville, counsellors were confident that they knew which clients were job-ready. Gueron's random assignment study proved that it wasn't possible to predict success in advance: the job market often threw up surprises.

Taking over as MDRC president in 1986, Gueron became better at explaining to people who ran social programs why random assignment was fair. In one instance, a county commissioner continued random assignment after the research ended, seeing it as a just and unbiased way of choosing who would be assisted.[25]

Others weren't so warm. In 1990 Florida legislator Ben Graber tried to shut down MDRC's evaluation of 'Project Independence', an employment program. Random assignment, Graber said, was treating welfare recipients like 'guinea pigs'. He foreshadowed legislation that would ban the use of control groups. The media was quick to pick up the story. The *Miami Herald* editorialised that randomisation was 'misguided, wasteful, cold-hearted, and just plain dumb'. The *St. Petersburg Times* editorial called it 'a cruel joke' which would spend millions of dollars to deny mothers with small children the job training they deserved. Within weeks, politicians in other states were announcing their opposition to randomised trials. The *Washington Times* predicted: 'Public protest precipitates end of welfare experimentation'.[26]

Testifying in Florida, Gueron focused on the fact that the program had never been properly evaluated. 'If we had a readily available wonder drug to help people be self-sufficient and off of welfare, I'm sure there isn't a person in this room who would not use it. If Project Independence is that, I assume you would put more money into it. Since we don't know that and the funds are not there, you would be wise to get the answers first.'[27] The legislature approved the trial. A few years later, the evaluation results were in: the employment program saved the taxpayer about as much as it cost to run. It wasn't a wonder drug, but it was worth continuing. The Florida press had compared Gueron's team to scientists pulling the legs off spiders, but they had fought back, and managed to produce the definitive evaluation of Project Independence.

Before the use of randomised evaluation, debates over social programs often featured conflicting studies, using a tangle of approaches. When the experts diverged, policymakers and the public were torn. As economist Henry Aaron remarked, 'What is an ordinary member of the tribe to do when the witch doctors disagree?'[28] In the Florida case, the official in charge of Project Independence came to Gueron after commissioning three non-randomised studies, all of which used different methodologies and arrived at different conclusions. 'The only way to get out of the pickle of these duelling unprovable things,' he decided, 'was to get an evaluation of unquestioned quality.'[29] To Gueron, randomised evaluation was a powerful communications tool because of its simplicity. 'Anyone could understand the basics of the analysis. There was no fancy statistical footwork.'[30]

In the late 1960s, Gueron recalls, 'researchers knew in theory the power of random assignment. They just didn't believe it would be useful to evaluate real-world social programs and address important policy questions.'[31] But over her career Gueron successfully deployed policy experiments in courtrooms, schools, community colleges, job training centres and community organisations. Over time, she ceased warning her colleagues that 'no one wants to be in a random assignment study'.[32] MDRC was turned down more often than accepted, but the popularity of social experiments steadily grew. They were straight-forward, and made it harder to hide failure.

'The key thing about random assignment,' Gueron concludes, 'is that it is the epitome of transparency. You flip a coin. You create two groups or more. You calculate average outcomes. And you subtract . . . That power is to be treasured, and contrasted with many prior and other evaluations that have led to disputes among experts about methodology, which is the death knell for research having an impact on policy.'[33] The chief lesson she draws from her career: 'Fighting for random assignment is worth it.'

5

LEARNING HOW
TO TEACH

O scar the Grouch gives children permission to feel sad. Big Bird questions everything. Mr. Snuffleupagus is the imaginary friend. Count von Count loves mathematics. Grover embodies self-confidence. Ernie delights in practical jokes. Bert has an utterly different personality to Ernie, but is his best friend nonetheless. Kermit the Frog is always a gentleman.

In 1967, Joan Cooney began to plan a television show unlike any other: a collaboration between creative designers and child science experts. At a time when children were watching shows like *Looney Tunes* and *The Flintstones*, this would be a television program that followed its own academic curriculum. Most unusually, the Children's Television Workshop would use evidence to shape the show. The idea of combining research with television production was, Cooney says, 'positively heretical'.[1] And so it was that an unorthodox team of designers and social scientists created *Sesame Street*.

In its first year, *Sesame Street* was evaluated in a randomised trial, which compared a treatment group (children who were encouraged to watch the program) with a regular control group. Unfortunately, the researchers hadn't reckoned on the show's popularity. With more than one-third of American children tuning in to each episode, there wasn't much difference in viewing rates between the two groups.[2]

So the next year, researchers took a different approach – focusing on cities where *Sesame Street* was only available on cable and then randomly providing cable television to a subset of low-income households, whose children were encouraged to watch Big Bird and friends. This time, there was a big difference in viewing rates between the control group (without *Sesame Street*) and the treatment group – and a significant difference in vocabulary.[3] Children who watched *Sesame Street* had the same cognitive skills as non-viewers who were a year older.

In the past half-century, over a thousand research studies have been conducted on *Sesame Street*, many of them feeding back into the show's development.[4] In one experiment, the show's designers wanted to find out how best to teach preschoolers the functions of their eyes, nose and mouth. Groups of young children were randomly assigned to watch either a test video featuring Grover interacting with a little girl named Chelsea, or a video with Elmo pointing out body parts on the Mona Lisa painting. When tested afterwards, children who had been allocated to watch the video with Grover had a better grasp of how their body parts worked than children who watched the video with Elmo. The researchers concluded that the painting was too abstract a teaching tool, and that children learned body parts best in a segment featuring both a Muppet and a human actor.

In teaching children about the concepts of animate and inanimate objects, a randomised study showed that preschoolers became confused when the show included both plants and animals. Children could understand why a chicken was in a different category from a rock – but adding a tree created too much confusion. After testing different variants of the 'What's Alive?' segment, the show designers removed the tree and aired a segment simply comparing animals with inanimate objects.

Another question was how many letters of the alphabet should be taught in each episode. *Sesame Street* designers randomly assigned preschoolers to watch episodes with two 'Letters of the Day' or with one 'Letter of the Day'. They found that doubling the letters wasn't an effective way to teach. Asked afterwards to correctly identify letters, children who watched episodes with two letters were less likely to know either of them than children who had watched an episode with just one letter.

Research even determined which subjects went to air. A pilot program about the death of storekeeper Mr Hooper showed that it gave children a better understanding of death, without adverse reactions. But a pilot about the divorce of Mr Snuffleupagus's parents left some children in the test audience with the mistaken impression that all parental arguments invariably lead to divorce. *Sesame Street* aired the show about death, but the program about divorce was never broadcast.

*

How we understand childhood is inextricably linked to the question of whether it's worth investing early in helping children. Indeed, we often put the spotlight on what young children are unable to do. They can't feed themselves, walk or kick a ball, and they make lousy dinner party guests. The word 'infant' derives from the Latin adjective *infans*, meaning 'not speaking'. Inadvertently, we see children as defective adults. We think the role of parents and educators is to correct their mistakes, keep them out of trouble and help them grow up to be perfect, like mum and dad (or so we tell ourselves!).

Psychologist Alison Gopnik advocates a different view. If a family were a corporation, she says, children would be the research and development division, while adults would be the production and marketing departments. 'They [children] think up a million new ideas, mostly useless, and we take the three or four good ones and make them real.'[5] From this perspective, creating environments where children can play creatively is vital to ensuring we thrive as a species. It also shapes how we think about children from disadvantaged backgrounds, and whether their life chances are predetermined or malleable.

In 1958 another psychologist, David Weikart, took up the job of being director of special education in Ypsilanti, Michigan.[6] At that time, schools were segregated, and all the African-American students in the town attended one primary school – the Perry School. Weikart noticed that the school was run down. Instead of a playground, it had a field filled with thistles. Many of the African-American students ended up repeating grades, entering special education or leaving school early.

Yet when Weikart gave a presentation to school principals about these problems, users responded defensively. One sat with arms tightly folded; others stood by the window smoking; a few left the room. When he pressed them to act, they said there was nothing they could do. Black students were just born that way. So Weikart came up with an alternative solution: 'Because I couldn't change the schools ... well, obviously you do it before school.'

In the late 1950s the only institutions that looked anything like preschools were nursery schools, focused purely on play. By contrast, Weikart was interested in the work of psychologists such as Jean Piaget, which suggested that young children's minds are actively developing from the moment they are born. But when it came to early intervention, Weikart noted, 'There was no evidence that it would be helpful. There wasn't data.' So he decided to put Piaget's theories to their first rigorous test.

66

In 1962 the Perry Preschool opened, for children aged three and four. Twenty-eight families had expressed interest in enrolling their children. From these, the researchers had chosen thirteen to attend preschool, while fifteen remained as a control group.[7] The selection was random – literally made by the toss of a coin. Over the next four years, the experiment would grow to 123 children (fifty-eight who attended, and a control group of sixty-five).

Former Perry Preschool teacher Evelyn Moore remembers how the program pushed back against the prevailing wisdom that a child's intelligence was fixed, and that many of the children in the community were 'retarded'. She saw something different – these children knew the names of baseball players. They recalled the words to songs. And their parents had hope. When Moore visited the families at home, she saw that almost all had pictures on the wall of two men – John F. Kennedy and Martin Luther King.

The preschool curriculum was highly verbal. Children were taught to draw, to make up stories and to complete increasingly complicated puzzles. Teachers asked open-ended questions, in a teaching technique known as 'verbal bombardment'.[8] They visited a farm, a fire station and an apple orchard, where they picked apples and cooked them into apple sauce. Months later, in winter, they went back to the orchard to see the seasonal change. When Evelyn Moore asked the children where the apples had gone, one child reflexively replied, 'Teacher, I didn't take 'em.'

Decades later, one participant, 'David', recalled how Perry Preschool wove education throughout the daily experience: 'even during the playtime there seemed to be a learning component to it. I understand it now as relationship building, playing games with others, getting used to interacting with others.'

The Perry Preschool program lasted only two years, but over the coming decades researchers tracked the outcomes for those who had participated, and for the randomly selected control group. In the early years they found that those who had attended preschool did better on IQ tests – but this effect faded over time.[9] Then in the teenage years they began to notice other impacts. Seventy-seven per cent of pre-school participants finished Year 12, compared with 60 per cent of those in the control group. By the time they were in their twenties, those who had been to preschool were more likely to own a car, own a home and have a steady job. They were also less likely to use drugs and less likely to be on welfare. By age forty, 28 per cent of those in the preschool group had been to jail, compared with 52 per cent of the control group.

The leading economic analysis of the program estimates that for every $1 spent on Perry Preschool, the community gained between $7 and $12.[10] By far the biggest benefit came from reduced crime, show-ing that if you target early intervention at people with a fifty-fifty chance of going to prison, you can change the lives of participants at a reasonable cost to the broader community.

In the decades since, randomised evaluations of early childhood programs for extremely disadvantaged children have continued to show benefits.[11] From 1972 to 1977, 111 infants in North Carolina participated in the Abecedarian experiment, which provided five days a week of care for children from four months of age all the way until they entered primary school. When they grew up, participants were more likely to attend university, more likely to be employed as adults, and tended to wait longer before having children of their own.[12] By the time the participants were in their mid-thirties, it had been three decades since the program ended. And yet those who had been part of the Abecedarian Project had significantly lower blood pressure.[13]

Other randomised trials to help young children have focused on parenting strategies. 'Triple P', a positive parenting program designed at the University of Queensland, works with parents over about eight sessions to build up skills in praising children, creating engaging activities, setting rules and managing misbehaviour. Randomised trials have shown Triple P to be effective at making parents feel more confident in their parenting skills, and at reducing the amount of misbehaviour that parents observe.[14]

Seeing these results in the mainstream community, a team of education researchers in Brisbane worked with Indigenous social workers to develop a culturally appropriate version of Triple P, and then tested it via a randomised trial.[15] The experiment involved fifty-one families, the sort of sample size that often makes it impossible to discern true policy impacts from background statistical noise. However, in this case the effect of Triple P was so large that it led to a statistically significant drop in the share of children who showed behavioural problems. Psychologists administered a test that asked about thirty-six problematic behaviours. As a result of Triple P, children reported six fewer of these behaviours – moving the average child in the sample out of the 'clinical range' and into the 'normal range'.

In Ireland, which has one of the highest rates of child poverty in the advanced world, a twelve-session positive parenting program called the Incredible Years Basic Parenting Programme has shown similarly powerful results in children aged three to seven.[16] Targeted at some of the most disadvantaged children in Ireland, the early findings of the randomised trial suggest that intervening in the 'incredible years' could ultimately have incredible results for the community, reducing crime, welfare spending and health-care bills.[17]

Some parenting interventions begin when the children are just infants, with home visits by nurses in the first months of a child's life.[18] These programs typically target children who might be 'at risk': because the parents are poor, because the babies had low birth weight, or because social service agencies are concerned about the family's wellbeing. Nurses provide counselling, offer advice on getting babies to sleep and remind parents of the importance of talking and singing to their newborn. Randomised evaluations have found that home visits from nurses lead to better parenting and improvements in child cognition. There is also evidence that nurse home visits reduce the number of women who suffer from physical or sexual violence at the hands of their partners.[19]

But a careful synthesis of the evidence also pointed to the value of randomised trials in getting a realistic measurement of the effects. It found that non-randomised studies tended to overestimate the benefits of nurse home visits by a factor of three to six.[20] It's hard to be sure precisely what went wrong with the non-randomised studies, but one possibility is that they compared parents who asked for a home visit with those who did not request one. If parents who wanted a nurse to come to their home were a little more motivated, then this would likely skew the result in favour of home visits.

Neuroscience has provided a powerful motivation for early intervention. As early childhood researcher Dana Suskind puts it, our liver, lungs and heart work perfectly from day one. Only the brain is partially developed at birth.[21] And yet there is also a risk that neuroscience will be misused – either to justify any early intervention, or to suggest that disadvantage in the early years causes irreversible damage. Some people mistakenly jump from the fact that the brain is four-fifths of its full size by age three to conclude that all early years programs are great value for money. One shocking brain scan showing the underdeveloped brain of a three-year-old pops up frequently in PowerPoint presentations and TED talks by advocates, but no one seems to know where the image comes from, let alone the circumstances of the child's upbringing. In Europe, the '1001 critical days' movement has argued that this period determines how a child functions throughout life – sometimes going so far as to claim that 'age two is too late'.[22] The movement would do better to focus on rigorously analysing what works, rather than alleging that it's 'game over' once a child becomes a toddler.

In Melbourne, half a century after David Weikart set up the Perry Preschool, a group of researchers are applying a scientific approach to understanding how to design an effective early childhood program for children at risk. The Early Years Education Program is Australia's first randomised trial of high-quality early learning for extremely disadvantaged children.[23]

Walking into the early years centre in West Heidelberg, I'm struck immediately by how homely it feels, with soft lighting, rugs and couches. The play area looks fresh, and there are chickens and guinea pigs in cages. Inside, the educators exude calm and confidence. Most have more than a decade's experience in early childhood. At the youngest ages, there are only three children for every adult.

Like a hospital intensive care unit, the aim of the centre is to repair trauma. Severe challenges like drug abuse and family breakdown have led to an atmosphere of 'toxic stress' in the lives of the infants and toddlers who attend. A four-year-old boy, 'Will', has been excluded from two childcare services because of biting, swearing, spitting and urinating in the playroom.[24] Will's mother endured three violent relationships, and Will himself was sexually abused at the age of three by one of his mother's partners. His mother regularly smacks him and shouts at him, and Will still wears nappies because he is too frightened to use the toilet.

Left in this situation, Will could easily end up in child protection, on welfare or in jail. Over the course of his life, he might experience extreme hardship, as well as costing the community hundreds of thousands of dollars. And yet the West Heidelberg centre isn't cheap either. Will benefits from highly qualified educators, small group sizes and a kitchen that provides him with two meals a day. The early signs are good: Will has been put in charge of caring for the chickens and collecting their eggs. But only a rigorous analysis will help us know if the benefits to Will and the other children at the centre justify the expense.

Talking with parents involved in the Early Years Education Program, I'm struck by the tension that they felt during the randomisation process.[25] A mother told me she held her breath as the news came through on the telephone. Parents are told when they apply that their odds of getting a place are 50/50. To some, it feels like a lottery, but places in the centre are limited and families who are not chosen are still able to access regular childcare. As one researcher observes to me, 'A 50 per cent chance is better than many of these families get in many other parts of their lives.'

Without randomisation, there's invariably the risk that those who attend the centre will be the children with the most motivated parents, whose children might have had better outcomes regardless. Because the researchers are confident that they have a credible comparison group, they hope to follow both groups for the next fifty years: to understand whether a great early childhood education really does transform lives.

*

Among education researchers, randomised evaluations have traditionally been viewed with suspicion. There is no shortage of discontent about the current state of knowledge, and much has been spent on educational evaluations. But as one analysis pointed out a decade ago, 'not much has been learned about what works'.[26] Prominent education researchers have tended to reject randomised trials, wielding arguments that the world is too complex, control groups are unethical, or randomised trials are politically unfeasible.[27]

Making schools work better is a truly complicated task. From their first day of class to Year 12, students spend around 16,000 hours at school. But that's only a small fraction of their waking hours, so it's perhaps not surprising that around half the variation in student performance is determined by families, not schools.[28] Teachers have always had to deal with young people's backchat, indolence and hormones. Today, they must also hold the attention of children who are avid users of smartphones, tablets and gaming consoles.

Schools, too, are facing challenges in attracting and retaining staff. Half a century ago, schools were one of the main employers of working women, who faced much worse gender discrimination in other occupations. Now, high-achieving women have promising career options in business, medicine and law. Consequently, the academic standards of new teachers have slipped backwards.

The results are showing up in test scores. Over the past century, intelligence tests administered across the population have shown a steady increase, decade on decade. But it now looks like the 'Flynn effect' – named after New Zealand social scientist James Flynn – may be driven mostly by the fact that we are getting more education rather than because our schools are improving. Over the past two decades, in the Programme for International Student Assessment, the OECD has administered standardised tests to a sample of 15-year-olds. In many advanced nations, test results are getting worse. Average test scores in advanced countries have fallen in mathematics, reading and science.[29] How do we turn these trends around?

Randomised trials of school-based programs can produce some surprises. In recent years, the US Department of Education devoted over a billion dollars annually to an after-school program known as the 21st Century Community Learning Center initiative.[30] Children attend the centres for up to four hours of after-school programs, which can involve everything from tutoring to drama to sports. An early evaluation of the program drew positive conclusions about its effectiveness. Surveying teachers, researchers found that children who attended the centres had made improvement over the year in their academic performance, motivation, attentiveness and classroom behaviour.[31]

This sounds promising, until you stop and think for a moment about the counterfactual. In effect, the researchers were assuming that from one year to the next, children make no improvement in their understanding of the subject matter or ability to learn. They were attributing any improvement in how students think or behave to the after-school program. This meant that the evaluators were putting a heavy thumb on the scales in favour of the program.

Then a team of economists at Mathematica, a policy research organisation that specialises in randomised trials, released the results of their evaluation. Rather than comparing students to how they were a year ago, the Mathematica evaluation randomly assigned primary school students to attend an after-school program or to the control group (which generally meant being at home with a parent or relative).

The results were starkly different from the earlier evaluation. Children who attended after-school programs were significantly more likely to misbehave at school – engaging in behaviour that led to detention, to their parents being called to school, and to discipline problems.[32] Attending an after-school program raised the chances of a child being suspended from 8 per cent to 12 per cent: perhaps because going to an after-school centre raised the odds that children would fall in with the wrong crowd. Ultimately, there was no evidence that the after-school program improved academic outcomes, but plenty of evidence that it worsened behaviour.[33] A program costing American taxpayers over a billion dollars a year was failing to improve student learning and creating disciplinary problems.

Unfortunately, the story does not have a happy ending. A group of advocates, the most prominent among them the former Californian governor Arnold Schwarzenegger, have successfully lobbied to maintain federal funding for 21st Century Community Learning Centers. Schwarzenegger felt no obligation to discuss the data or explain why he thought the Mathematica study was flawed. Instead, he airily argued, 'It would be a mistake, let me repeat, a big mistake, to use that study as justification to reduce current funding levels for after-school programs.'[34] The US Congress decided to keep funding the program. Congress might otherwise have chosen to spend the money in ways that have been proven to help low-income children. For example, a billion dollars could provide home visits from nurses for 88,000 first-time mothers, high-quality early childhood programs to 96,000 preschoolers, intensive reading support to 295,000 third-graders, or an evidence-based program to reduce teen pregnancy to 1.3 million teens.[35]

In the United Kingdom, the Education Endowment Foundation (EEF) has commissioned over a hundred evaluations, many of them randomised, to test what works in the classroom. Among those randomised evaluations that produced positive results are personal academic coaching, individual reading assistance, a Singaporean-designed mathematics teaching program, and a philosophy-based intervention encouraging students to become more engaged in classroom discussion.[36]

Because the EEF is running a large number of randomised trials, its evaluation experts are also working to ensure that researchers can compare the size of the results. Just as when buying a car, the right question isn't 'How good is it?' but 'What do I get for my money?' Resources will always be scarce in education, so knowing which programs are the most efficient is vital.

One way that the EEF compares programs is by looking at how much it costs to improve a pupil's performance by the equivalent of one month's learning.[37] Even among effective programs, they found wide divergence. To get a one-month improvement for one student, personal academic coaching cost £280, individual reading assistance cost £209, the mathematics teaching program cost £60, and the philosophy-based intervention cost £8.[38] So while all the programs 'worked', some were a whopping thirty-five times more cost-effective than others.

In some cases, the EEF trialled programs that sounded promising, but failed to deliver. The Chatterbooks program was created for children who were falling behind in English.[39] Hosted by libraries on a Saturday morning and led by trained reading instructors the program gave primary school students a chance to read and discuss a new children's book. Chatterbooks is the kind of program that warms the cockles of your heart. Alas, a randomised trial found that it produced zero improvement in reading abilities.

Another EEF trial tested the claim that learning music makes you smarter. One former president of the National Association for Music Education insisted: 'Music enhances knowledge in the areas of mathematics, science, geography, history, foreign language, physical education, and vocational training.'[40] Most studies of this question have compared those who choose to study a musical instrument with those who do not. But children who take up the violin at age three might already be different – more driven, more cognitively gifted or with pushier parents – than those who do not. In the EEF study, 900 students were randomly assigned either to music or drama classes, and then tested for literacy and numeracy.[41] The researchers found no difference between the two groups; suggesting either that learning music isn't as good for your brain as we'd thought, or that drama lessons are equally beneficial.

Across the Atlantic, even fewer educational interventions have been found to be supported by rigorous evidence. In 2002 the United States established the What Works Clearinghouse, a federal body responsible for assessing the scientific evidence on which education interventions are most effective – looking at everything from science teaching to assisting students with disabilities. In its first decade, nine in ten of the randomised trials commissioned by the What Works Clearinghouse failed to produce positive effects.[42] Wags began calling it the 'Nothing Works Clearinghouse'.[43]

Over the years since, the Clearinghouse has managed to garner bipartisan support. As well as commissioning new studies, the body is also responsible for sifting through the available evidence – looking at what the best evaluations conclude. To get the highest rating, studies must use random assignment.[44] Given the decentralised nature of US school education, the What Works Clearinghouse serves as a resource for educators and parents alike.

While many new programs don't work, some have produced significant impacts. In one experiment, the Bill & Melinda Gates Foundation conducted a randomised trial of coaching programs for teachers. Each month, teachers sent videos of their lessons to an expert coach, who worked with them to eliminate bad habits and try new techniques. By the end of the year, teachers in the coaching program had seen gains in their classroom equivalent to several additional months of learning.[45]

With technology proliferating in schools, randomised trials are exploring whether hardware and software can help children learn faster. Giving free computers to schoolchildren tends not to have much of an impact on students' literacy and numeracy scores.[46] But experiments evaluating online learning tools have found sizable impacts, particularly for mathematics.[47] By turning problems into games, breaking down skills into digestible chunks and providing rapid feedback, applications such as ASSISTments and SimCalc have boosted achievement in arithmetic, algebra and calculus. Randomised trials have backed some unconventional strategies to raise school performance. In Israel, a randomised trial in forty low-achieving schools saw students offered a $1500 payment for passing their final exams. The payment raised school completion rates by more than one-third.[48] In the UK, weekly text messages to parents about the dates of upcoming tests and what students were learning that week boosted the performance of high schoolers.[49] Relative to a randomised control group, the text messages (costing £6 per pupil) improved mathematics performance by a month of additional learning per year. Another cost-effective intervention sent letters to parents whose children were missing a lot of school (on average, seventeen days per year).[50] Because parents underestimated their children's absences, simply telling them the statistics on how many days their children missed had the effect of cutting absences by one-tenth.

Massive impacts have also been observed in a randomised evaluation of the Promise Academy, an unusual school in New York's Harlem district. Outcomes for young people in Harlem were dreadful: a study once found that life expectancy for young men born in Harlem was lower than for those born in Bangladesh.[51] Cocaine, guns, unemployment and family breakdown created an environment where disadvantage was perpetuated from one generation to the next. Founded in 2004, the Promise Academy has an extended school day, with classes running from 8 am to 4 pm, and after-school activities often continuing until 7 pm. There are remedial classes on Saturdays, and the summer break is shorter than in most schools. The result is that students spend nearly 50 per cent more time in school than the typical child. The school operates on a 'no excuses' model, emphasising grit and perseverance. It is assumed that every child will go on to university. Both students and teachers are heavily monitored, with a strong focus on test score gains.

The Promise Academy is one of 6900 public charter schools in the United States. When such schools have more applicants than places, they assign spots based on a lottery. Like a Powerball draw or the Vietnam draft, these charter school lotteries are carried out publicly.

A few use computer algorithms. Others write students' names on pieces of paper and draw them out of a box. In some cases, schools borrow the same equipment used by gambling lotteries, assigning students a number and then drawing the balls out of a cage. The documentary *Waiting for Superman* shows the selection process for two Harlem schools, where there are twenty applicants for every lottery place. As students are selected, we see their parents screaming for joy. Afterwards, we see the tears on the faces of unsuccessful parents. Those who miss out include Bianca, a kindergarten student whose mother works multiple jobs in the hope of Bianca getting to college; and Francisco, a first-grader who is struggling with his reading.

From the ecstasy and heartbreak of the lottery comes a clear comparison. Researchers followed students like Bianca and Francisco, and compared them with students who had won a place in the Promise Academy. They found that the school had a massive impact on performance. Across the United States, the average black high school student is two to four years behind his or her white counterparts. Students who won a lottery to attend the Promise Academy improved their performance by enough to close the black–white test score gap.[52] As lead researcher Roland Fryer points out, this overturns the fatalistic view that poverty is entrenched, and schools are incapable of making a transformational difference. He claims that the achievements of the Harlem Children's Zone are 'the equivalent of curing cancer for these kids'. 'It's amazing,' he muses. It should be celebrated.'[53] In a nation where racial gaps persist everywhere from home ownership to life expectancy, programs like this one offer the potential for fulfilling the founding promise that 'all men are created equal'.

Passion for social reform can go along with rigorous assessment of interventions. The Thirty Million Words Initiative is named after a 1995 study which suggested that disadvantaged children might hear 30 million fewer words by their fourth birthday than children from affluent backgrounds.[54] The institute's founders thought that one way of overcoming that gap might be to provide parents with feedback about how well they were doing in chatting with their children. When the study was carried out over two decades ago, the only way of counting words was to have a researcher in the room. But today voice recognition devices can do the job. For around $400, a digital device called LENA (for 'language environment analysis') sits in a child's pocket and counts how many words parents and children say to one another. So the Thirty Million Words Initiative is carrying out a randomised trial to see whether giving parents daily data on how much they have been speaking with their children will encourage them to do more of it. So far, the results are promising.[55]

The best non-government organisations are always looking for ways to put their programs to the test, and so improve what they do. They know that a lousy outcome for a program is ultimately a great result for the community, because it means we can stop spending money in ways that don't work.

Randomised trials are at their best when the results make us a little uncomfortable. As someone who tends to regard exam results as a useful indicator of student aptitude, I was troubled when I read a study carried out in Chicago that provided primary school students with an unexpected incentive just before the test started.[56] Immediately before the exam began, some students were told that if they beat their score on the last test, they would receive a prize. Even small rewards increased students' scores by the equivalent of several months' learning. The youngest students were most susceptible to a cheap trophy, while older students responded to $20 in cash. The incentives were especially effective if the researchers placed the prize on the student's desk and said that it would be taken away if they failed. Conversely, prizes had little impact if the researchers promised to hand them over in a month's time. Since students only learned about the prizes a few minutes before the exam, the sizable results suggest that most Chicago school students aren't trying their hardest on the typical test. In turn, this implies that test scores are a rougher measure of ability than researchers had previously thought.

Carrying out randomised evaluations can even be done on the largest of programs. As we'll see in Chapter 7, researchers in developing countries have used randomised trials to test the benefits of changes as massive as opening new schools in a village or doubling teacher pay in a school.

But sample size isn't the only thing that matters – it's also whether you're testing something that might reasonably be expected to work at all. In New York, a randomised trial across more than 600 schools set out to test whether teacher merit pay was effective. But rather than rewarding individual teachers, the system depended on the performance of an entire school. Given that the typical New York school has sixty teachers, it was very unlikely that any single teacher's efforts would affect their school's final results. If that wasn't enough, the school outcome was based on a complex formula that was extremely difficult for most teachers to understand.[57] Unsurprisingly, the experiment found no impact of merit pay on test scores.[58] This is an accurate assessment of that kind of merit pay plan, but should not be extrapolated to conclude that merit pay never works.[59]

A similar problem arose with the Project STAR experiment, a randomised trial of class size reductions. Conducted in Tennessee in the late 1980s, the experiment showed that pupils scored better in smaller classes.[60] However, it has been suggested that this impact was due to the fact that the treatment group teachers knew that if the study showed a positive effect, then class sizes would be reduced permanently across the state.[61] If this critique is true, then this suggests that class size reductions do have the potential to produce learning gains, but only if teachers face strong incentives to produce better outcomes.

*

At the college level, randomised experiments are proliferating. In Ohio and North Carolina, researchers worked with tax preparation company H&R Block to identify low-income families with a child just about to finish high school.[62] Half of these families were randomly offered assistance in completing a financial aid application. From the perspective of the tax preparer, this process took about eight minutes and cost less than $100 (including the cost of the software). But it made a significant difference to the families. Two years later, the children of those who had received help applying for financial aid were one-quarter more likely to be enrolled at university.

Because children whose parents did not attend university often lack basic information about the college application process, modest interventions can have large impacts. In Ontario, a three-hour workshop for Year 12 students raised college attendance rates by one-fifth, relative to a randomised control group.[63] In regional Massachusetts, peer support provided by text message raised the odds that Year 12 students would enrol in college.[64] In Chile, a randomised trial that provided information about earnings made poor students more likely to enrol in courses with higher earning potential.[65] Among low-income, high-achieving US high school seniors, an experiment that gave students more information about college quality markedly increased the odds that they chose an institution to which they were well-matched.[66]

Randomistas have even shed light on the direct benefits of attending university. Under normal circumstances, it's impossible to know the counterfactual to attending college. But in the Netherlands, an unusual randomised trial provided one answer. With medical schools massively oversubscribed, the Dutch government decided to allocate places based on a lottery. This makes it possible to compare the earnings of the few fortunate students who are admitted with their less *gelukkig* counterparts. It turns out that a spot at medical school boosts earnings by 50 per cent, equivalent to around €1 million in lifetime earnings.[67]

Admission isn't all that counts. Fail to finish a degree, and you're less likely to enjoy its benefits. Across advanced countries, only four out of ten bachelor's students graduate on time.[68] Even three years after they were supposed to have walked across the stage, just seven out of ten have a bachelor's degree. Is there anything randomised trials can teach us about improving university completion rates?

As it turns out, there is. In one experiment, personalised coaching increased completion rates for at-risk students.[69] Another showed that a combination of academic support services and financial incentives reduced dropout rates – though only for female students.[70] Given that college dropout is expensive for institutions and for individuals, both these programs seem to represent good value for money.

There is something fitting about applying the philosophy of 'test, learn, adapt' to improving education. But can the same philosophy that helped make *Sesame Street* one of the world's most effective educational television programs be applied to police and prisons?[71] Is it feasible or practical to reduce crime and incarceration through randomised trials?

6

CONTROLLING
CRIME

.

A house in suburban Canberra had been the target of multiple burglaries. For the sixth time, someone had broken in through a window, and stolen items from the bedroom of the family's nine-year-old son.[1] But this time the culprit had been caught in the act. It was the nine-year-old boy from next door – nabbed with a pillowcase full of Lego.

When police officer Rudi Lammers was called to the scene, he decided not to simply follow the usual processes for dealing with young offenders. Instead, he sat down with the two nine-year-olds and asked the victim, 'What do you think we should do?'

The reply surprised him. The victim tipped out half the Lego from the pillowcase, and gave the rest to the thief. Then he said, 'Any time you want to play Lego, come over. But can you come through the front door? Because Dad gets really cranky when you come through the window.'

Decades later, Lammers was approached by a man in a Canberra club who whispered in his ear, 'Do you know who I am? I'm the Lego boy – that experience changed my life.' The former child thief had stopped stealing after that incident, and now ran a building company.

In an informal sense, Lammers was practising 'restorative justice conferencing' – bringing offender and victim together to discuss what the perpetrator should do to repair the harm they have caused. Restorative justice is common in traditional societies, including among the Maori in New Zealand, Native Americans and Indigenous Australians. Since the late 1980s, criminologists have argued that by engendering shame and recompense, restorative justice could be a better deterrent than fines or jail time. But when it first began, many regarded restorative justice as silly or soft.

Since the late 1990s, places as diverse as Indianapolis, London and Canberra have been running experiments in which offenders were randomly directed either into restorative justice or the traditional judicial process. Some kinds of cases – such as family violence or fraud – aren't suitable for restorative justice, but the experiments covered a wide range of other crimes, including assault, robbery and car theft.

Combining the results of ten restorative justice experiments from around the world – a process known as meta-analysis – researchers concluded that it does cut crime.[2] In the two years afterwards, offenders who went through the restorative justice process were significantly less likely to commit another crime. For society, the benefits more than covered the costs. In the London experiment, the gains from crime reduction were worth fourteen times more than the cost of running the restorative justice process. And in a result that surprised some theorists, restorative justice seems to work particularly well for violent crimes.

Results from the Canberra experiment showed that restorative justice also helped victims. Compared with those cases that were randomised to go to court, victims of violence were less likely to fear that the offender would hurt them again if their case went through restor-ative justice. Under restorative justice, victims were five times more likely to get a sincere apology. Victims of violence were also asked if they would harm the offender if they got the chance. When cases went to court, nearly half the victims said afterwards that they still wanted to take revenge – compared with less than one in ten cases that went through restorative justice. Since many crimes are motivated by revenge, this suggests that restorative justice may help avoid tit-for-tat cycles of violence.[3]

In criminal justice the instinctive solution is not always the one that produces the best results. In the United States, the violent crime rate has halved since the early 1990s.[4] Meanwhile, the incarceration rate has almost doubled, with nearly 1 per cent of American adults behind bars.[5] Black men who do not finish high school have a two in three chance of going to jail at some point in their lives.[6] As Senator Cory Booker noted in 2015, 'Right now, we have more African-Americans under criminal supervision than all of the slaves in 1850.'

Could randomised trials help reduce both crime and incarcera-tion? In this chapter, I discuss four kinds of criminal justice experiments: prevention, policing, punishment and prison. Creating a society with less crime and less punishment requires getting each of these steps right. Can randomised trials help us do it?

*

The exercise is called 'The Fist'. The young men are split into pairs. One is given a golf ball. The other is told he has thirty seconds to get the ball.

Immediately, students start grabbing, hitting and wrestling.

After the time is up, the teacher asks why no one simply asked for the ball. 'He wouldn't have given it,' says one. 'He would have thought I was a punk,' replies another.

Then the teacher turns to those with the ball, and asks how they would have responded to a polite request. 'I would have given it; it's just a stupid ball,' one replies.

The young men – from rough inner-city neighbourhoods – are participating in a crime prevention program called 'Becoming a Man'. The goal is to shift teenagers from acting automatically to thinking deliberately, recognising that the right strategy on the street might be the wrong approach in the classroom. For example, a young man in a high-crime neighbourhood who complies with requests like 'give me your phone' may be seen as a soft target for future crimes. By contrast, if the same young man fails to comply with a request by his teacher to sit down in class, he may be suspended from school.

'Becoming a Man' doesn't tell youths never to fight. Unlike children in affluent suburbs, teenagers growing up in high-poverty neighbourhoods may need to act tough just to stay safe. So the program's role-play exercises encourage teenagers to choose the right response for the situation. Making eye contact could be fatal when walking past a rival gang member, but is essential in a job interview. Based on cognitive behavioural therapy, 'Becoming a Man' aims to get youths to slow down, judge the situation and deliberately choose whether to comply, argue or fight back.

Does it work? From 2009 to 2014, researchers in Chicago carried out two randomised trials, in which teenagers were randomly assigned into 'Becoming a Man' programs or after-school sports.[7] 'Becoming a Man' cut arrests by a large amount: between one-third and one-half. Some researchers now think that reducing 'automaticity' – the tendency of young men to instinctively lash out – may do more to improve the lives of young men than standard academic remediation and job training programs. Edinson, a Year 12 student at Amundsen High School, summed up the program's philosophy:

'A boy has problems. A man finds solutions to his problems.'[8]

Remarkably, the effects of cognitive behavioural therapy seem to show up in other contexts too. In war-torn Liberia, researchers recruited nearly a thousand of the most violent men in the nation's capital, and then randomly offered some of them the chance to complete a short course designed to reduce automaticity and improve self-awareness.[9] A year later, men who had gone through cognitive behavioural therapy were less likely to deal drugs, steal or carry a weapon. The effect was particularly strong for those who had received a second randomised treatment – a US$200 cash grant. Together, the impact of therapy and a one-time payment halved the number of crimes from sixty-six to thirty per year.

One of the things I like about the Liberian experiment is that Chris Blattman and his co-authors admit they were surprised by their own results. Because the cash grant was a one-off payment, they hadn't expected it would have any impact on long-term behaviour. The research team are now exploring the mechanism through which a temporary payment can change lives.

There's a lot we don't know about the world, so being surprised by experimental findings is perfectly healthy. Indeed, we should be deeply suspicious of anyone who claims they know what works based only on theory or small-scale observation. As the economist John Maynard Keynes once put it, 'When the facts change, I change my mind. What do you do, sir?'[10]

Programs that divert troubled young people away from offending can have a huge impact on their life trajectories. In Chicago, African-American high schoolers randomly assigned to get an eight-week part-time summer job were 40 per cent less likely to commit a violent crime. The effect persisted for more than a year after the job ended.[11] When prevention programs work, they not only save young people from having to go through life with a criminal record, they also save victims from the pain and cost of crimes that are averted, and save taxpayers the cost of paying for more jails.

*

In the early 1970s, a Michigan bowling alley ran an advertisement that said: 'Have Some Fun. Beat Your Wife Tonight.'[12] It reflected the fact that family violence was considered normal at that time. Abused women often found themselves being asked, 'What did you do to provoke him?' Social workers urged women to stay with abusive men for the sake of their children. Hospitals looked the other way as they patched up injuries. Safe shelters were rare. When responding to a family violence call, officers sometimes laughed at the victim. They seldom removed the man from his home. Police typically took a 'speak softly' approach, aiming to defuse the tension. One state's police manual advised officers, 'Don't be too harsh or critical.'[13]

By the late 1970s, police attitudes had begun to shift. The Battered Women's Movement emerged to challenge the idea that violence in the home should be treated more leniently than violence on the street.[14] A study of spouse killings found that most had been preceded by at least five police call-outs in the year before the murder.[15] Some argued that lives could have been saved if the police had been tougher, while others thought that arrests would make little difference. Many victims were unwilling to sign complaint statements, fearing that the stigma of arrest could lead the man to take revenge later.

Patrick Murphy, president of the US Police Foundation, argued that police responses were based on little more than 'hunch, supposition, tradition'. So in 1981 the Foundation engaged in an unusual experiment with the city of Minneapolis, seeking 'through scientific inquiry ... to supplant tradition with fact in resolving the question: How can the police deter future domestic violence?'[16]

In the Minneapolis Domestic Violence Experiment, officers were given a special pad of report forms which listed three kinds of responses: arrest the perpetrator, send the perpetrator away from the home for eight hours, or provide advice to the couple. The three responses – arrest, send or advise – appeared in random order throughout the report pad. In cases of family violence where the victim was not seriously injured, officers were to follow the action indicated on the top page of the pad.

The results were unequivocal. Measured either by police reports or victim surveys, households where the perpetrator was arrested saw about half as much violence in the following six months as those in which police officers sent the perpetrator away or provided advice to the couple.[17] Reading reports of the study, the New York police commissioner immediately told his officers to make an arrest if a victim of family violence wanted to press charges.[18] Within months, Dallas, Houston and Minneapolis had changed their policies too.[19] A year after the study came out, the national rate of arrest in family violence cases had risen from 10 per cent to 31 per cent.[20] Two years later, it was 46 per cent.

In subsequent years, replication studies produced a more nuanced finding, suggesting that the effect of arrest on family violence was stronger when perpetrators were employed than when they were jobless.[21] But the shift in policing practice for family violence would almost certainly not have been as sharp without a randomised trial. Understanding the best way for police to respond to family violence remains critical. Globally, half of all female homicide victims are killed by their partners or family members.[22] As a United Nations report notes: 'With bitter irony, women run the highest risk of being killed by those who are expected to care for and even protect them.'[23]

One of the leading academic investigators on the Minneapolis

Domestic Violence Experiment was Lawrence Sherman, then in his early thirties. The child of a Baptist minister and a YMCA worker, Sherman says, 'I was brought up with a strong sense of social justice.'[24] He finished his undergraduate degree in Ohio in half the usual time – two years rather than four – then found himself in the late 1960s in front of the draft board, as a conscientious objector to the Vietnam War. While others in his position had fled to Canada or been jailed, Sherman confidently told the draft board that he could avoid military service by taking on any government job, and he planned to undertake a research fellowship with the New York Police Department. 'The draft board wasn't pleased,' he recalled. 'Then again, they weren't so upset when the police headquarters was bombed the weekend before I started work, and they realised I was just as likely to be killed in New York as in Vietnam.'[25]

Through his work with police departments, Sherman became fascinated with understanding why some policing strategies worked while others were ineffective. His answer was to forge a new discipline: experimental criminology. This broke fresh ground not only for police forces, but also for the discipline of criminology itself. 'For most of its history,' Sherman observes, 'criminology has been essentially a descriptive or observational science, sort of like astronomy.'[26] Astronomers study the movement of celestial bodies; they do not try to change their trajectories. Sherman thought criminology should be more like medicine – striving to make sick people healthier, or, better still, intervening before they became sick in the first place. A core focus of criminology, he believed, ought to be figuring out how to cut crime. Experimental criminology was a significant departure from the thinking of people like Frenchman Émile Durkheim, who took the view that crime was inevitable because it was 'bound up with the fundamental conditions of all social life'.[27] Durkheim wanted to explain crime. Sherman wanted to reduce it.

In Kansas City, the early 1990s saw a boom in crack cocaine. Dealers relied on 'crack houses' – abandoned homes that could be used to sell their product. The city's police force wanted to find out the effect of shutting down crack houses. So they worked with Lawrence Sherman to design an experiment.[28]

To begin with, the police needed to verify complaints that a home was being used to sell drugs. An undercover officer or informant went to the house and bought crack cocaine using sequentially marked bank notes. Then Sherman's team came into the picture. In the police station were a series of numbered envelopes, each containing a note that said either 'raid' or 'no action', according to the results of a random number generator. If the note said 'raid', the police filed a search warrant request with a local judge. If it said 'no action', the evidence was put to one side.

The raid was conducted by an eight-man tactical team from the Street Narcotics Unit. To be sure they had the right house, they sometimes sent in another undercover agent to buy drugs. A few years earlier, a raid on the wrong house had led to bad publicity for the unit, and they wanted to be sure they had the correct home.

Immediately after the confirmation buy, the Street Narcotics Unit began the raid. An unmarked van drove up to the front of the house, its side door opened and an officer used a battering ram to break down the front door. Officers poured into the house, sometimes using flash-bang grenades to disorient those inside. Everyone was ordered to lie face-down and was handcuffed. Outside the house, police were waiting to catch anyone who jumped out a window or dashed through the back door. Nearby residents came out of their homes to see what was going on, sometimes applauding and cheering the officers. Everyone in the crack house was taken to the police station for questioning, and the home was searched for drugs. Sometimes new buyers would arrive while the house was being searched, then quickly flee when they realised what was going on.

At the end of the eight-month experiment, Kansas police had randomly raided ninety-eight crack houses, with about the same number left alone as a control group. Looking at crime reports for the two sets of neighbourhoods, Sherman and his team saw that the raids had an immediate effect on crime. Two days after the raids, there were half as many reported offences in the city blocks that had been raided than in the control neighbourhoods. But the impact quickly evaporated. Within a fortnight, crime rates in the raided areas were no different from those in places for which the randomised envelope had read 'no action'.

But while raids failed to produce a sustained reduction in crime, experimental criminologists found other evidence that 'hot spots' policing – concentrating resources on the areas that produce the most calls for help – could cut crime.[29] In Jersey City, police cracked down on a subset of the most dangerous street corners. Intersections randomly chosen for the crackdowns saw larger reductions in crime than the otherwise identical corners randomly chosen to be the controls.[30] In Philadelphia, an experiment found that two- to three-kilometre foot patrols, short enough so that police repeatedly passed the same points, massively cut crime in dangerous neighbourhoods. Shifting from traditional approaches such as car patrols to hot spots foot patrols could avert four violent crimes a week.[31]

Does this kind of approach simply shift the crime elsewhere? One way to answer the question is to look at the areas surrounding the hot spot and see if crime has increased in those streets. In both Jersey City and Philadelphia, researchers saw little evidence that the criminals had simply shifted their operations a few blocks away. Carried out appropriately, hot spots policing does seem to reduce overall crime.[32] A majority of US police forces currently use the approach, with a fresh wave of studies now looking at the kinds of hot spots policing that work best.[33] One of the latest findings is that 'problem oriented policing' – an approach in which police work with community leaders to address the underlying causes of crime – may be a more effective form of hot spots policing than strategies that simply focus on arrests.[34]

Perhaps you're not surprised by the results on hot spots policing. After all, some street corners in Philadelphia produce ten times as many crimes as others, so it makes intuitive sense that a 'flood the zone' approach might reduce offending rates. But high-quality evaluations of policing programs don't always produce the expected result. Take, for example, Neighbourhood Watch, which promotes citizen involvement in crime prevention through encouraging incident reporting, marking property and conducting surveys on security. Anecdotal reports from Neighbourhood Watch organisers almost invariably report that the program has a substantial impact on reducing crime. Low-quality evaluations told a similarly positive story. But the randomised trials show zero impact. As experimental criminologist Lawrence Sherman puts it: 'One of the most consistent findings in the literature is also the least well-known to policymakers and the public. The oldest and best-known community policing program, Neighbourhood Watch, is ineffective at preventing crime.'[35]

*

We've looked at prevention and policing. Now let's look at punishment. As we have seen, not every form of punishment that sounds good actually does good. In the case of Scared Straight, the program was a tale worthy of an Academy Award. Yet when tested in rigorous evaluations, Scared Straight turned out to increase crime rates. A short experience of jail put youngsters at risk, and ended up making them more likely to commit offences in the future.

When it comes to punishing crimes, most people's minds turn to prison. But prison is only one way in which societies punish their wrongdoers. Over the centuries, punishments have included every-thing from the guillotine to the pillory, chain gangs to house arrest.

But does the punishment fit the crime? When it comes to dealing with addicts, there's a temptation to take a zero-tolerance approach. Psychological research suggests that drug users tend to evoke a visceral response of disgust, which can make it harder for people to support rational policies that reduce rates of drug abuse and drug-related crime.[36] From Richard Nixon's War on Drugs to Chinese labour camps for drug users, societies across the globe have often opted for a 'tough on drugs' policy.

In our prisons today, many prisoners are locked up for crimes committed while using narcotics. New drugs – such as crack cocaine or crystal methamphetamine – often cause a spike in crime. As anyone who has tried to quit smoking knows, it isn't easy to stop using an addictive drug. Yet the traditional court system is set up to punish crime, not help people kick the habit.

In 1999 Australia was in the midst of a heroin epidemic. Use of the opioid had risen fourfold over the decade, and almost 150,000 people were shooting up regularly.[37] New South Wales premier Bob Carr, who had lost his younger brother to a heroin overdose, announced that his state would trial a controversial alternative: the Drug Court. Drug Courts aim to treat addiction outside the jail system. Offenders who successfully complete the one-year program are typically put on a good behaviour bond.[38] Failure generally means going to jail.

The Drug court wasn't the first in the world, but it was still radical for Australia.[39] To address the critics, the state government decided they had to have strong evidence of its effectiveness. So they set up a trial. A group of eligible offenders – who had committed non-violent crimes and were willing to plead guilty – were randomly assigned either to the Drug Court or to the traditional judicial process. Those people were then matched to court records in order to compare reoffending rates over the next year or more.

The study found that for every 100 offenders who went through the traditional court system, there were sixty-two drug crimes committed in the year after release.[40] For those who went through the Drug Court, there were eight drug crimes committed in the subsequent year. It showed that even a citizen who didn't care about the wellbeing of drug users should support the Drug Court, since it reduced crime at a cost about the same as that of the traditional system. Randomised evaluations of drug courts elsewhere have reached similar conclusions.[41] Director of Public Prosecutions Nicholas Cowdery admitted that he had evolved from being a sceptic to a strong supporter: 'the Drug Court of NSW is a success'.[42]

Today, the NSW Drug Court remains an unconventional part of the judicial system. Its style is informal, and the focus is on whether offenders are managing to break their drug habit. Testing can occur multiple times a week. Admitting to drug use attracts one sanction. Getting caught lying about drug use attracts three sanctions. Fourteen sanctions and you go to jail.

When participants move forward – by finding a job, staying off drugs or graduating from the program – the judge leads the courtroom in a round of applause. As senior judge Roger Dive notes, 'You can see how much encouragement the participant gets from that applause. You can see how crestfallen are the ones who have fallen back and aren't applauded. It's all-important to them.'[43] When one man, a former heavy user and dealer, graduated from the program to the applause of the courtroom, he wept. 'You were the first people who gave me a chance.'[44]

The Drug Court has also maintained its evidence-based philosophy. In 2010 the court conducted another randomised trial this time to see whether there was value in bringing Drug Court offenders before the judge twice a week rather than once a week. The evaluation found that more intense judicial scrutiny halved the chances of a positive drug test.[45]

On the other side of the Pacific Ocean, another judge had been thinking about similar challenges. Appointed to the bench in 2001 after a stint as Hawaii's US attorney, Steven Alm was immediately struck by the way in which his state punished probation violators. Probation officers would let slide the first ten to fifteen violations – such as failing a drug test – before recommending that a person be sent to prison. Those running the system were frustrated that most breaches went unpunished. Reasonably enough, offenders saw the system as arbitrary. When a breach landed them behind bars, they blamed the probation officer, the judge and an unfair system.

Looking at the ad hoc enforcement of probation violations, Alm thought about how we treat children. When the rules are clear and promptly enforced, kids are less likely to be naughty than when the rules are arbitrary and unpredictable. 'I thought about how I was raised and how I raise my kids. Tell 'em what the rules are and then if there's misbehavior you give them a consequence immediately. That's what good parenting is all about.'[46]

In the case of parolees, Alm devised a system known as Hawaii's Opportunity Probation with Enforcement, or HOPE. When offenders fail a drug test or miss a probation appointment, a judicial hearing is held as soon as possible – typically within seventy-two hours. If the judge is satisfied that there has been a breach, the parolee is immediately jailed for a few days. The approach aims to be swift, certain and proportionate. As Alm puts it, it's 'Parenting 101'.

Buoyed by promising results, an external team devised a randomised evaluation. The study found that those who were assigned to the HOPE program were less likely to miss probation appointments, spent half as much time in jail, and were half as likely to commit a crime in the following year.[47]

Conversations with the parolees also revealed an intriguing aspect of the program: offenders preferred it. An overwhelming majority felt that it helped them stay off drugs and improved their family relationships. Many saw the court system as an ally in rehabilitation, rather than the enemy. In the early days of the program, a researcher spoke to a man who was serving a short jail spell for failing a drug test. The probationer told the interviewer: 'Judge Alm, he's tough, but he's fair. You know where you stand.'[48] Programs based on the HOPE model are now operating in more than thirty US states.[49]

Fairness is at the heart of the HOPE program, but the irony is that its randomised evaluation was arbitrary. Like every randomised experiment, assignment to the treatment or control groups was purely based on chance. Like the Australian Drug Court trial, participants were given no choice about whether they would be part of the study. The principle of equal justice requires that the same offence receives the same punishment. Yet once they were in the experiment, otherwise identical offenders were randomly assigned to different punishments.

Is this ethical? I believe so. While those designing new criminal justice programs anticipate they will produce better outcomes, they do not know for sure that being in the treatment group is better than being in the control group. In fact, while the treatment group did better in the HOPE and Drug Court experiments, the control group did better in the Scared Straight and Neighbourhood Watch experiments.

One way of thinking about the ethical issue in randomisation is that it turns on what we know about a program's effectiveness.[50] Adam Gamoran, a sociologist at the University of Wisconsin–Madison, agrees that if you are confident that a program works, then it is unethical to conduct a randomised trial. But if you are ignorant about whether the program works, and a randomised trial is feasible, Gamoran argues that it is unethical not to conduct one.

When it comes to randomised experiments on punishment, the results are frequently unpredictable. As we have already seen, the results of the Scared Straight experiments demonstrated that a short stint in jail makes a young person more likely to commit crimes, not less likely. Likewise, studies of militaristic 'boot camps' find that they reduce reoffending rates only when they are designed to teach inmates new skills, not simply make life as tough as possible.[51]

*

Finally, let's look at prisons, the institutions that currently house over 2 million Americans. The rapid growth of the jail population has been most dramatic in the United States, but similar trends can be seen in other countries. Over the past few decades, the United Kingdom has seen a significant fall in violent crime rates and a marked rise in incarceration. The same is true in Australia, where the imprisonment rate is now the highest in the nation's history.[52]

While some have claimed that bigger jails have made our streets safer, most experts disagree. That's because the rise in imprisonment has been driven largely by tougher sentencing practices – such as California's 'three strikes' laws – which have been shown not to have much of an impact on criminal behaviour.[53] Mark Kleiman, a leading researcher on the HOPE evaluation, argues that most people about to commit a violent crime are living day by day, and that raising the maximum sentence from ten to twenty years isn't likely to have much of a deterrent effect. In Hawaii, HOPE succeeded not because it was punitive, but because it was predictable. If you want to deter crime, focus on certainty, not severity.[54]

Prison can potentially also reduce crime through the 'incapacitation effect' – a fancy way of saying that you can't steal my television while you're doing time. But because crime tends to be a young man's game, very long sentences don't do much to incapacitate people who would otherwise be menacing the population. Grey-haired inmates are becoming increasingly common. Reviewing the evidence, an expert US National Academy panel concluded: 'Most studies estimate the crime-reducing effect of incarceration to be small.'[55] Rather, mass imprisonment risks creating further disadvantage, as released offenders struggle to find legal work, and to integrate back into their families and communities.

If only we had randomised evidence on the impact of prisons. Then again, it's hard to imagine that any prison authority would agree to run an experiment to answer this question. Courts and parole boards aim to dispense equal justice, not rely on luck. To have enough statistical power would require thousands of prisoners. There would need to be big differences in the sentences of the two groups, based on nothing more than chance. The cries of unfairness would be deafening.

Or so you might think. In 1970 the California parole board agreed to run just such an experiment. That year, 3000 prisoners who were coming up for release were divided into two groups. Using a random table of numbers, half of the prisoners had their sentence shortened by six months, while the rest served their regular term. After release, the authorities looked to see who reoffended. They found no difference between the two groups, suggesting that another six months behind bars didn't reduce recidivism.[56]

Prisons are meant to serve four purposes: to rehabilitate inmates, to incapacitate them from harming the community, to make an example of them so as to deter potential wrongdoers, and to exact retribution on behalf of society. But the evidence – including from the California study – increasingly suggests that longer sentences may only serve one of these purposes: retribution. A five-year jail term costs society five times as much as a one-year sentence, but it's doubtful it has five times the deterrent effect. If the aim is to make society safe, it's better that we write our laws with thoughtful minds, not angry spleens.

*

If you've ever been the victim of a crime, you'll know how tough it is to take a dispassionate view. But passion-driven policy often leads to laws like the 'three strikes' rule that saw Leandro Andrade sentenced to fifty years in jail when he stole $153 of videotapes from stores in Ontario, California.[57] Andrade had previously been convicted of drug and burglary offences, so the videotapes were his third strike. He will be eighty-seven years old when released, and his incarceration will cost taxpayers over US$1 million.

When 'Laura Norder' shows up on the ballot paper, she wins a lot of votes. But as experimental criminologists have shown, our gut feel isn't much of a guide to what actually works to improve community safety. Whether it's prevention, policing, punishment or prison, the challenge isn't just to carry out rigorous research, it's also to do a better job of conveying the expert consensus to the public. Since 2011 the US Department of Justice has run the website CrimeSolutions.gov, which gives its highest rating to programs and practices backed by randomised experiments. Experimental criminologists such as Lawrence Sherman are slowly gaining the upper hand – but it'll be a long time before we can finally put all those failed crime-fighting ideas behind bars.

7

VALUABLE EXPERIMENTS
IN POOR COUNTRIES

L ariat Alhassan ran a business selling paint in Abjua, Nigeria.[1] Business was passable, but she didn't know how to expand. Alhassan sold the paint out of the boot of her car, travelling to meet her customers. To land bigger orders, she needed to have a showroom, but she couldn't afford one without more sales.

In 2011, Alhassan heard an ad on the radio, inviting entrepreneurs to apply for a new competition. The advertisement told business owners: 'It may be small today, but it won't be after YouWiN! the youth enterprise and innovation competition.' At first, Alhassan thought YouWiN! must have been a scam. It turned out to be a radical approach devised by the finance minister, Ngozi Okonjo-Iweala. As Okonjo-Iweala put it, 'We had a large unemployment problem ... especially with young graduates. And these are people who are ripe to be encouraged as entrepreneurs.' So the Nigerian government ran a competition for entrepreneurial small businesses. Based on a short business plan, the government gave successful firms up to 10 million

Naira (about US$64,000). The amount was equivalent to about a decade's wages for the typical Nigerian.

Enter David McKenzie, a New Zealand–born development economist now working at the World Bank. To test the impact of YouWiN! grants on businesses, McKenzie persuaded the Nigerian government to randomise grants across some of the semi-finalists. The government announced 1200 winning businesses, with a majority chosen randomly by McKenzie. As the podcast *Planet Money* documented, one of the successful firms was Lariat Alhassan's paint selling business. She used the money to hire staff, buy a delivery truck and rent a showroom.

Alhassan wasn't the only winner who made good use of the money. Three years after the grants were distributed, McKenzie's randomised trial compared the lucky winners with unlucky losers. He estimated that entrepreneurs who won a grant were more innovative, grew faster and took on more staff.[2] Dividing the employment impact by the total cost of the program, each additional job cost the government $8500, making it far more effective than most similar programs. Reading the results, a prominent development economist asked, 'Is this the most effective development program in history?'[3]

Perhaps no area of policy has seen such a rapid growth in randomised trials as development economics. In the 1990s there were fewer than thirty randomised experiments from developing countries published globally each year. In the 2010s there have been at least 250 randomised development studies published annually.[4] Two-thirds of all impact evaluations in development economics now use randomisation.[5] Randomised trials are proliferating across organisations such as the World Bank, the Bill & Melinda Gates Foundation, the UK Department for International Development and the US Agency for International Development. As Yale's Dean Karlan put it, 'There are hundreds and hundreds of randomized trials going on, and ten years ago that just wasn't the case.'[6]

Part of the drive towards randomisation has been a recognition that there may not be a single answer to alleviating global poverty. There was a time when many development theorists thought the solution was simply for developing nations to be able to borrow on the international capital markets. Then there was a notion that the problem was over-population, and that providing free condoms would quickly raise living standards. After that came a push for debt forgiveness, on the principle that once countries were freed from their crushing loan repayments, they would grow quickly. Proposed by well-meaning idealists, none of these schemes lived up to their initial promises.[7]

The Greek poet Archilochus once wrote: 'A fox knows many things, but a hedgehog one important thing.'[8] In development, the randomistas are the foxes, and grand planners the hedgehogs. Where the planners have proposed a single reason why millions of people go to bed hungry each night, those who advocate randomised trials in development are searching for multiple solutions. Hedgehogs are confident they know what works. Foxes aren't sure, but they're sniff-ing everywhere.

Because the randomistas take an eclectic approach, tracking their progress is invariably messy. In this chapter I have sought to provide some order by grouping randomised trials in development into four groups: experiments that aim to create more business activity, experi-ments that seek to make government work better, experiments that try to improve health, and experiments whose goal is to raise educa-tional standards.

*

In helping entrepreneurs build businesses, we have already seen from the YouWiN! experiment that access to cash can be crucial. If a smart youngster in Sweden has a brilliant idea for a start-up, she can prob-ably borrow money from friends, family or a bank. An equally bright innovator in Somalia might not have access to any of these funding sources. But designing a financing system that works in a poor nation is no easy task. If you've ever lent money to someone who failed to repay the debt, you know the central challenge for a bank: how do you distinguish the conscientious from the crooked?

In 1976 Muhammad Yunus, a university professor in Bangladesh, lent US$27 of his own money to a group of poor village women who made bamboo furniture. As Yunus recounts, they repaid the loan and their businesses became more profitable. So he set up a bank to provide 'microcredit' – loans as small as a few dollars.

Fast-forward two decades, and microcredit was among the hottest trends in development. Yunus's Grameen Bank had grown into a multi-billion-dollar organisation. The prime minister of Bangladesh argued that microcredit would 'allow the world's poorest people to free themselves from the bondage of poverty and deprivation to bloom to their fullest potentials'.[9] Internationally, microcredit won supporters from the left for its focus on poor women and from the right for its emphasis on personal responsibility. A pair of supporters wrote: 'If a social evangelist had a choice of picking one tool, one movement with the goal of emancipating the poorest women on earth, the microcredit phenomenon wins without serious competition'.[10]

As US president, Bill Clinton provided development assistance to microcredit programs and championed Muhammad Yunus for the Nobel Peace Prize.[11] Awarding the prize to Yunus in 2006, the Nobel committee praised him for developing 'micro-credit into an ever more important instrument in the struggle against poverty'. U2's Bono wrote: 'Give a man a fish, he'll eat for a day. Give a woman microcredit, she, her husband, her children, and her extended family will eat for a lifetime'.[12]

Yet it turned out that the bold claims for microcredit were largely based on anecdotes and evaluations that failed to distinguish correlation from causation. By the 2000s, researchers had begun carrying out randomised trials of microcredit programs in Bosnia, Ethiopia, India, Mexico, Morocco and Mongolia. Summarising these six experiments, a team of leading development economists concluded that microcredit had no impact on raising household income, getting children to stay in school, or empowering women.[13] Microcredit schemes did provide more financial freedom, and led people to invest more money in their businesses, but it didn't make them more profitable.

Part of the reason that microcredit struggled to change lives is that it offered relatively small sums of money at high interest rates. Whereas the Nigerian entrepreneurs got to keep their YouWiN! prizes, microcredit borrowers had to pay back their loans with interest rates that sometimes exceeded 100 per cent. Microcreditors defended themselves by pointing out that they were cheaper than the knee-breaking loan sharks who came before them. But even the world's best companies would struggle to pay 100 per cent interest rates and make a profit. As Dean Karlan puts it, there just aren't that many golden-egg-laying geese around.[14]

As the gloss has come off microcredit, some economists believe that there may be larger benefits from helping people save than from helping them borrow. A survey of recent randomised trials finds that savings programs tend to boost income and wealth, increase spending on health care and education, and provide a buffer against unexpected shocks.[15] Contrary to the past views of Bill Clinton and the Nobel Prize committee, the world's poorest seem to have a greater need for bank accounts than credit cards.

'The rich are different from you and me,' wrote F. Scott Fitzgerald. 'Yes,' responded Ernest Hemingway, 'they have more money.'[16] In recent years, some researchers have explored an even simpler approach: giving cash to the poor. Working across Ethiopia, Ghana, Honduras,

India, Pakistan and Peru, a research team tested the impact of providing the very poor with a package that included assets (typically livestock), income support, bank accounts and business training.[17] A year after the end of the program, its effects could still be clearly seen. Compared with randomly selected households that did not get the resources, recipients were making more money from farming. They were less likely to be hungry or stressed, worked harder, and felt that they had higher status in their communities. Similar results have been found in a Ugandan program that gave cash to ultrapoor women. The impacts are not as transformative as in the Nigerian YouWiN! experiment, but appear promising nonetheless.

These results have led a group of US philanthropists to create a charity called GiveDirectly.[18] As the name suggests, the organisation has one simple mission: to enable donors to give cash to the extreme poor. GiveDirectly is about to embark on a randomised experiment in Africa, in which it will give at least 6000 villagers a dollar each day, guaranteed for a decade.[19] If successful, this could radically reshape how we think about aid.

For good reason, many programs to help businesses are focused on money. But we shouldn't underrate the value of motivation. In a recent randomised trial, villagers in rural Ethiopia were shown four videos over the course of an hour.[20] Each depicted people in poverty who managed to better themselves through hard work, goal-setting and careful decision-making. The villagers who watched the videos were extremely poor – with most making less than a dollar a day. They faced a raft of challenges, including illiteracy, corruption, sickness and bad roads.

One video told the story of Teyiba Abdella, beginning with glowing accounts from her neighbours.[21] Abdella used to carry big loads even when she was pregnant, one neighbour says. But her life is getting better and better, another tells us. And then Abdella herself comes on the screen: a tall Ethiopian villager. We hear about how she used to carry 50 kilograms of flour on her back for three hours to walk to the market. Before she could afford a donkey, Abdella tells us, 'I used to work like a donkey.' Now, as well as flour, she sells eggs and chickens. The ten-minute clip finishes with her husband saying how proud he is of Abdella, a 'role model to her fellow villagers'.

Could hearing stories like Abdella's motivate someone to change their life? When the researchers followed up six months later, they found that just that one hour of watching motivational videos had made a lasting difference. Those who watched the videos had higher aspirations and greater savings rates, and were more likely to enrol their children in school. Summing up their findings, the research team admitted: 'The extent and nature of their response has surprised us.' Yet the result doesn't seem to be a one-off. On the other side of the continent, a randomised trial in Togo found that personal initiative training for entrepreneurs boosted profits by almost one-third (a significantly larger impact than traditional business training).[22]

*

Poor countries are often poorly governed. The countries with the worst infrastructure are Congo, Chad and Yemen.[23] The most corrupt nations are Somalia, South Sudan and North Korea.[24] The most fragile states are the Central African Republic, Congo and South Sudan.[25] Lacking money and well-trained public servants, it's hardly surprising that governments in developing countries don't operate with Swiss efficiency. But perhaps randomised trials can help these governments decide how to allocate their scarce resources.

In China, researchers have used randomised experiments to learn about how government responds. In an experiment across more than 2000 counties, a request for help in obtaining *dibao*, the basic social payment for those unable to find work, was posted on government web forums.[26] In some counties, researchers simply posted a deferential request for help. In other counties, the request went further, adding either a threat of collective action ('If you can't help, we'll try to figure out what we can do together about this situation') or a threat of tattling ('If this problem cannot be addressed, I'll have to report it to upper-level government officials'). Both threats increased by about one-third the chances that local Chinese officials provided some kind of response.

Just as threats provoke better behaviour, bribes can lead to worse behaviour. A novel Indian experiment looked at what happened when a randomly selected group of young men were offered a cash incentive to obtain their driving licences quickly.[27] To get the money, many in the study hired 'agents', who paid bribes to the testing authority. Shortly afterwards, the researchers gave everyone in the study a surprise driving test. Their focus was on how many people were incompetent behind the wheel, and yet had a licence. It turned out that those offered the cash incentive were 18 percentage points more likely to have their licence and yet be unable to drive.

My initial reaction to the licence study was to think that it was unethical, on the basis that the researchers were putting dodgy drivers onto the streets of Delhi. When I chatted about the findings with study author Sendhil Mullainathan, he acknowledged that I wasn't the first to feel uneasy. But since everyone in the study got free driving lessons afterwards, he pointed out, 'every single participant – treatment or control – was a better driver as a result of being in the experiment'. Multiple ethics boards approved Mullainathan's research, because they understood the value of rigorously studying corruption in India.

Licensing corruption thrives because going down the honest route to get an Indian driving licence is a Kafkaesque nightmare. Without the help of an agent, the typical applicant makes three trips to the regional transport office and speaks with eight bureaucrats. If you don't pay a bribe, getting an Indian driving licence typically takes more than five hours. When an experiment is the best way to shed light on a serious problem, we have to weigh the risk of doing a randomised trial against the risk of continued ignorance. I will return to these ethical issues in more detail in Chapter 11.

Other randomised trials in development work closely with governments. When Fabiola Vázquez Saút, mayor of the Mexican city of Acayucan, found that council only had money to pave about half the streets, she saw an opportunity to avert some voter anger, and learn about the impacts of road paving. Rather than selecting the roads herself, she let researchers from Oxford and the University of Toronto randomly choose which streets to upgrade. The Acayucan experiment created something unusual – the world's first study of the true impact of public road building on property values.[28] Comparing homes on paved streets with those on unpaved streets, researchers found a considerable increase in value. Indeed, the increase in home values was as large as the cost of the street works. Households responded to their newfound wealth by buying home appliances and motor vehicles, contributing to a fall in material poverty.

In Kenya, economists worked with the national electricity utility to randomly give some households a discount on their connection fee.[29] By varying the subsidy, the researchers were able to see how much households valued being connected to the grid. Unlike the Mexicans and their road experiment, Kenyan households seemed to place a much lower value on an electricity connection than it cost to provide it. Much as we might like to think about turning the lights on for households that now make do with kerosene lamps, it may be that scarce development dollars are better directed towards roads, schools or health clinics than to electrification in remote areas.

One researcher who has been at the vanguard of conducting experiments with governments in low-income countries is Karthik

Muralidharan, an economics professor at the University of California, San Diego. Energetic, fast-talking and engaging, Muralidharan has persuaded several governments to conduct randomised trials at a scale that would only have been dreamt about a generation ago. When he heard that the Indonesian government planned to spend US$5 billion to double teacher pay, Muralidharan and his co-authors persuaded government officials – working with the World Bank – to agree to implement the policy early among a randomly selected group of a few thousand teachers.[30] The study concluded that those teachers who had their pay doubled were happier, but there was no discernible impact on student outcomes.

In the Indian state of Andhra Pradesh, Muralidharan worked with the government to randomise the rollout of biometrically identified smartcards.[31] From 2010 onwards, India began issuing its citizens with smartcards that were encoded with their fingerprints and photograph, and linked to a newly established bank account. Muralidharan and his co-authors found that the program had precisely the effects intended: more eligible citizens accessed the program, payments were received more quickly, and less money was siphoned off by corrupt officials. In each case, the study's estimates are extremely precise, since the experiment comprised a whopping 19 million people – more than the entire population of Chile.

*

Ill-health is perhaps the most tangible marker of global poverty. Just as new drugs are routinely tested through randomised trials, public health researchers are increasingly using randomised trials to create a safer environment in developing nations. One disease that has received significant attention is malaria, one of the world's nastiest killers. As the Anopheles mosquito feeds from an infected person, it takes in the parasite. When it bites a new victim, they may contract malaria.[32] Malaria claims the life of a young child every two minutes, which means that five children have died of the disease since you started reading this chapter.[33]

Because mosquitos are most active at night, a simple solution is to sleep under a bed net. But the challenge for aid workers has been how best to increase the uptake of bed nets. Some people argued that if you simply give out free bed nets, recipients won't value them. New York University's William Easterly warned that free nets 'are often diverted to the black market, become out of stock in health clinics, or wind up being used as fishing nets or wedding veils.'[34] So from 2000 to 2005, the World Health Organization focused on subsidising the cost.[35] Nets were distributed at a cost of about US$2 to $3, with part of the money retained by the local salesperson.

As it turns out, economic theory isn't much help in deciding how to set the right price to maximise the take-up of bed nets. It could be that people who are most willing to pay for a product are those who need it the most. Perhaps paying for a product is a signal of quality, which leads the buyer to make more use of it. There's also a theory about the 'power of free', which sees people consume more when the price falls to zero. You probably see some of these theories at work in your own life. If you overeat at the buffet, you've fallen victim to the power of free. But if you open the most expensive bottle of wine at the start of the night, you're using price as a signal of quality. Like I said, theory doesn't provide a decisive answer.

It took a series of randomised experiments to answer the question.[36] Offer people a free bed net, and almost everyone takes one. Raise the price of a bed net from zero to just 60 cents, and the take-up rate falls by two-thirds. When the researchers visited the villages, those who received a free bed net were equally likely to be sleeping under it as those who had paid a subsidised price. Free distribution also did a better job of protecting those people most at risk of malaria.

As the results of the randomised trials became clear, the World Health Organization switched its policy to favour free distribution of bed nets.[37] In sub-Saharan Africa, two out of three children now sleep under an insecticide-treated net, compared with just one in fifty in the year 2000. Widespread take-up of bed nets is saving hundreds of thousands of children's lives annually – and randomised trials have shown how best to achieve the goal.

Getting the prices right is a central challenge in development economics. Further randomised trials have explored the question of whether free is best for a number of other interventions, including deworming tablets for children and water disinfectant for families. In both cases, the best price turns out to be zero, with coverage rates increasing substantially when households pay nothing.[38]

Indeed, when it comes to vaccination, the ideal price may even be negative. A trial in India showed that families were more likely to get their children vaccinated when they received food and metal plates worth about US$3.[39] With more children being vaccinated, health centres could cut the cost per child – even after subtracting the cost of the products they gave away.

But giveaways aren't always successful. After a visit to Argentina, businessman Blake Mycoskie decided he wanted to do something about the lack of decent footwear in developing nations. A talented entrepreneur, Mycoskie had founded and sold four companies by his thirtieth birthday. Now he was affected by the poverty he saw in villages outside Buenos Aires: 'I knew somewhere in the back of my mind that poor children around the world often went barefoot, but now, for the first time, I saw the real effects of being shoeless: the blisters, the sores, the infections.'[40]

To provide shoes to those children, Mycoskie founded 'Shoes for Better Tomorrows', which was soon shortened to TOMS. The company made its customers a one-for-one promise: buy a pair of shoes, and TOMS will donate a pair to a needy child. Since 2006, TOMS has given away 60 million pairs of shoes.[41] It has inspired others companies to apply the one-for-one model to eyeglasses, soccer balls, condoms, toothbrushes, flashlights and medical scrubs.[42]

Six years in, Mycoskie and his team wanted to know what impact TOMS was having, so they made the brave decision to let economists randomise shoe distribution across eighteen communities in El Salvador. The study showed that the canvas loafers didn't go to waste: most children wore their new shoes most of the time.[43] But the children's health wasn't any better, as the TOMS shoes were generally replacing older footwear. Free shoes didn't improve children's self-esteem, but did make them feel more dependent on outsiders.

These were shocking findings. Corporate philanthropy wasn't an add-on for TOMS – it was the firm's founding credo. Now a randomised trial showed that among recipients in El Salvador, free shoes weren't doing much to improve child outcomes, and may even have been fostering a sense of dependency. Yet rather than trying to discredit the evaluation, TOMS responded promptly. As lead researcher Bruce Wydick wrote:

> TOMS is perhaps the most nimble organization any of us has ever worked with, an organization that truly cares about what it is doing, seeks evidence-based results on its program, and is committed to re-orienting the nature of its intervention in order to maximize results. In response to children saying that the canvas loafer isn't their first choice, they now often give away sports shoes … In response to the dependency issue, they now want to pursue giving the shoes to kids as rewards for school attendance and performance … Never once as researchers did we feel pressure to hide results that could shed an unfavourable light on the company. By our agreement, they could have chosen to remain anonymous on the study; they didn't …

For every TOMS, there are many more, both secular and faith-based, who are reticent to have the impacts of the program scrutinized carefully by outside researchers. Instead of demonstrating the effectiveness of their program on the poor to potential donors, many organizations today continue to avoid rigorous evaluation, relying on marketing clichés and feel-good giving to bring in donor cash. TOMS is different, and we applaud them for their transparency and commitment to evidence-based action among the poor.[44]

Ultimately, the TOMS randomised trial doesn't look like a failure at all. Blake Mycoskie's goal in establishing the firm was to improve the health of poor children. The company evaluated its approach. It didn't work. So it changed tack. If all donors were as big-hearted and open-minded as TOMS, there would be less poverty in the world.

Other experiments have looked at ways to reduce the road toll. If you want to get a vivid sense of the dangers of driving, open up the World Health Organization's page on the topic. Immediately a timer starts counting down with the caption 'A road user will die in ...'[45] Every twenty-five seconds, the timer reaches zero, another number is added to the death toll, and the counter resets. Annually, that's 1.25 million traffic deaths.

Across the globe, Africa has the highest traffic fatality rates of any continent. Part of the reason is dangerous driving. In Kenya, where travel by *matatu* or mini-bus is common, the average passenger reports experiencing a life-threatening event in a mini-bus every three months.

To encourage passengers to speak up when drivers are behaving recklessly, a team of researchers worked with *matatu* companies to place stickers in the buses with slogans such as 'A careless *matatu* driver is your wake-up call! Stand up. Speak up.'[46] In case anyone missed the message, the sticker also included a photograph of a severed foot. Comparing 1000 randomly selected *matatus* with stickers with 1000 that did not have stickers, the researchers found that a sticker provided the social licence to passengers to speak out against risky driving. They estimated that a simple sign – costing virtually nothing – halved the accident rate. If randomistas promoted their results with bumper decals, this one might say 'Study shows safety stickers save souls'.

Defecating outdoors might not seem as dangerous as a speeding bus, but it turns out to be just as life-threatening. Because one-third of the world's population lack access to a toilet, many people do their number twos in the open, contaminating nearby lakes, rivers and drinking wells. This leads to diarrhoea and parasite infections, which are particularly likely to be fatal for young children.

Initial strategies to reduce open defecation focused on building toilets, but it quickly became clear that in many cases these new facilities were not being used by villagers. So a movement known as Community Led Total Sanitation sprang up. This strategy begins with locals taking the facilitators on a 'walk of shame' – a tour to look at where people defecate. The facilitators then discuss with the community how that faeces makes its way back into the food and water supply. The aim of the project is to generate a sense of disgust, and persuade locals to (in the words of one campaign song) 'Take the poo to the loo'.

In randomised trials covering over 400 villages across India, Indonesia, Mali and Tanzania, sanitation education reduced open defecation rates and increased the share of households that installed their own toilets.[47] Strikingly, children were taller in the treated villages, because they had avoided the stunting effect of faeces-borne diseases. And because the researchers found similar results in all four nations, we can be pretty confident that the program would work in other countries too.

*

Finally, let's look at how randomised trials are shaping schooling in low-income nations. While better educated children earn more as adults, a perennial challenge has been to ward off parents' temptation to withdraw their children from school to help feed the family. How can governments create a better incentive for parents to keep their children enrolled?

One persuasive answer came from a randomised trial in Mexico in 1997, when the government of President Ernesto Zedillo decided to change the way subsidies were provided to poor households. Rather than make food and energy cheaper, the Zedillo government chose to experiment with giving cash to poor households, on the proviso that their children regularly attended health clinics and remained enrolled in school. The program – then known as Progresa – was to be rolled out across 500 Mexican villages. But Santiago Levy, a former economics professor serving as deputy Mexican finance minister, devised a short, sharp randomised trial.[48] Rather than doing the rollout in an ad hoc manner, the government deliberately chose to implement Progresa in half the villages in May 1998, and the other half in December 1999.[49] This provided a brief experiment – lasting just eighteen months – in which the two groups could be compared.

The impacts on children were sizable. Thanks to Progresa, secondary school children were 15 per cent more likely to attend school. Preschool children were 12 per cent less likely to be sick. Toddlers were less likely to be stunted. Progresa households also ate more healthily, and were more likely to go to the doctor at the right times. When the government changed in 2000, Progresa became the first major Mexican social program to survive across administrations. President Vincente Fox changed the name to Oportunidades, but then supported the expansion of the program. It is now known as

Prospera. Similar programs – known as conditional cash transfers – currently operate in over sixty countries.[50]

For developing country governments and donors, Progresa didn't just provide evidence that conditional cash transfers worked; it also showed that randomised trials could be done quickly and simply. From the standpoint of the Mexican government, it would never have been possible to give every village access to Progresa at the same time – so why not randomise the rollout and learn something about the program's effects?

Other randomised trials are ambitious not because of their sample size, but because they randomise things that we might have thought were impossible to test. In Afghanistan, a recent education experiment asked the question: what happens when you build a village school? Previously, the conventional wisdom had been that students were better served by higher-quality regional schools than lower-quality village schools.

But was it really ethical to randomly assign schools to villages? To run their study, a team of researchers worked with a charity in north-west Afghanistan that planned to open thirty-one schools over a two-year period.[51] Because they knew it would not be possible to open all the schools in a single year, the charity was willing to randomly determine which village schools would open in the first year and which would open in the second year.

At the beginning of the study, no one had access to a village school. After two years, everyone in the experiment had access to a village school. But one year into the experiment, the effects could be studied. At that point, the early-adopter villages served as the treatment group, and the late-adopters as the control. The study received ethics approval because every child in the experiment ended up with access to a village school. The rollout was no slower than it would have been without a randomised trial.

The results of the study were unexpected. Regional schools, spanning a few villages, had better staff than village schools. Teachers in regional schools were formally trained, while the village school was often run by just one teacher, who hadn't finished high school. But to get to a regional school, pupils had to travel an average of 5 kilometres each way.

The researchers found that village schools did more to boost educational attainment, chiefly because they had significantly higher attendance rates. The difference was particularly marked for girls, who were 52 percentage points more likely to attend school when a village school was opened. As one village elder observed, 'The way is long, so there should be one or two people in the family to take the girls to school ... and bring them back which is the main reason why they don't let them go.' This massive difference in attendance meant that the impact on test scores was significant and positive. Having access to a village school boosted student performance by approximately a full grade level, relative to regional schools.[52] As filmmaker Woody Allen once put it, 80 per cent of life is showing up. The Afghan randomised trial disproved the conventional wisdom about village schools.

Randomised trials have even been used to inform that most taboo aspect of education – sex education. Should children be taught to use contraception, or counselled to avoid all horizontal refreshments? The question is particularly relevant in Africa, where more than 20 million people are HIV positive, and over 4000 people contract the disease each day.[53]

In 2009, on a visit to Cameroon, Pope Benedict XVI said that HIV/AIDS is a tragedy that 'cannot be overcome through the distribution of condoms; on the contrary, they increase it'. Instead, the Pope argued for 'the humanisation of sexuality, spiritual renewal which brings with it new ways of behaving'.[54] Within days, the comments had been condemned by the United Nations, France and Germany. An editorial in *The Lancet* called them 'outrageous and wildly inaccurate' and called on the Pope to retract his words.[55] But to many Africans, the world's most senior Catholic was merely reflecting the way their schools delivered sex education. In Kenya, the 'Nimechill' campaign (partly funded by the US government) urged young people to make a two-fingered 'peace' sign to show their desire to abstain from sex until marriage. Young people who were tempted to have casual sex were encouraged to join a 'chill club' or pledge to 'keep it locked'. The official sex education textbook urged students to 'Avoid sex' and 'Say NO to sex before marriage'.

Does it work? Six years after Pope Benedict's Cameroon visit, a team of researchers published their randomised evaluation of Kenya's abstinence campaign. The ABCD campaign – 'Abstain, Be faithful, use a Condom … or you Die' – turned out to have absolutely no impact on pregnancy rates.[56] Five years after receiving the education program, one-third of teenage girls had fallen pregnant – precisely the same proportion as in the control schools. Kenya's abstinence campaigns were just as ineffective as the US programs we saw in Chapter 3.

But while Kenyan teens didn't seem to respond to a simple 'no sex' message, a more nuanced information campaign was successful in shaping behaviour. In Western Kenya, students were shown a video about the risks of relationships with older men, commonly known as 'sugar daddies'.[57] Their teacher then wrote on the board the HIV rates among men of different ages: 4 per cent for teenage boys, compared with 32 per cent for men in their thirties.[58] In effect, the girls were told, they were eight times more likely to contract HIV from a sugar daddy than from a boy their own age. In schools that were randomly selected to learn about the sour side of 'sugar daddies', girls were nearly one-third less likely to become teenage mothers, and more likely to use condoms. Perhaps Pope Francis might shift the focus from criticising condoms to decrying sugar daddies.

*

'If I can predict what you are going to think of pretty much any problem,' argues Esther Duflo, 'it is likely that you will be wrong on stuff.'[59] Since childhood, Duflo wanted to do something to reduce global suffering. Growing up in Paris, she recalls watching television coverage of the Ethiopian famine in the 1980s. Duflo's mother, Violaine, a paediatrician, would travel each year to Africa – returning with images of the child victims of war that she had treated.

Initially, Duflo studied history at the elite École Normale Supérieure in Paris. But her turning point came when she spent a year working with economist Jeffrey Sachs in Moscow, helping advise the Russian government. 'I immediately saw that, as an economist, I can have the best of both worlds. You can be there but keep your principles intact and say exactly what you think, and go back to your studies if you are ejected. What you are doing is meaningful and pertinent and maybe will change something.'[60]

It didn't take Duflo long to make her mark on the economics profession. Tenured at twenty-nine, she has been awarded the Clark Medal (often a precursor to the Nobel Prize) and a MacArthur Foundation genius grant. With Abhijit Banerjee, Duflo founded the Abdul Latif Jameel Poverty Action Lab, or J-PAL, based at the Massachusetts Institute of Technology. Through her work at J-PAL, Duflo has been responsible for hundreds of randomised trials, including several in this chapter: business training, microcredit, subsidised anti-malaria bed nets, and vaccination incentives.

Duflo's favourite hobby is rock climbing – a sport that rewards bravery, tenacity and flexibility. So it perhaps isn't surprising that she tends to reject the idea that we can simply guess the best way up the mountain. Instead, Duflo prefers to start with a range of strategies, and put them to the test. 'When someone of good will comes and wants to do something to affect education or the role of women or local governments,' she says, 'I want them to have a menu of things they can experiment with.'[61] Sure, she admits, policies sometimes fail. But generally it is because people are complex, not because there is a grand conspiracy against the poor.

Like her mother, Duflo spends a considerable amount of time each year in developing countries – travelling to places like India, Kenya, Rwanda and Indonesia to work with her research collaborators and see J-PAL's experiments firsthand. She knows that some studies will confirm the effectiveness of an anti-poverty program, while other evaluations will highlight defects. 'One of my great assets,' she says, 'is I don't have many opinions to start with. I have one opinion – one should evaluate things – which is strongly held. I'm never unhappy with the results. I haven't yet seen a result I didn't like.'[62]

In business, governance, health and education, randomistas like Esther Duflo are providing answers that help to reduce poverty in slums and villages across Africa, Latin America and the Asia-Pacific. Invariably, these results are messier than the grand theories that preceded them. That's the reality of the world in which we live.

But it's not all chaos. Just as biologists and physicists build up from the results of individual experiments to construct a model of how larger systems operate, randomistas have sought to combine the results of multiple experiments to inform policymakers. J-PAL doesn't seek just to run randomised trials, but also to synthesise the evidence. In the case of schooling, J-PAL runs the ruler across dozens of programs designed to raise test scores in developing countries.[63] It gives high marks to programs that increase the authority of the local school committee, that encourage teachers to show up (in one case by having them take a daily class photo) and that track students by achievement levels. But J-PAL gives a failing grade to free laptops, smaller class sizes and flipcharts.

At Yale University, Innovations for Poverty Action plays a similar role to MIT's J-PAL centre, conducting randomised trials and summarising their results for decision-makers. A recent publication explores what works to boost financial inclusion.[64] Monthly text messages reminding clients of their goals boosts savings. ATM cards have no impact on women's savings behaviour. Rainfall insurance makes farmers more productive. Microcredit does not increase the numbers of small businesses.

This kind of scorecard approach is not without its critics. One challenge is that combining studies across the developing world may miss important local differences. When I summarised J-PAL's findings on schooling and Innovations for Poverty Action's findings on financial literacy just now, I neglected to tell you that these experiments were conducted in different countries, including Ghana, Peru and Indonesia. These places vary greatly in their poverty levels, racial mix, literacy levels and so on. Indeed, when researchers run the same experiment in different places, there generally turns out to be a good deal of variation.[65]

Another challenge is that apparently similar interventions might turn out to be different in design or implementation. Text messages reminding people to save more money may work only if worded a particular way. Giving more power to school committees could range from letting them look at the school budget to allowing them to fire teachers.

To illustrate the challenges of generalisability across developing country randomised trials, Karthik Muralidharan uses the example of textbooks.[66] For many charitable donors, seeing a classroom of students sharing a single textbook led to an obvious conclusion: giving textbooks would raise student performance.

In four different experiments, students in schools that were randomly selected to receive textbooks did no better on exams than students in schools without textbooks. But as Muralidharan points out, closer examination of the four studies reveals four different reasons why textbook distribution failed to make a difference. In Sierra Leone, textbooks reached the schools but were put in storage rather than being distributed to the children.[67] In India, parents cut back their spending on education in response to the free textbook program.[68] In Tanzania, teachers had little incentive to use textbooks in their lessons.[69] In Kenya, textbooks only helped the top fifth of students; the rest of the students were unable to read.[70]

Knowing all that, how would you respond to someone who asked: 'Do free textbooks help students?' You might just say, 'no.' Or you could say, 'Maybe – but only if they aren't put in storage, if parents don't spend less on schooling, if teachers use them, and if students are literate.' Together, the studies illustrate four different ways that a promising program can fail. They are a reminder of the need for randomistas to produce deeper knowledge. As Princeton's Angus Deaton puts it, the best experiments don't just test programs, they help us understand 'theories that are generalizable to other situations'.[71]

The challenge of taking research findings from one specific part of the world and applying them in another is not unique to randomised trials. In fact, it's not even unique to statistical research. Any time we generalise about humans in the world, we have to remember that people and programs differ. A drug that works on people of African ancestry may be less effective on people of European ancestry. Fire-fighting strategies that are effective in Madagascar may not work in Mali.

In Chapter 11, I'll return to the topic of replication. But it is also worth pointing out that the alternative to using one kind of evidence is not necessarily another, better kind of evidence. As comedian

Stephen Colbert sardonically noted of President George W. Bush, 'We're not members of the factinista. We go straight from the gut.' As the saying goes, you can't reason someone out of a position if they didn't reason their way into it in the first place.

Randomised trials may not be perfect, but the alternative is making policy based on what one pair of experts describe as 'opinions, prejudices, anecdotes and weak data'.[72] As the poet W.H. Auden once put it, 'We may not know very much, but we do know something, and while we must always be prepared to change our minds, we must act as best we can in the light of what we do know'.[73]

8

FARMS, FIRMS
AND FACEBOOK

English scientist John Bennet Lawes had a problem. In 1842 he had been granted a patent for a product called 'super-phosphate', made by treating bones or mineral phosphates with sulphuric acid. He established a factory, and was ready to produce this new artificial fertiliser. But when he tried to sell 'J.B. Lawes's Patent Manures', farmers told Lawes that they didn't see why they should buy fertiliser when their crops already grew perfectly well with animal manure. To persuade his customers, Lawes ran an experiment. On his family estate in Hertfordshire, just north of London, he divided a field into twenty plots and randomly assigned them to receive no fertiliser, chicken and cow manure, or ammonium sulphate.[1] Then he planted winter wheat on each of the plots. Each year the wheat was harvested, and the amount produced by each plot was recorded.

It didn't take long for the field to show dramatic differences. Within a couple of years, Lawes observed, 'the experimental ground looked almost as much as if it were devoted to trials with different seeds as with different manures'.[2] Lawes' fertiliser sales took off, and by the time of his death in 1900 his estate was worth £565,000 (£55 million in today's money). Since then, global production of phosphate-based fertilisers has grown from around 100,000 tonnes per year to over 40 million tonnes per year.[3] Hertfordshire became a major research centre, hosting some of the world's leading experimental scientists, including Ronald Fisher, whose story we heard earlier. The experiments begun by Lawes continue today, making them the world's oldest continuously running ecological experiment.

Globally, randomised experiments have been critical to farming success. In 1890 the rust fungus obliterated much of the Australian wheat crop, and the colonies had to import wheat. In response, a mathematician-turned-farmer by the name of William Farrer used experiments to find a rust-resistant variety of wheat. Critics mocked his 'pocket handkerchief wheat plots'.[4] But after trying hundreds of different breeding combinations, Farrer created a new 'Federation Wheat' based not on reputation or appearance, but on pure performance.

Agricultural trials of this kind are often called 'field experiments', a term which some people also use to describe randomised trials in social science. Modern agricultural field experiments use spatial statistical models to divide up the plots.[5] As in medicine and aid, the most significant agricultural randomised trials are now conducted across multiple countries. They are at the heart of much of our understanding of genetically modified crops, the impact of climate change on agriculture, and drought resistance.

*

Gary Loveman was in his late thirties when he decided to make the switch from Harvard to Las Vegas. A junior professor at the time, he took up an offer to become the chief operating officer at Harrah's casino. The CEO of Harrah's was preparing to step down and wanted

Loveman to succeed him in the top job. Former professors aren't most people's idea of a casino manager, and Loveman had no intention of becoming a typical casino manager. One of the things that attracted him to the betting businesses was the ready availability of data. And yet casinos were often run by gut feeling: 'What I found in our industry was that the institutionalization of instinct was a source of many of its problems.'[6]

For as many problems as possible, Loveman set about running randomised trials.[7] How to get interstate customers to come more often? Randomly choose a group to receive a discounted hotel offer and compare their response with those who aren't randomly selected. How to keep high-rollers happy? Randomly experiment with incentives like free meals, free hotel rooms, exclusive access to venues, and free chips. How to get waiters to sell more drinks without becoming obnoxious? Randomly adjust the salary bonuses paid to casino staff. How to stop unlucky first-timers walking away? Randomly trial consolation prizes. (Loveman claims that the casino does not target gambling addicts.[8])

Asked whether it was difficult to set up a constant stream of experiments, Loveman replied, 'Honestly, my only surprise is that it is easier than I would have thought. I remember back in school how difficult it was to find rich data sets to work on. In our world, where we measure virtually everything we do, what has struck me is how easy it is to do this. I'm a little surprised more people don't do this.'[9] He said that Harrah set out three cardinal sins: 'It's like you don't harass women, you don't steal and you've got to have a control group. This is one of the things that you can lose your job for at Harrah's – not running a control group.'[10]

Loveman is part of a growing band of business randomistas.[11] In 1994 Nigel Morris and Rich Fairbank started the credit card company Capital One. Their philosophy was explicitly experimental. Should credit card offers be sent in white or blue envelopes? Mail out 50,000 of each, and see which gets the higher response rate.[12] Could the website be tweaked? Create two versions, randomly direct visitors to each and see which is best.

Capital One's biggest innovation was to be the first major firm to offer customers free balance transfers from other credit cards. It ended up being highly successful, but Morris and Fairbank didn't need to bet the company on it. Instead, they randomly selected a small group of customers, offered them free balance transfers and compared their behaviour with other Capital One customers.[13] Capital One is now the eighth-largest bank holding company in the United States. Fairbank describes his firm as 'a scientific laboratory where every decision about product design, marketing, channels of communication, credit lines, customer selection, collection policies, and cross-selling decisions could be subjected to systematic testing using thousands of experiments'.[14]

At Kohl's, one of the largest department store chains in the United States, an experiment helped resolve a split on the board regarding opening hours.[15] In 2013 the company was aiming to cut costs, and considering opening an hour later. Some managers liked the idea, while others expected the drop in sales would outweigh the cost savings. So the firm ran an experiment with 100 of its stores. The verdict: big cost savings with a small loss of sales. Bolstered by rigorous evidence, the firm pushed back opening hours across more than a thousand stores.

On 15 January 2014 the dating website OkCupid ran an unexpected experiment with its customers: it declared 'Love is Blind Day', and removed all photos from the website. Three-quarters of users immediately left the site. But then the company noticed something else. Among those who remained, people were more likely to respond to messages, conversations went deeper and contact details were exchanged more often. Racial and attractiveness biases disappeared.

As company co-founder Christian Rudder put it, 'In short, OkCupid worked better.'[16]

Then, after seven hours, OkCupid restored access to photos. Conversations immediately melted away. As Rudder puts it, 'The goodness was gone, in fact worse than gone. It was like we'd turned on the bright lights at midnight.'[17]

Having access to OkCupid, Rudder points out, makes it possible to analyse 'a data set of person-to-person interaction that's deeper and more varied than anything held by any other private individual.'[18] It also makes it possible to run experiments. Because Love is Blind Day wasn't a randomised trial, its impact had to be assessed by comparing it with user patterns at the same time of the week.

But other OkCupid experiments are random. In a blog post titled 'We experiment on human beings!', Rudder explains how the website tested the impact of its match quality scores.[19] Take a pair of people who are a bad match (with a 30 per cent match rating). When told the truth, there was a 1.4 per cent chance they would strike up a conversation. But what if OkCupid told them they were a terrific match (displaying a 90 per cent match rating)? In that case, the odds of the pair striking up a conversation were 2.9 per cent: more than twice as high. The results of the randomised experiment showed that 'the mere myth of compatibility works just as well as the truth.'[20]

Some firms remain reluctant to run experiments, with managers stymied by bureaucratic inertia, or fearing that an experiment will demonstrate that they don't have all the answers (the truth: they don't).[21] But in other industries, experiments are everywhere. Running a randomised experiment in business is often called 'A/B testing', and has become integral to the operation of firms such as eBay, Intuit, Humana, Chrysler, United Airlines, Lyft and Uber.

Money transfer firm Western Union uses randomised experiments to decide what combination of fixed fees and foreign exchange mark-ups to charge consumers. Quora, a question-and-answer website, devotes a tenth of its staff to running randomised trials, and is conducting about thirty experiments at any given time.[22] As one writer puts it, 'We talk about the Google homepage or the Amazon checkout screen, but it's now more accurate to say that you visited *a* Google homepage, *an* Amazon checkout screen.'[23] Another commentator observes that 'every pixel on the [Amazon] home page has had to justify its existence through repeated testing of alternative layouts.'[24] Among the largest restaurants, retailers and financial institutions in the United States, at least a third are running randomised experiments.[25]

But these experiments don't always go according to plan.

*

In 2000, tech-savvy users of online bookseller Amazon discovered something curious: movie prices were changing. A customer who looked at the DVD of *Men in Black* might see it priced at $23.97. But if the same person then deleted their cookies (small files on your hard disk that allow websites to track your browsing patterns), and went back to Amazon's website, then the same DVD might be offered for sale at $27.97. The four-dollar difference was random – part of an Amazon experiment to see how price-responsive their customers were.

The experiment probably didn't last long enough to teach Amazon much about price-responsiveness, but when the news broke, they did quickly learn how their customers felt about random price changes. Amazon users called it a 'bad idea' and a 'strange business model'. One person posted on a discussion forum: 'I will never buy another thing from those guys.'[26] Los Angeles actor John Dziak said he felt betrayed. 'You trust a company, then you hear they're doing this kind of stuff, your trust wavers, and you go somewhere else.'[27]

A week later, Amazon admitted that it had embarked on a five-day randomised price test, involving sixty-eight DVD titles, and testing discounts of up to 40 per cent. The company announced that it was ceasing the experiment, and would refund to 6896 customers an average of $3.10 as a result of the random price test.[28] Amazon would keep on running randomised experiments in areas such as website design, but the company promised to no longer run pricing experiments on its customers.

But pricing experiments remain ubiquitous.[29] Randomly varying prices in mail-order catalogues for women's clothing, researchers found that when retailers end prices with the number nine (such as $9.99 or $39), demand jumps by up to one-third.[30] Although the rational thing to do is to round up, our brains have a tendency to round down, making things priced with nines seem cheaper than they really are. In fact, customers seem to be so bad at processing prices that the study finds higher demand at a price of $39 than $34. Perhaps it shouldn't come as a surprise that a survey of consumer prices estimates that about half of all published prices end in nine.

Customers also seem to make predictable mistakes when shopping online. One randomised experiment on eBay tested what happened when the seller dropped the minimum bid by $1 but raised the shipping cost by $1.[31] It turned out that for the products they were selling – CDs and Xbox games – buyers tend to ignore the shipping costs. If you're buying a product on eBay and you suddenly notice that it has an exorbitant shipping cost, you might be dealing with a seller who keeps up to date with the latest randomised trials.

Another trick that companies use to increase their profits is to offer products with a special status. In an experiment in Indonesia, a major credit card company randomly offered customers an upgrade to one of two products. Some were offered a 'platinum' credit card, featuring airport lounge access, discounts on international fashion brands and a higher credit limit. Other customers were offered a card with all the same features, but without the 'platinum' branding.

Customers were significantly more likely to accept the offer of a high-status platinum card, and more likely to use it in visible settings, such as restaurants.[32]

Other experiments take place in stores. Working with a single US retail store for sixteen weeks, a team of researchers tested whether shoppers were more likely to buy a bottle of hand lotion when the shelf sign said '33 per cent off' or when it said '50 per cent more free'.[33] The two descriptions are mathematically identical, but they found that the product was nearly twice as popular in the weeks when it was sold using the larger '50 per cent more free' tagline.

With only one store, there's a limit to how much we can generalise results. Moreover, the experiment has to be run by randomly turning the promotion on and off. But with multiple stores, it can be done in a single week. Working with a chain of eighty-six supermarkets, a group of researchers compared the impact of single-unit discounts (e.g. 50 cents) with multiple unit promotions (e.g. two for $1).[34] In half the stores, customers saw single unit discounts, while in the other half, they saw multiple unit promotions. Measuring sales across a variety of products – from canned soup to toilet paper – the researchers find that multiple unit promotions have a psychological 'anchoring' effect, leading customers to spend one-third more.

But just as there are lousy products, there are dud promotions too. In 2003 a team of marketing professionals worked with CVS, the largest pharmacy chain in the United States, to identify product promotions that they thought weren't working.[35] The company then agreed to run a major experiment. For fifteen product categories, they would stop promotions in 400 randomly selected stores.

Three months later, the evidence was in. By axing the promotions, CVS sold fewer products but at higher prices. Across the 400 stores that ran the experiment, profits were up. Not surprisingly, CVS soon put the changes in place across all its 9000 stores. A simple randomised trial likely increased the organisation's annual profits by more than $50 million. If your favourite CVS discount suddenly disappeared in 2003, it's likely because the company figured out that the promotional price wasn't attracting enough new buyers.

Randomised trials have even looked into what happens when customers are invited to 'pay what you want'. A German study found that most of the time, customers pay less than the price that the company would normally charge.[36] But because the quirky pricing scheme attracts new customers, it can end up paying off in the form of higher profits.

*

I'm sitting in a conference room in the Coles headquarters in Hawthorn East, several kilometres outside the centre of Melbourne. The building is the epicentre of the $30 billion Coles supermarket empire. There are people wearing Coles uniforms, Coles products, and a Coles-branded cafe in the middle of an atrium emblazoned with Coles advertisements. It's like Disneyland for retailers.

The reason for my visit is to learn about how one of Australia's biggest supermarkets uses randomised trials. Coles owns FlyBuys, the nation's largest loyalty card program. Each year, one in three Australians swipes a FlyBuys card. As well as earning points at Coles, Target and Kmart, all FlyBuys users get promotions on their checkout dockets, emails offering special discounts, and coupons mailed to their home.

Well, not quite all of them. To be precise, 99 per cent.

The FlyBuys loyalty card has an inbuilt randomised trial, they explain to me. One in every 100 customers is in the control group. Their cards work just the same as everyone else's, but FlyBuys doesn't send them any promotional material.

'Can you tell whether my FlyBuys card is in the control group?' I ask, pulling it out of my wallet.

'Sure, I just look at the last two digits,' replies one of the data ana-lysts from Coles.

'What's the number for the control group?'

'Sorry, it's a secret.'

I can't blame them for not wanting to give it away – but it's too tantalising not to ask.

For Coles, the FlyBuys control group provides a clear and unam-biguous performance benchmark for their promotions. If the promotional program is working well, then sales per customer should be higher among the 99 per cent who get promotions than among the 1 per cent who do not. The better the promotions, the bigger the gap.

I asked whether the management team and the board ever worry that FlyBuys are leaving money on the table by taking one in 100 cus-tomers out of the promotions. Not at all, they reply. Without a randomised control group, 'how do you know you're having an impact?'

Coles also uses randomised trials to test all kinds of aspects of their marketing. Should discount coupons be tear-off or loose? Are people more likely to open an email with a quirky header like 'Bonzer Offer'? Should special offers be cash discounts or FlyBuys points? How does a 1000-point reward compare with a 2000-point reward? Do countdown clocks make people more likely to go to a store?

But it's their response to my question about the FlyBuys control group that sticks in my head as I leave the Coles mothership. If you don't have a randomised control group, 'how do you know you're hav-ing an impact?'

*

With over 3 billion passengers flying every year, planes account for 2 to 3 per cent of worldwide greenhouse gas-emissions. For the airlines themselves, fuel is a massive expense. If you're running an airline, about one-third of your costs are on jet fuel. And yet it turns out that pilots' decisions can make a significant difference to how much fuel a plane uses. By not carrying too much fuel, updating the route based on new weather information, or turning off an engine when taxiing off the runway, pilots can cut their fuel use considerably.

But how to get pilots to save fuel? Virgin Atlantic Airways teamed up with economists to see whether providing better feedback to pilots on their fuel use would make them more efficient.[37] Working with the pilots' union, the researchers reassured pilots that they would not be ranked against each other. 'This is not, in any way, shape or form, an attempt to set up a "fuel league table",' the letter told them. Despite knowing this, pilots who received monthly reports on their fuel efficiency ended up guzzling less gas than pilots who did not receive such reports. The feedback was purely private, yet it led pilots to tweak their behaviour. With an experiment that cost less than US$1000 in postage, Virgin cut its annual fuel usage by about 1 million litres.

Other personnel experiments have focused on low-wage jobs. In an experiment in the Canadian province of British Columbia, tree planters were either paid a fixed daily wage or an amount per tree. When paid a fixed wage, they planted about 1000 trees a day. When paid for each tree, they planted about 1200 trees each day.[38] A randomised experiment in the US state of Washington found similar results for workers in fruit orchards.[39] The Washington state study had an interesting twist, however. Flat-rate workers were resentful when they realised their colleagues were earning piece rates. So perhaps piece-rate workers did better because they were being compared against disappointed colleagues.

If you've ever picked fruit, you'll know that your productivity depends on the quality of the crop as much as on how hard you're working. In one set of experiments, a team of British researchers forged a relationship with a strawberry farmer who was trying to set the right pay rates.[40] In one setting, workers were simply paid a fixed sum per kilogram. In another setting, workers' pay rates depended on the total amount everyone picked that day. If everyone's output was high, the managers reasoned, the fields must be bountiful. So as total pickings rose, the farmer lowered the rate per kilogram (though all workers were paid above the minimum wage). But the workers didn't take long to cotton on – or strawberry on. Under the second pay scheme, working hard had a collective cost. So the strawberry pickers slowed down, particularly when they had a lot of friends in the picking team. This meant they picked fewer kilograms, but kept the pay rate per kilogram higher. By contrast, the simple piece-rate pay scheme didn't create perverse incentives, and turned out to significantly increase total output.[41]

Pay isn't all that matters. Studies of supermarket checkout workers, strawberry pickers and vehicle emissions inspectors find that more productive co-workers raise everyone's performance.[42] Social incentives matter too. In a randomised experiment of condom sellers in urban Zambia, a team of researchers compared the effect of bonus pay with social recognition of star employees.[43] In that setting, it turns out that the promise of being publicly recognised has twice as large an impact as financial rewards. Who knew that being 'condom seller of the month' could be such an incentive?

But other kinds of 'recognition' can have the opposite effect. In a randomised experiment run on workers on Amazon's online Mechanical Turk platform, some employees were given feedback about their relative ranking, compared to their co-workers.[44] Telling workers their place in the pecking order turned out to reduce productivity. If you're a boss, these experiments are a reminder that the most productive people in the workplace are bringing in a double dividend. They also suggest that you might want to promote 'most valued employee' awards, but sack worker league tables.

Randomisation is particularly critical when studying employees. That's because people behave differently when they know they're being watched. If I tell you that I'm going to measure your productivity for a day, you'll probably spend less time surfing Facebook. This is known as the 'Hawthorne effect', after a famous study of workers in the Hawthorne Works factory in the 1920s. As it turns out, there are now questions over precisely what was going on in that study.[45] But there is no doubt that Hawthorne effects are real, just like placebo effects in medicine. For example, Virgin Atlantic's experiment showed significant differences between pilots who received personalised fuel usage reports and those who did not. But there was another impact too. All the pilots were told at the outset that the airline was conducting a fuel use study. Just knowing that they were being watched made pilots in the control group 50 per cent more likely to fly efficiently.

*

While many randomised trials in business have studied tweaks, some have looked at more dramatic changes. One of the big debates in business has been whether management consulting firms are change agents or charlatans. Reviewing the history of the industry, Matthew Stewart's *The Management Myth* concludes that management consulting is more like a party trick than a science.[46] Another critic calls it 'precisely nine-tenths shtick and one-tenth Excel'.[47]

If we want to know the impact of management consultants on firm performance, it isn't enough to compare firms that use consultants with those that don't. That kind of naive comparison could be biased upwards or downwards, depending on why firms engage consultants. If hiring a consultant is a sign that the management team is thinking big, then we might expect those kinds of firms to outperform their competitors, even in the absence of outside help. Alternatively, if hiring a management consultant is the corporate equivalent of calling in the doctor, then we might expect a naive comparison to show that consultants were associated with underperformance.

To tackle the question, Stanford's Nicholas Bloom and his collaborators worked with twenty textile plants in India.[48] Fourteen were randomly selected to receive five months' worth of management consulting advice from Accenture, an international management consulting firm.[49] Afterwards, productivity was one-tenth higher in the firms that had received management advice. Although the advice was free, the productivity boost was large enough that companies would have made a profit even if they had paid for it at the going rate.

So if you run a medium-sized firm, should you stop reading now and phone the management consultants? Not necessarily. International surveys of management quality tend to rate India very low. Bloom and his team include photographs in their report of what the factories looked like before the intervention. They show tools scattered on the floor, garbage left in piles, machines not maintained and yarn left in damp sacks. It isn't hard to see how outside consultants were able to help managers clean up the plants, shift to computerised systems and ramp up their production. But with a better-run firm, the gains from calling in Accenture, McKinsey or Boston Consulting might be a good deal smaller.[50]

Bloom's management consulting experiment also illustrates a curious fact about randomised trials: under the right conditions, the number of treatment and control groups can be remarkably small.[51] With similar factories, a major intervention and plenty of output data, Bloom and his team could be confident that they had measured statistically significant effects – meaning that the results were unlikely to be a mere fluke in the data.

Sometimes the statistics allow randomistas to find significant effects in small samples. But occasionally the problem is the reverse. This turns out to be a difficulty plaguing experiments that test the impact of advertising. Since the early 1980s, US cable television companies have had a product called 'split cable', making it possible to deliver different advertisements to households watching the same program. Market researchers such as AC Nielsen then work with a panel of households to log everything they buy (these days, participating households have a handheld scanner and just scan the barcodes of every new product).

Online, running randomised experiments is even simpler. Web retailers select a large group of people, randomly send half of them an advertisement for their product, and then use cookies to follow how people behave. In some cases, companies are even able to link up online ads with purchases made in person.

But while setting up a randomised advertising trial is easy, measuring the effect is hard. Our shopping patterns are volatile: we switch brands, buy on impulse and only occasionally buy big products (think about the last time you chose a new credit card, or bought a vacuum cleaner). Advertising is ubiquitous, so most advertisements have no impact on most people. Estimating the true impact of advertising on customers is a needle-in-a-haystack problem.

Combining 389 'split cable' experiments, one study concluded: 'There is no simple correspondence between increased television advertising weight and increased sales.'[52] In general, the estimates suggest that advertising works, but struggle to tell a lousy campaign from a successful one. To illustrate the problem, the researchers turn to the most-watched advertisements in America: television ads shown to Super Bowl viewers. Airing a thirty-second Super Bowl ad costs $5 million, nearly 5 cents per viewer. Even if an advertiser could use 'split cable' techniques to individually randomise across all 110 million Super Bowl viewers, the firm would have to buy dozens of ads to generate a measurable impact. No product in America, the researchers conclude, has a big enough advertising budget to find out whether Super Bowl ads really work. They dub this finding 'the Super Bowl impossibility theorem.'[53]

If anything, the problem is even worse when it comes to measuring the impact of online advertising. Pooling twenty-five online advertising experiments, which each randomised advertisements to about a million users, a recent study concludes that it is 'exceedingly difficult' to discern what works. Their typical campaign had a sample size of 1 million people. The researchers estimate that it would have to cover 9 million people in order to reliably distinguish between a wildly profitable campaign and one that merely broke even.

Difficult as it is to measure the impact of online ads, randomised trials are still the best option. The alternative is to compare people who were targeted with an ad against similar people who weren't targeted.[54] This can go badly wrong when the advertisement is served up based on internet searches. Suppose we run a non-randomised study of the effect of Nike ads, looking only at young and healthy people. Now imagine that people in the study who searched for 'running shoes' were shown Nike ads, and their purchasing patterns compared against those who did not search for running shoes. Would we really credit the advertisements for any difference in buying habits? Or would it be more sensible to think that people who searched for running shoes were already more likely to buy Nikes (or Asics or Brooks, for that matter)? If you've ever had the experience of searching for a toaster and then seeing toaster advertisements on your screen for the next week, you'll know how ubiquitous microtargeting has become. In that environment, randomisation gives firms the best chance of finding out the true effect of their online marketing campaigns.

*

Google's first randomised experiment was conducted on 27 February 2000.[55] Curious about whether the firm should give users more than ten search results, they randomly assigned 1 in 1000 users to receive twenty results, and another 1 in 1000 users to get thirty results. The company couldn't have gotten a bigger rebuff. Doubling or tripling the number of results slowed the loading times and caused many users to leave the site. They stuck with the top ten.

Today, Google is conducting hundreds of randomised experiments on its users: seeking to fine-tune its search algorithm and the way its results are presented.[56] In some cases, these involve tiny tweaks – such as increasing the amount of white space around the first search result, bolding query words in the search results or making slight adjustments to the graphics.

When choosing the colour for its toolbar, Google designers noticed that users were slightly more likely to click through if the toolbar was presented as a greenish-blue colour than if it was coloured plain blue. More click-throughs meant more advertising revenue for the company, so modest improvements had significant revenue implications. Seeing the results, Marissa Mayer, then a vice-president at Google, suggested that they go further. Mayer proposed randomly splitting users into forty equally sized groups. Each group would then see the toolbar in a slightly different shade of blue. The company could then simply choose the colour based on whatever generated the highest click-through rates. Science, not gut instinct, determined the result. With billions of clicks, even a small difference means big bucks. According to journalist Matthew Syed, a Google executive estimated that finding the perfect colour for the toolbar added US$200 million to the company's bottom line.[57]

At other times, Google tests bigger changes, such as new features or products. But not every new idea at Google gets trialled with live traffic. Indeed, the company estimates that for every idea that gets trialled, there are three others that were considered and rejected before reaching the trial stage. Even among those that are trialled, only one in five leads to a change in the product. In other words, Google's ideas have a failure rate of nineteen out of twenty.[58] As co-founder Eric Schmidt observes, 'This is a company where it's absolutely okay to try something that's very hard, have it not be successful, and take the learning from that.'[59]

Some people say that when you have a really big sample, you don't need randomised trials. Instead, they claim, you can just look for patterns.[60] But Google most likely has more data than any other organisation in the world, yet still conducts oodles of in-house experiments. Google's scientists have access to around 15 exabytes of data, and around 40,000 searches each second. If Google still gets value from randomised trials, then the same must go for every other researcher on the planet.

At Netflix, the same data-driven culture prevails. People who sign up for a free trial are randomly assigned to different treatments aimed at turning them into paying customers.[61] Regular users are often placed in experiments to test new aspects of the website. As Netflix's data boffins note, gut feel doesn't definitively tell you what to offer someone who has just finished watching *House of Cards*. Should it be the shows that are most similar, most popular or most trendy? As they admit, 'using our own intuition, even collective intuition, to choose the best variant of a recommendation algorithm also often yields the wrong answer'.[62] Better personalisation and recommendations allow Netflix to keep more of its customers. The company estimates that improving its algorithms has saved it over US$1 billion a year.[63]

Perhaps because Google's and Netflix's experiments are directed at improving the quality of their websites, they haven't attracted much criticism. For Facebook, the experience was much less positive when it partnered with psychology researchers to carry out a social science experiment on its users.[64] For a single week in January 2012, Facebook randomly altered the emotional content in the News Feeds of 700,000 users. Software analysed each post by a Facebook friend, compared it against a list of positive and negative words, and classified it as negative, positive or neutral. People in the experimental treatment either saw 10 per cent fewer negative posts or 10 per cent fewer positive posts.[65] The study only affected what people saw in their News Feed; they could still view all the posts by going to a friend's Wall or Timeline.

The researchers then watched to see how users responded. They found that there was a small but noticeable impact: when people see more negativity in their friends' posts, their own posts become more negative. Reading negative material also led to social withdrawal. When you see negative posts, you're less likely to use Facebook the next day. Before the experiment, some had theorised that Facebook might be driven by a combination of jealousy and schadenfreude. If social comparisons dominate, successful friends should make us morose, while their bad news should make us feel fortunate. The reality turns out to be simpler: our moods follow those of our friends. Positive and negative emotions are contagious.[66]

Like Amazon's pricing experiments, Facebook's emotional manipulation experiments caused a media firestorm. The researchers were criticised by the British Psychological Society, the Federal Trade Commission was asked to investigate, and the academic journal *Proceedings of the National Academy of Sciences* published an editorial 'expression of concern'.[67] Sheryl Sandberg, then Facebook's chief operating officer, told users: 'It was poorly communicated and for that communication we apologize. We never meant to upset you.'[68]

Given that I'm both a randomista and a former professor, you might expect me to side with companies that collaborate with academics to conduct social science experiments. But I can readily see where the complainants are coming from. If you're a Facebook user, there's a chance you unwittingly took part in their 2012 emotional manipulation study. You wouldn't have known it then, and you wouldn't know it now. And unlike a tweak to the Google algorithm, we can't be confident the Facebook experiment left its users unscathed. For experiments of this kind, large firms may want to consider encouraging a subset of users to opt in to become 'A/B testers', perhaps offering them a perk in exchange for their pioneering spirit. Such a model would give companies the confidence that their guinea pigs at least knew they were in a maze, while giving users who find experimentation a bit 'creepy' the chance to say no.

9

TESTING THEORIES
IN POLITICS AND
PHILANTHROPY

Residents of East Rock, Connecticut, take Halloween
seriously. On a typical night, around 500 children
descend on each house that offers candy to trick-or-
treaters. But in 2008 the costumed children came upon
an unusual home, owned by economist Dean Karlan. The left side of
the porch was decorated with campaign posters and a life-size cut-
out of the Democratic presidential candidate, Barack Obama. The
right side of the porch featured the Republican candidate, John
McCain.[1]

East Rock is a heavily Democratic neighbourhood, so it was no
surprise that when children were told that they could pick up one
piece of candy from either side of the house, four out of five chose the
Democratic side. Then the economist homeowner tried something
else. Randomly selected children were told that they could get two
pieces of candy from the Republican side, or one piece from the

Democratic side. In other words, they were offered a sweet induce-ment to go against their political preferences.

It turned out that whether children in a Democratic-voting neigh-bourhood were willing to take candy from a Republican depended on their age. Those aged between four and eight tended to stick to their ideology. Older children, aged nine to fifteen, mostly switched to the Republican side if it meant twice the candy. Four years later, a repeat experiment for Halloween 2012 (this time featuring Barack Obama versus Mitt Romney) produced similar results.

These Halloween experiments suggest that there may be some truth in the cliché about young people voting with their hearts and older people voting with their wallets. It's also a reminder that ran-domistas like Dean Karlan are endlessly imaginative in their quest to test theories with the toss of a coin.

Indeed, in his first presidential race, Barack Obama's team was using randomised trials to evaluate campaign strategies. In Dec-ember 2007, when visitors first went to the Obama website, they saw one of several images, including a colour image of Obama, a black-and-white family photo or a video of Obama speaking.[2] Then they were encouraged to subscribe to campaign emails using various mes-sages, including 'Join Us Now', 'Learn More' or 'Sign Up'. Take a moment to guess which combination of image and message you think worked best. Is it the colour photo, the black-and-white photo or the video? Would you imagine it is best to ask supporters to *Join*, *Learn* or *Sign Up*?

There are reasons to like each of the combinations, but on the Obama campaign team, people's instincts tended to gravitate to the video and the message 'Sign Up'. They were expert campaigners, but most of them turned out to be wrong. After rotating the variants across 300,000 web visitors, the campaign found that the combina-tion of the black-and-white photo and 'Learn More' garnered 41 per cent more email addresses. Over the course of the campaign, the Obama team estimated that this one experiment garnered nearly 3 million more emails, 280,000 more volunteers and US$60 million more in donations. The experts had assumed that people were more likely to sign on when they saw a video. But as campaign digital adviser Dan Siroker told one interviewer, 'Assumptions tend to be wrong.'[3]

In this chapter, I'll discuss the growing use of randomised trials in politics and philanthropy, starting with campaigns to get people to the ballot box, then moving on to randomised trials on fundraising, and concluding with a recent spate of experiments where politicians are the unwitting subjects of randomised experiments.

*

In countries where voting is voluntary, a huge amount of effort goes into persuading people to go to the polls. These 'get out the vote' campaigns are conducted both by nonpartisan civic groups (who are keen to raise overall turnout), as well as by candidates (whose aim is to increase turnout among their own supporters).

In the 1924 US presidential election, political scientist Harold Gosnell noticed that a huge amount of effort was being made to get citizens to vote.[4] The National League of Women Voters and the Boy Scouts were knocking on millions of doors, reminding people of their civic duty to cast a ballot. Turnout was indeed higher in 1924 than it had been in 1920. But when it came to the question of what part of the increase had been caused by the doorknocking efforts, Gosnell argued that the only candid answer was 'we do not know'.

To find out, Gosnell embarked on what was probably the first randomised trial in political science – investigating the impact on voter turnout of sending letters to homes in Chicago.[5] Only by having a credible control group, Gosnell pointed out, could we truly know what impact the mailings had on voting. His studies estimated that those who received a letter were between 1 and 9 percentage points more likely to vote.

Nearly a century later, direct mail has much less impact on voters than in Gosnell's day. But he understood – as some campaigners still do not – that randomised trials are one of the best ways of measuring what works in a political campaign. In their bestselling book *Get Out the Vote*, two leading political randomistas, Alan Gerber and Donald Green, point out that campaigns are often still run by grizzled veterans who know a lot about inputs – the various tactics that can be used – but not much about outputs – the number of extra votes they garner.[6] The greybeards have plenty of anecdotes but no control groups. For example, campaign veterans might point out that a candidate spent a lot of time making telephone calls, and then got a swing towards her. The problem is that it's hard to know the counterfactual: what would have happened if she hadn't hit the phones?

Similarly, campaign veterans might point to a part of the electorate where extra street stalls were held, and note that the candidate's vote was higher in those suburbs. Again, how do we know that those suburbs wouldn't have favoured the candidate for other reasons? In the past, campaigns have massively overestimated the impact of voter contact on turnout by asking people what contact they had with politicians and whether they voted. The problem is that contact with politicians isn't random. Campaigns pursue citizens who are more likely to vote, and those citizens who seek out their local candidates are the kinds of people who were always more likely to vote. So simply looking at the correlation between contact and turnout doesn't tell you much.[7]

Yet the myths persist. As a politician, I meet plenty of campaign veterans with their own secret sauce. I've met 'experts' who are convinced that partisan letters work best when paired with doorknocking, that telephone calls work best in the final week of the campaign, or that posters outside the election booth make a huge difference. But ask them about their evidence base and it's quickly apparent that their war stories lack a control group.

Steadily, however, campaigns are beginning to shift their strategy towards an approach that is more curious, open-minded and data-driven. Modern political strategists are less likely to think that they know all the answers, and be more open to being proven wrong. They have less confidence in any particular campaign technique, but more confidence that they know how to sort effective campaigns from bad ones.

Following in Gosnell's footsteps, researchers have now published more than a hundred studies on the impact of various campaign strategies on increasing voter turnout. In the United States, this is facilitated by the fact that whether or not a person voted in a particular election is public information (though which candidate they voted for remains secret). So if campaigners want to boost turnout, they can start with a list of 20,000 people on the electoral roll, send a letter to 10,000 of them before the election and then look at the voter files afterwards to see whether there are turnout differences between the two groups.

Now that the randomistas have been running turnout experiments, we have a wide range of findings on different techniques to get people to the polls. So let's run through the evidence, starting with traditional approaches (television, radio, letters, phone calls and door-knocking), and finishing with newer strategies (emails, text messages and online advertisements).

In his 2006 campaign for Texas governor, Rick Perry allowed a group of political scientists to randomise the placement of his radio and television advertisements. Over a three-week period, Governor Perry's ads – which began 'I've never been more proud to call myself a Texan' – were assigned across eighteen media markets by researchers. The academics then tested the impact via telephone surveys.[8] The experiment showed no effect of his radio advertisements. In the case of television, the maximum volume of advertisements – costing us$3 million a week – increased Governor Perry's support by 5 percentage points. But the following week, there was no detectable impact on voter preference. By contrast with product commercials, at least political advertisements have a measurable impact.[9] But the fact that the effect has disappeared a week after seeing the ad is a reminder that few ads are memorable.

The history of political advertising has produced a handful of famous advertisements – such as Ronald Reagan's 'Morning in America' segment, or the attack ad on Michael Dukakis for releasing Willie Horton from jail – but they are the exception. Most political advertising – like Rick Perry's riff on Texan pride – is pretty forgettable. The Perry study suggests that a last-minute television blitz would indeed increase a candidate's share of the vote. Conversely, it also implies that a one-week 'television blackout' period prior to polling day would entirely eliminate the effect of television ads on the election campaign.

How about letters? When sent by non partisan groups, direct mail has a small but positive impact on turnout. Experiments have now been conducted in low-stakes and high-stakes elections, with researchers sending up to eight pieces of mail to each household. Combining the results of fifty-one randomised experiments conducted in the United States between 1998 and 2014, Alan Gerber and Donald Green concluded that each additional letter raises turnout by about 0.5 percentage points.[10] Put another way, nonpartisan groups need to post 200 letters to get one more person to the polls.

A remarkable 2006 Michigan study suggests that this impact could be magnified using 'social pressure'.[11] Relying on the fact that voter turnout is public, researchers experimented with three kinds of letters that ramped up the social pressure: first, one that told people that their voting behaviour would be monitored by university researchers; second, a letter that set out the household's past voting behaviour and promised to update it after the election; and third, a letter that listed the turnout of neighbours living on the same block. Each boosted turnout, with the 'neighbours' mailing increasing turnout at a massive rate of one extra voter for every twelve letters.

Most other studies have reinforced these findings, although one study in a small city in Texas failed to find any effect of social pressure.[12] One intriguing theory for this is that in some settings, the threat to tell the neighbours whether you voted might serve to anger people rather than to embarrass them into voting. Other randomised trials take a more positive approach to social pressure, by thanking people for voting in previous elections, or promising to put citizens with perfect voting records on a public 'honour roll'.[13] These kinds of letters raise turnout, but not by as much as the threat to shame non-voters.

While letters can persuade people to vote, this effect seems to be restricted to mailings from groups that are interested in raising civic participation. When letters are sent by those with a stake in the outcome, they have little or no impact. Summarising nineteen US randomised experiments sent by Democratic candidates, Republican candidates and advocacy organisations, Gerber and Green find that such groups would need to send 10,000 letters to persuade one more person to vote.[14] This estimate is so imprecise that it cannot reliably be distinguished from zero, leading Gerber and Green to conclude that 'partisan mail has no effect on turnout'.[15]

Another relatively cheap campaign technique is the 'robocall'. These are carried out by a computer, which automatically dials telephone numbers and then plays a message to the person or answering machine that picks up. Across randomised trials covering more than a million people, Gerber and Green suggest that robocalls perhaps get one more voter for every 1000 people who hear the message.[16] But as with partisan direct mail, the effect is so small that that the true impact may be zero.

A more personal approach is for real people to make the calls. This has traditionally been done by groups of pizza-munching volunteers gathered together in an office. But some campaigns have also experimented with using commercial phone banks. Across a series of randomised trials, both volunteers and paid workers have successfully increased turnout, but the impacts vary a lot. Chatty calls seem to be more effective than delivering a short, formal message.[17] Phoning closer to election day seems to have a bigger impact. And volunteers seem to outperform commercial callers. On average, Gerber and Green estimate it takes thirty-eight completed phone calls to get an additional person to the polls.[18]

Knocking on the door of a stranger and asking for their vote is hard work. Over the years, I've done plenty of doorknocking for others' campaigns and my own. On different occasions, I've got frozen, sunburnt, drenched by rain and swooped by magpies. Most people who answer the door are perfectly pleasant, but I've accumulated enough insults to make a bushranger blush.

Doorknocking is certainly tougher to do than sending letters or making phone calls. But is it more effective? In an attempt to increase voter turnout rates among minority citizens, the California Votes Initiative ran over a hundred experiments, with tens of thousands of people being contacted.[19] In two-thirds of those experiments, citizens who had been contacted were more likely to vote. Similar results have been observed in large-scale experiments involving Democratic and Republican candidates, as well as those involving nonpartisan groups in Britain, and partisan groups in France.[20] On average, Gerber and Green estimate, one additional person votes for every fourteen householders who speak with a face-to-face canvasser.[21] For a candidate, these results suggest that knocking on a person's door is nearly three times as effective as calling them on the telephone, and probably 700 times more effective than sending them a letter. Given this, political scientists have lately been puzzling as to why campaigns spend only about one-twentieth of their budgets on personal campaigning.[22]

Finally, there's the effect of campaigning online. A truism of campaign reporting is that every election in the twenty-first century has been described as 'the first truly online election'. And while it is true that citizens are steadily getting more information from email, the web and social media, it doesn't follow that campaigns run through these platforms are likely to get people to vote a particular way (or at all).

In the case of email, campaigns by non partisan groups to get people to the polls have generally been ineffective. For example, a non-profit group that aimed to increase turnout among US college students sent over 200,000 emails, with no statistically significant increase in voter turnout.[23] Similarly, partisan emails sent to New York City Democrats had no impact on whether recipients voted.[24] The only way an email will get you to the ballot box, randomised trials suggest, is if it comes from one of your friends, or from the electoral commission itself.[25] A similar pattern comes from text messages, which seem to work only when voters have opted in to receive them, or when they are sent by the officials in charge of the election.[26]

Much the same is true of online advertisements. In recent years, Facebook has crowed that partisan ads on their platform could shift as many as one in five voters, Google has claimed that its ads made a significant difference in Senate races, and a bevy of journalists have written about the power of internet advertising to change the shape of an election.[27] Most recently, the Republican National Committee's Gary Coby boasted that the Trump campaign tested 40,000 to 50,000 variants of their Facebook advertisements every day of the 2016 presidential election campaign.[28]

Facebook facilitates easy A/B testing, but the outcomes that the platform measures are views and clicks, not votes. This matters because in experiments involving both Democratic and Republican candidates, Facebook ads raised candidates' name recognition, but didn't make people any more likely to vote for them.[29] And in experiments involving more than 300,000 voters, Facebook ads placed by Rock the Vote – a popular nonpartisan group – had no impact on behaviour.[30]

As with emails, online advertisements seem to change behaviour when your friends are involved. On the day of the 2010 mid-term congressional elections, Facebook ran a massive experiment on 61 million of its US users.[31] People were shown one of three messages: an 'I voted' button with pictures of their friends who had clicked it (social pressure message), an 'I voted' button with statistics on how many people had pressed it (informational message), or no message at all (control). Matching the data with voting records, the researchers found that for every 250 people who got the social pressure message, one additional person voted. By contrast, those who got the informational message were no more likely to vote than the control group. People don't vote because millions are voting – they vote because their closest friends are voting.

In general, the results from randomised experiments on political campaigning are a reminder of how hard it is to change whether or how people vote. But a savvy randomista could still swing a close election. In recent decades, there have been dozens of state, local and national elections where the winning margin was less than one vote in 1000. They include the 2000 presidential election, which saw George W. Bush beat Al Gore by 537 votes in the critical state of Florida. In politics, even the smallest edge can mean the difference between victory and defeat.

*

Another set of randomised trials have focused on how to fundraise. Working with charities and political parties, researchers have run a series of experiments looking at which strategies work best when asking for donations. In one experiment, researchers in North Carolina sent charity workers out asking for money to support an environmental centre at the local university.[32] The workers randomly varied whether they simply asked for donations, or whether they told householders that donors would also have the chance to win a prize. With a prize on offer, nearly twice as many people participated, and about 50 per cent more money was raised.

The researchers also noted another difference between household behaviour: when the charity worker was an attractive woman, men were more likely to donate. (As Aristotle once noted, 'Beauty is a better introduction than any letter.') While you could argue that this ranks as the least surprising finding ever to emerge from a randomised experiment, it is interesting that the size of the prize effect and the beauty effect are about the same.[33]

While some charity workers can brighten the day, an intriguing experiment suggests that many are unwanted. Prior to a fundraising drive for a Chicago children's hospital, certain households were randomly sent flyers which listed the precise time that they would be doorknocked.[34] Knowing who was knocking reduced the share of people opening the door by up to one-quarter. In some cases, the flyer included a 'do not disturb' checkbox, which cut down giving by nearly one-third. Again, the experiment provides an insight that theory couldn't deliver. Some scholars have argued that giving is primarily motivated by the desire to enjoy a warm inner glow. If this were true, householders should have been more likely to open the door when they knew the person on the other side would be asking for money. The fact that people hide from charity collectors suggests that many donors are simply yielding to social pressure.[35]

Working with the Salvation Army's 'Red Kettle' Christmas drive, economists tested the lengths to which we will go to avoid guilt.[36] The researchers chose a Boston supermarket with two main entrances, and randomly placed a bell-ringer on one of them. On average, the Salvation Army worker collected 33 cents a minute. Next came the ask. Salvation Army workers began saying 'please give' to each shopper. This had two effects. Average donations shot up to 55 cents a minute, and the number of people shooting out the other door rose by one-third. Now, the team placed a Salvation Army bell-ringer on the alternative exit. Faced with two bell-ringers politely asking for donations, and no guilt-free way of escaping the supermarket, Bostonians gave at the rate of 99 cents a minute. By maximising guilt while minimising the opportunity to avoid it, the Salvation Army tripled donations. Red Kettle donations were one part generosity, two parts guilt-avoidance.

Other randomised trials have helped charities refine the way they fundraise. When people are told that a 'lead donor' has already committed money, they are more likely to donate.[37] In situations as diverse as a fundraising drive for a German opera company and a capital campaign for a Florida environmental policy centre, people who receive letters that mention a lead donor gave between 50 per cent and 100 per cent more. Such seed money seems to provide a signal that the charity is worthy of support.

Another effective strategy is to offer matching donations – for example, telling people that if they donate $1 then a matching donor will give an extra $1 (or an extra $2 or $3). In a randomised mail experiment conducted with a US civil rights charity, people turned out to give one-fifth more when they were told that it would be matched.[38] However, increasing the match rate – for example from $1 to $3 – had no impact on donors' generosity. This is a puzzling result for economists, since a higher match rate effectively reduces the 'price' of charitable giving. For example, a $1 match means that it costs 50 cents to get $1 to a charity, while a $3 match means that it only costs 25 cents to get $1 to a charity. The randomised results are also at odds with what many fundraising experts had argued. For example, a handbook written by 'one of America's most successful and respected fundraisers' assured readers that when compared to a 1:1 match, 'a richer challenge (2:1) greatly adds to the match's attractiveness'.[39] The theory sounds sensible, but it took a randomised evaluation to find out that it was bunkum.

An unexpectedly successful strategy turned out to be the 'once and done' campaign, in which aid charity Smile Train promised donors 'Make one gift now and we'll never ask for another donation again'.[40] The strategy ran contrary to standard fundraising wisdom, which suggested that charities should focus on building a relationship with their strongest supporters. It turned out that donors liked the option of opting out of future mailings, but most did not tick the box to take themselves off the mailing list. 'Once and done' increased total fundraising by nearly 50 per cent.

Other randomised charity experiments have confirmed popular theories. An international aid organisation found that request letters which included a modest gift (four postcards drawn by Bangladeshi street children) nearly doubled their donations.[41] A university business school discovered that offering alumni an exclusive invitation to a popular economics talk more than doubled their donations.[42] A New Zealand art gallery concluded that donations were 50 per cent higher on days when their gift box was seeded with a smattering of banknotes than when it started off empty.[43]

Then there's the question of whether charities can raise more money by suggesting a particular amount. If you've ever seen a street performer hold out their hat and say, 'Notes only, please!' you'll have a sense of why it might raise or lower the total take. Charity suggestion experiments include radio phone-a-thons which suggest different amount to callers, appeals that name a single figure, and letters which suggest three possible amounts. The conclusion: picking the optimal suggested amount is hard. Depending on the dollar amount chosen, studies have found instances in which suggested figures have both raised and lowered total donations.[44]

As charities have become more scientific about their fundraising, the appetite has grown for high-quality studies on why, how and to whom we give. In 2012 the John Templeton Foundation donated nearly US$5 million to the University of Chicago to establish the 'Science of Philanthropy Initiative'. As director John List describes it, 'Each time we set up these partnerships, we form an experimental relationship where we teach the partner how to think about experimentation: how to think about randomisation of mail solicitations, how to think about randomisation within a phone-a-thon, how to think about how to randomise different techniques for large donors.'[45]

In the political realm, one study tested whether people were more likely to donate money in order to stop something bad or to enable something good. A randomised experiment with a pro-choice lobby group found that people were more likely to give money when they perceived a threat.[46] Barack Obama's 2012 presidential campaign reached a similar conclusion. Randomised testing of email subject headers found that a fundraising appeal titled 'Do this for Michelle' raised about $700,000, while 'I will be outspent' raised $2.6 million.[47] Given that politics is a zero-sum contest, it's likely that many of the insights on political fundraising aren't yet public. But there is some sharing of ideas among ideological bedfellows. For example, Dan Wagner, who led Obama's 2012 data science team, went on to found Civis Analytics, which offers analysis to progressives, including Justin Trudeau's successful 2015 campaign for the Canadian prime ministership.

*

On 2 February 2001, a public meeting was held in the West African village of Tissierou by supporters of presidential candidate Sacca Lafia.[48] Villagers were informed that Lafia was the first candidate from that region since 1960. 'If elected,' they were told, 'he will help promote the interests of the Borgou-Alibori region, by building new schools, hospitals and roads and more importantly, hiring more Bariba people in the public administration.' It was a direct appeal to the self-interest of the local community.

The next day, the same campaign team visited the nearby village of Alafiarou. Again, they held a meeting on behalf of Lafia – but this time the message was different. They told the crowd: 'If elected, he will engage in a nationwide reform of the education and health-care systems, with emphasis on building new schools and new hospitals and running vaccination campaigns. In conjunction with other opposition leaders, we will fight corruption and promote peace between all ethnic groups and all the regions of Benin.' It was a high-minded appeal to good public policies aimed at building a better country.

Across Benin, presidential campaign teams were giving similar speeches. The leading contenders for president had agreed to work with social scientists to devise two kinds of speeches for their candidates: pork-barrelling or nation-building. For decades, political scientists had tried to understand when each kind of campaigning was effective. Now, these theories were being put to the test.

After the election, voters in the different villages were surveyed, and a curious result emerged: pork-barrelling speeches tended to boost support among male voters, while nation-building speeches appealed more to female voters. A unique experiment had dug up a finding that had barely been discussed by previous studies: Benin men tended to think local, while women were more likely to think national.

A growing number of experiments are being run with – or on – politicians. Following the Benin experiment on electoral speeches, researchers in Sierra Leone tested the impact of election debates. Working in randomly selected districts, they organised candidate debates.[49] In Sierra Leone, elections had generally consisted of 'giving out bags of rice and T-shirts'. Debates were a novelty. Sometimes candidates who had never spoken in public before did well. In other cases, candidates bombed. As debate organiser Saa Badabla put it, 'If someone performed badly, people would say: "In Parliament they're going to be talking about laws. How can it be that this person would go?"'[50]

In constituencies where debates were held, candidates worked harder. Citizens learnt more about the issues. Exposure to a debate made voters 9 percentage points more likely to support the candidate whose top priority issue aligned with theirs. After the election, researchers also saw a change in behaviour among elected members, with those in debate districts holding twice as many public meetings during their first year in office. Particularly in areas wracked by ethnic conflict, researchers now think that election debates may be a vital tool in encouraging a culture of disagreement over important issues without resort to violence.

Are US politicians racist? In one study, researchers sent thousands of state legislators a simple email asking about registering to vote.[51] To test for racial bias, the researchers randomly varied whether the emails came from Jake Mueller, a typically white name, or DeShawn Jackson, a strongly African-American name. The experiment found that the black name received 5 per cent fewer replies overall.[52] White politicians were more likely to respond to white voters, while black legislators were more likely to respond to black constituents. Another randomised study in South Africa produced a similar result.[53]

Over recent years, US elections have become eye-wateringly expensive. As a rule of thumb, successful candidates need to spend over US$1 million to win a House seat, US$10 million to win a Senate seat, and nearly US$1 billion to win the presidency.[54] As one campaign finance expert wryly notes, such sums are not raised at bake sales.[55] And yet experts have differed on the extent to which donors get better treatment from politicians. To test this, one lobbying organisation sought to line up meetings with 191 members of the US Congress.[56] They were working on behalf of a group of people who had all donated money to their local congressperson. But in some of the cases, the meeting was requested for a 'constituent', and in others for a 'donor'. Those who self-identified as donors were three to four times more likely to get a meeting.

Other studies have looked at whether giving politicians additional information can change how they vote. In a New Mexico experiment, some state politicians were sent information about their constituents' attitudes.[57] In a New Hampshire experiment, some politicians were sent a lobbying email.[58] In both studies there was an impact on the floor of the legislature, suggesting that some representatives can be swayed by just one poll or a single lobbying activity. The ability of small interventions to shape results was backed up by a randomised experiment which sent out warning letters to US state politicians about the consequences of making misleading statements. Legislators who got the letter were less likely to receive a negative fact-checking rating.[59]

Now, you might think that a politician telling you about political experiments is a bit like a pet rat saying that its cage could really use some mazes. Some of my parliamentary colleagues might raise an eyebrow at the prospect of encouraging researchers to experiment upon us. But the fact is that randomised studies have cast new light on how the political process operates. If politicians are providing worse services to minority race constituents and better services to donors, then the public has a right to know about it.

*

In 2008, as they went to the polls to overwhelmingly elect America's first black president, California voters also supported a ballot measure striking down same-sex marriage. Gay and lesbian activists were shocked and upset. From defeat at the ballot box, community leaders began exploring the best way of reducing prejudice.

Many ideas were floated, but the activists ultimately chose a strategy centred around honest, vulnerable conversations. Campaigners would go door-to-door, sharing their stories of discrimination, and inviting householders to do the same. The approach was known as 'deep canvassing', and aimed to break down discrimination by creating a greater sense of empathy towards gay and lesbian people. David Fleischer, who now directs the leadership program at the Los Angeles Lesbian, Gay, Bisexual and Transgender Center, says that it worked because it connected to people's values: 'When we were nonjudgmental and vulnerable with them and when we exchanged our lived experiences about marriage and gay people, that's when we started changing people's minds.'[60]

At the end of 2014, deep canvassing received its strongest affirmation. An article in *Science*, one of the world's top academic journals, reported that a randomised experiment in California had found that a twenty-minute conversation with a gay canvasser could shift attitudes towards same-sex marriage.[61] The results were splashed across the media.

In Florida, two young scholars, David Broockman and Joshua Kalla, were working on a similar study – this time exploring whether deep canvassing could change attitudes to transgender people. But when they looked closely at the data from the *Science* study, they found a range of irregularities.[62] Eventually Broockman and Kalla concluded that one of the authors of the original study – a graduate student – had fabricated the results. His senior collaborator, Donald Green, asked *Science* to withdraw the paper, sorrowfully concluding:

'There was no data, and no plausible way of getting the data.'[63]

To Fleischer, who had campaigned for over thirty years on lesbian and gay rights, the news came as a shock. He personally phoned journalists who reported on the study to say that there was no longer evidence for deep canvassing. The graduate student on the study 'had lied to us. Taken advantage of us. And I also wanted to point out to people we were not going to give up.'[64]

With the California study now discredited, Broockman and Kalla found themselves working on the frontier of knowledge. Their Florida study was now the first randomised evaluation of deep canvassing. Three months after canvassers had gone door-to-door, households were surveyed by telephone. When Broockman analysed the data, he backed away from his screen, and said, 'Wow, something's really unique here.'[65]

The Florida study not only confirmed the value of deep canvassing, it also showed results that were more powerful than the faked California results.[66] One way of benchmarking the size of the effect is to compare it with the steady evolution in attitudes to transgender people that has taken place over time. Asked to rate their view of transgender people on a scale from 0 to 100, the average American's attitude has warmed by 9 points over a fifteen-year period. But the campaigners had a bigger impact still: a single conversation with a canvasser caused Floridians' attitudes to transgender people to warm by 10 points. Just a ten-minute personal conversation took householders more than fifteen years forward in their attitudes towards transgender people.

The new research also suggested that social change had more to do with the style of the conversation than the background of the canvasser. While the bogus California research had purported to find effects only from gay campaigners, the Florida study showed that both transgender and non-transgender canvassers were able to shift attitudes. As Fleischer put it, 'Our ability to change voters' hearts and minds has been measured, this time for real.'[67]

Not every story of academic misconduct has a happy ending, but one reason the fabrication came to light is that randomised experiments are, in their essence, extremely simple. That simplicity makes it easy to compare results across studies, and shows up questionable findings. Had the Californian analysis involved a bunch of clever statistical tricks, the fraud might never have been uncovered. Randomised trials are so simple that anyone can run one. In fact, let's look at how you might do just that.

10

TREAT
YOURSELF

For a few days in July 2017, people searching Google for 'randomised trial', 'A/B testing' or 'RCT' might have seen an ad pop up in the sidebar. At the bottom of the ad were the words 'A new book due in 2018' and a link to my publisher's website.

But it was the first part of the ad that mattered. Web surfers were randomly shown one of twelve possible book titles, including *Randomistas: Experiments That Shaped Our World, Randomistas: The Secret Power of A/B Tests* and *The Randomistas: How a Simple Test Shapes Our World*. My editors and I each had our favourite titles, but we had agreed to leave the final decision to a randomised experiment. The medium that brought you cat videos, the ice bucket challenge and Kim Kardashian would choose this book's title.

A week later, over 4000 people had seen one of the advertisements, and we had a clear winner. People who saw *Randomistas: How Radical Researchers Changed Our World*, were more than twice as likely to click the ad as those who saw *Randomistas: The Secret Power of Experiments.* The worst performing title (not a single person clicked on it) was *Randomistas: How a Powerful Tool Changed Our World.* The experiment took about an hour to set up, and cost me $55. For this edition, we tweaked the winning subtitle to *How Radical Researchers Are Changing Our World.*

A few years earlier, I had written a book on inequality for the same publisher. My editor wanted to call it *Fair Enough?* My mother suggested *Battlers and Billionaires.* After running Google ads for a few days, we found that the click rate for my mother's title was nearly three times higher. My editor graciously conceded that the evidence was in, and *Battlers and Billionaires* hit the shelves the following year.

Were these experiments perfect? No way. Since I was trying to sell books, the ideal experiment would have randomised book covers – perhaps on Amazon or in a bookstore. But that would have taken more time and money than I had available. Figuring that people searching about a topic were sufficiently similar to people who would buy books about that same subject seemed a reasonable assumption.

Anyone looking to run a better email campaign or redesign a website has dozens of online tools at their fingertips, including AB Tasty, Apptimize, ChangeAgain, Clickthroo, Kameleoon, Optimizely, SiteSpect and Webtrends. Retailers using the Amazon platform can even use Splitly, which randomly changes product descriptions and images. As we saw in Chapter 8, Amazon promised in 2000 never to run pricing experiments. But today, Splitly lets third-party retailers use the Amazon platform to randomly vary prices. The site claims to have generated nearly US$1 million in new sales through A/B testing on Amazon. Algorithms like these are one reason that Amazon's prices fluctuate wildly. To see this, check out the website CamelCamelCamel. com, which shows past prices for Amazon products sold by third-party retailers. In the years 2014 to 2017, the best price of the game Classic Twister ranged from $3.48 to $49.80.

When I taught introductory economics at the Australian National University, I ran a small randomised experiment on my students, testing whether dressing more formally had any impact on their ratings of the lectures. Through the semester, I randomly varied the days that I chose to don a jacket and tie, versus wearing something a little less formal. At the end of each lecture, I asked all students to rate it from 1 to 5. Crunching the data after my final presentation, I found no evidence that my students preferred a talk delivered in a tie. The lesson for lecturers: sweat the facts, not the fashion.

Self-experimentation has a long tradition in medicine. To prove that surgery didn't require a general anaesthetic, American surgeon Evan Kane injected himself with a local anaesthetic and then removed his own appendix. To prove that the polio vaccine was safe, Jonas Salk injected himself, and then his wife and children. To prove that the myxoma virus was fatal to rabbits but harmless to humans, Australian scientist Frank Fenner injected himself with enough of the virus to kill hundreds of rabbits. He was unharmed, though some Australians afterwards liked to call him 'Bunny'.

Some have pushed the limits even further. Addressing the 1983 Urological Association conference in Las Vegas, Giles Brindley announced to his audience that it was possible to produce an erection through direct injection. He then informed them that shortly before the lecture he had injected his penis with an erectile drug known as papaverine. On the screen, he showed slides of his penis in its flaccid state. Brindley assured the audience that no normal person would find giving a lecture to be an erotic experience. As one observer recalls, 'He then summarily dropped his trousers and shorts, revealing a long, thin, clearly erect penis. There was not a sound in the room. Everyone had stopped breathing.'

Single-patient experiments can be randomised, if the treatment is turned on and off. These 'single subject' or 'N of 1' experiments are becoming increasingly common in the case of drugs that are developed for rare diseases, or tailored based on the genetics of the patient. One ongoing experiment of this kind is a Dutch trial of treatments for rare neuromuscular diseases, which can affect just 1 in 100,000 people. Almost invariably, the most expensive drugs are those used to treat rare diseases. Single-patient trials are likely to be vital in helping health authorities decide whether drugs that cost hundreds of thousands of dollars per year are having the desired effect.

Like the pricing experiment in Chapter 8 – which involved just one store changing its prices from week to week – these N-of-1 experiments are a new way to use randomisation to learn about the world around us.

*

Because some of the most famous randomised trials involved a large number of people (like the conditional cash transfer experiment in Mexico), cost a lot of money (like the RAND Health Insurance experiments) or took many years (like the Perry Preschool experiment), randomising can sometimes seem too hard. That's why some of today's researchers are making it a priority to show that randomised experiments can be done quickly, simply and cheaply.

In 2013 the Obama White House, working with a number of major foundations, announced a competition for low-cost randomised trials. The aim was to show that it was possible to evaluate social programs without spending millions of dollars. From over fifty entries, the three winners included a federal government department planning to carry out unexpected workplace health and safety inspections, and a Boston non-profit providing intensive counselling to low-income youth hoping to be the first in their family to graduate from college. Each evaluation cost less than $200,000. The competition continues to operate through a non-profit foundation, which has announced that it will fund all proposals that receive a high rating from its review panel.

Simplicity is at the core of the approach taken by the behavioural insights teams which are emerging in central government agencies across the globe. In 2010 the British government became the first to establish a so-called 'Nudge Unit', to bring the principles of psychology and behavioural economics into policymaking. The interventions were mostly low-cost – such as tweaking existing mailings – and were tested through randomised trials wherever possible. In some cases they took only a few weeks. Since its creation, the tiny Nudge Unit has carried out more randomised experiments than the British government had conducted in that country's history.[9]

The Nudge Unit focused on 'low cost, rapid' experiments.[10] It found that letters asking people to pay their car tax were 9 percentage points more effective if they included a photograph of the offending vehicle, along with the caption 'Pay Your Tax or Lose Your Car'.[11] A personally scribbled note on the envelope along the lines of 'Andrew, you really need to open this' increased taxpaying by 4 percentage points. In an era of mass mailings, handwriting notes on envelopes is laborious, but every £1 spent on it garnered £200 in additional fines.[12] For late taxpayers, the Nudge Unit experimented with various appeals, ultimately finding the most effective message to be: 'The great majority of people in your local area pay their tax on time. Most people with a debt like yours have paid it by now.' Adding these two sentences increased the repayment rate by 5 percentage points.[13] This impact represents millions of pounds of additional revenue for an experiment that cost basically nothing.

Other interventions are similarly cost-effective. Britons owing money to the courts were twice as likely to pay up if they were sent a text message ten days before the bailiffs were scheduled to knock on their doors.[14] The texts averted 150,000 bailiff visits.[15] Overseas visitors were 20 per cent more likely to leave the country on time if they received a letter before their visa expired.[16] Jobseekers were nearly three times as likely to attend a recruitment event if the reminder text message was personalised and wished them good luck.[17] Online, the Nudge Unit tested how best to encourage people renewing their driving licences to sign up for the organ donor registry.[18] They randomly trialled eight different messages. One was a picture of smiling people and the words: 'Every day thousands of people who see this page decide to register.' Another had no photo, just the text: 'If you needed an organ transplant, would you have one? If so, please help others.' As Nudge Unit head David Halpern points out, it isn't immediately obvious which of these would be more effective. It took a randomised trial to prove that the 'would you have one?' message produced 100,000 more organ donors a year.

Foilowing the British model, Nudge Units have been established by governments in Australia, Germany, Israel, the Netherlands, Singapore and the United States, and are being actively considered in Canada, Finland, France, Italy, Portugal and the United Arab Emirates.[19] An Australian study run by the Nudge Unit in New South Wales found that simply stamping 'Pay Now' in red at the top of a letter raised payment rates by 3 percentage points, adding $1 million to government revenues and allowing over 8000 drivers to avoid having their licences cancelled.[20] Another study with St Vincent's Hospital in Sydney randomly tested eight variants of text message reminders. Compared with the standard message, it found a 3 percentage point improvement among patients who were reminded that attending the appointment avoided the hospital losing $125.[21]

BETA, the Australian government's Nudge Unit, has collaborated with over a dozen federal departments and agencies, including the Department of Foreign Affairs, the Australian Taxation Office and the National Disability Insurance Agency. Like his British counterpart David Halpern, BETA's founding head Michael Hiscox looked to initiate fast and simple studies, by tweaking existing programs.[22] Data collection can be the most expensive part of a randomised trial, so BETA tries not to run new surveys, but instead to use existing administrative records.

In today's 'big data' era, governments (and businesses) hold more information about us than ever before. From birthweight to exam results, welfare payments to tax returns, hospital admissions to criminal records, government databases are overflowing with personal information. In some countries, this information is linked together – indeed, Scandinavian governments have now ceased taking censuses, and rely solely on administrative data. Reasonably enough, citizens expect that their information will be held private. But this should not stop agencies from using existing data to measure the impact of randomised evaluations. If big data can help get information cheaply, randomised trials become a whole lot simpler.

*

Another source of simple randomised trials is lotteries. As we have already seen, randomistas have studied lotteries for desirable schools and for conscripts to fight in Vietnam. Economists have even looked at cash lotteries, estimating how an unexpected windfall changes people's lives. The typical answer is 'less than you might expect'. For example, a study of Dutch lottery winners found that a prize equivalent to two-thirds of a year's income leads people to upgrade their cars and buy new household appliances.[23] But six months after the lottery, winning households are no happier than their unlucky neighbours. In the United States, a study looked at whether lottery winners were more likely to send their children to university, and found an effect only with very large prizes.[24] Similarly, in Sweden, lottery winners were found to reduce their working hours, but only by a small amount.[25]

For many of the world's population, the biggest possible lottery win would be to move to a richer country. About 6 billion of the world's nearly 8 billion people live in developing countries, and surveys show that at least 2 billion of them would move to a developed nation if they could.[26] Facing excess demand for migration places, some advanced countries have used actual lotteries to decide who gets a spot. The argument for visa lotteries is that they place all applicants on an equal footing, regardless of their inside knowledge, wealth or personal connections.

As it happens, lotteries also provide a powerful way for researchers to estimate the impact of moving from one country to another.[27] Because migrants are self-selected, comparing the outcomes of movers and stayers could badly skew the results. Arnold Schwarzenegger isn't just another Austrian. Martina Navratilova isn't just another Czech. Ang Lee isn't just another Chinese person. If we want to know how shifting countries changes a person's life, then it's a mistake to compare migrants with those in their home country. Instead, we need a situation in which similar people apply to move, and only chance determines who get to migrate. Visa lotteries do just that.

One visa lottery study looked at workers at an Indian software company who moved to work in software companies in the United States.[28] Compared with unsuccessful applicants, those who won the visa lottery increased their earnings sixfold. Another analysis found that Tongans who won the visa lottery to move to New Zealand virtually quadrupled their earnings.[29] But victory had a price. The study monitored the extended families of successful and unsuccessful lottery applicants. The researchers found that winning the visa lottery was bad luck for those family members who stayed behind in Tonga. Migrants tended to be the breadwinners, so when they moved to New Zealand, incomes in their former Tongan households declined.

Importantly, the researchers were also able to compare the impact from the randomised experiment with what a naive analysis would have estimated. Comparing applicants with non-applicants – a common research strategy – would have produced the mistaken conclusion that migration *reduced* poverty among those Tongan families who sent a migrant to New Zealand. In other words, a study based on non-randomised data would have got the result exactly backwards.

Lotteries have also taught us something about religious observance. Every year, over a million Muslims perform the Hajj pilgrimage in Saudi Arabia. Participants often claim that travelling to Mecca fosters unity, but critics have feared that it could increase hatred towards non-Muslims. So a team of economists surveyed Pakistanis who had applied to that country's Hajj lottery.[30] Compared with those who missed out, lottery winners were more committed to peace, more accepting of other religions and had more favourable attitudes towards women. Pakistani pilgrims became more devout, but they were also more tolerant – most likely because the Hajj exposed them to people from around the globe.

Another simple form of randomised trial comes from randomised audits. In the United States, randomised taxpayer audits have been conducted since 1963, as a means of better targeting the Internal Revenue Service's compliance strategies.[31] The philosophy behind them is that tax avoidance has a habit of avoiding the eyes of the authorities. Rather than relying solely on informants and experts, a random audit looks at the level of compliance across the community, by randomly selecting something like 1 in 2000 returns for an in-depth check. The randomised audit approach embodies a sense of modesty, recognising that tax cheats can be hard to find. It's a bit like asking your friends to help look for your lost car keys: a fresh perspective can bring useful insights.

Randomised audits are politically controversial, which is why they have been discontinued in Australia, Sweden and (for a time) the United States.[32] But they aren't just about improving the system so we find more wrongdoers. They're also about reducing the number of times that the tax authorities chase someone up only to find they've done nothing wrong. One study estimates that better targeting compliance efforts will avoid tens of thousands of people being contacted by the tax authorities.[33]

For researchers, randomised audits are the best way of answering the question: who is most likely to underreport their income to the authorities? A recent study finds that taxpayers in the top 1 per cent failed to report 17 per cent of their true income, while low- and middle-income taxpayers omitted 4 per cent of their true income.[34] Only through a randomised audit study was it possible to uncover the fact that income underreporting was four times worse among the richest taxpayers.

Another straightforward use of audits occurs in Brazil, where the federal government randomly audits a sample of municipal governments to check their use of federal funds.[35] The audits revealed that nearly one-third of all federal funds were lost to corruption. Over time, municipal government audits have increased the numbers of mayors convicted for misusing their office, and reduced the incidence of corruption. Municipal audits are so popular among the Brazilian public that they are conducted alongside the national lottery.

*

Simple randomised trials can teach us a great deal about the world – but we have to be careful about experiments that are done in settings that are nothing like the real world. As Chicago economist Frank Knight once put it, 'The existence of a problem in knowledge depends on the future being different from the past, while the possibility of a solution of the problem depends on the future being like the past.'[36]

In this book, I've focused mostly on randomised experiments that test real-world practices – ranging from knee surgery to Drug Courts. By contrast, I haven't spent much time discussing the experiments that take place in scientific laboratories, where randomisation is intrinsic to the research. The people who play with test tubes may not think of themselves as randomistas – but in many cases, that's exactly what they're doing.

But a more controversial group of experimenters are those doing 'lab experiments' in social science. This often involves recruiting university students to answer hypothetical questions and play computer games. Rather less exciting than the games you might try on your Xbox or PlayStation, laboratory games are designed by social scientists to test behaviour in hypothetical settings.

Discussing the spectrum of experiments, economists Glenn Harrison and John List lay out four categories of randomised experiments.[37] First, natural field experiments, of the kind we've discussed in this book, where subjects are doing tasks they would normally do, and often don't know they are in an experiment. Natural field experiments could involve anything from providing support to disadvantaged students to changing the wording of a marketing letter.

Second, framed field experiments, where people know they are in an experiment, but the setting or commodity is natural. In one experiment, researchers set up a table at a sports card convention, and tested how collectors behaved in response to auctions for desirable sports cards.[38] Another framed field experiment, run in Sweden in the early 1970s, tested how much people were willing to pay in order to be the first to watch a brand-new television program.[39]

Third, artefactual field experiments. These are generally conducted in a university computer lab, but not with university students. Artefactual field experiments might involve games to test attitudes to risk among share market traders, or trustworthiness in the general population.

Fourth, conventional laboratory experiments. The typical laboratory experiment is run on university students, with an imposed set of rules and abstract framing. Conventional lab experiments include games that are used to test economic theories about fairness, altruism and attitudes to inequality.

From the researcher's standpoint, conventional laboratory experiments are simple to implement. Students are readily recruited – psychology students are often required to take part in experiments as a condition of their enrolment – and are generally paid a fairly low rate per hour. One of the downsides of this kind of simple study was summed up by Harvard psychologist Stephen Pinker, who once quipped: 'When psychologists say "most people", they usually mean "most of the two dozen sophomores who filled out a questionnaire for beer money".'[40]

Those students who volunteer for experiments are likely to be different from the student population at large. According to one comparison, students who sign up for lab experiments tend to spend more, work less volunteer more, and to have an academic interest in the subject of the experiment.[41] Additionally, students differ from people who are midway through their careers. For example, a study in Costa Rica had students and chief executives play the same set of trust games.[42] The business chiefs were significantly more trustworthy than the students.

A major concern of the laboratory setting is that its results will not generalise into the real world. When a professor is setting the rules of the game, people may react differently than in real life. For example, one lab experiment found that student subjects who had never given a cent to charity gave 75 per cent of their endowment to the charity in the lab experiment.[43] It's risky to draw broad conclusions from experiments that see real-life Scrooges becoming Oskar Schindlers the moment they enter the laboratory.

Admittedly, it's not always true that what happens in the lab stays in the lab. One psychology experiment tested whether it was possible to artificially generate interpersonal closeness.[44] University students were randomly paired up. Half the pairs were asked to make small talk, while the other half were given questions designed to build intimacy, such as 'What does friendship mean to you?', 'For what do you feel most grateful?' and 'What one item would you save if your house was burning?' The intimacy exercise worked so well that one pair of participants got married.

Like science experiments, we can get the best from social science laboratory experiments if we recognise their limitations. Recall that nine out of ten pharmaceuticals that work in the science lab fail to get approved for use on the general public. Similarly, we should generally regard social science laboratory experiments – whether run by psychologists or economists – as promising but not definitive.

*

Not all simple randomised experiments are good, but plenty of good randomised experiments can be simple. Economist Uri Gneezy tells the story of running an experiment to help a California vineyard owner decide how much to charge for his wines.[45] Gneezy and the business owner selected a cabernet that usually sold for $10. They then printed three versions of the cellar door price list, with the cabernet variously priced at $10, $20 or $40. Each day over the next few weeks, the winery randomly chose one of the three price lists. It turned out that the cabernet sold nearly 50 per cent more when priced at $20 than $10. The experiment took a few minutes to design and a few weeks to implement, but it boosted the winery's profits by 11 per cent. A full-bodied result with aromas of easy money – consume now.

In this chapter, I've given a taste of how you can run low-fuss randomised experiments in your personal life and within your own organisation. I hope it's encouraged you to think about becoming a randomista. If you do, let me know how it goes.

At a larger scale, we need to dispel the myth that all randomised trials need to be expensive and long-lasting. As Nudge Units have shown, tweaks can produce big gains. Such trials remind me of one of the maxims of writer Tim Ferriss: 'If this were easy, what would it look like?' Too often, we overcomplicate things by envisaging perfect schemes that are too hard to implement in practice. Like the Occam's razor principle in science, simple randomised trials can often teach us a great deal.

Unfortunately, some critics of randomised trials often take the same approach, shooting down randomised evaluation with a single riposte: 'It's unethical.' So let's now take a serious look at the ethical side of randomised trials and consider how we can ensure that randomised trials do as much good – and as little harm – as humanly possible.

11

BUILDING A BETTER
FEEDBACK LOOP

A s a young man, Luke Rhinehart decided he would start making decisions based on a dice roll. Periodically, he would write out a numbered list of possible things to do, roll a die and then follow its lead. Driving past a hospital one day, he saw two beautiful nurses walking along the side of the road. Feeling shy, Rhinehart drove on, but then decided that if he rolled an odd number, he would go back. The dice came up with 3. Rhinehart turned the car around, stopped next to the women and introduced himself. He gave them a lift, they arranged to play tennis the next day, and he ended up marrying one of the women, Ann.[1]

Rhinehart couldn't let go of the idea of making decisions based on rolling dice, so he began writing novels in which characters took randomisation too far. His most famous book, *The Dice Man*, was named the 'novel of the century' in 1999 by *Loaded* magazine. The main character does everything his dice tell him to. He ends up committing murder, arranging a breakout by psychiatric patients and organising a debauched 'dice party'.

Rhinehart was not the first writer to tackle randomisation in fiction. In 1941 Jorge Luis Borges wrote a short story titled 'The Lottery in Babylon', in which every major decision in the mythical society of Babylon is determined by a lottery. The lottery decides whether someone becomes an official or a slave, and whether an accused person is declared innocent or sentenced to death. Babylon, wrote Borges, 'is nothing but an infinite game of chance'.[2]

Borges' world may seem farfetched, but luck plays a significant role in real-life politics too.[3] In some cases, luck is even built into the system, as with the ancient Athenians, who chose each day's ruler by lottery, using a stone machine called the *kleroterion* (their equivalent of a modern-day Powerball machine). Because each person's rule only lasted a day, it is estimated that a quarter of Athenian citizens ruled the city-state at some point. Random election systems – known as 'the *brevia*' and 'the scrutiny' – were also used in late medieval and Renaissance Italy. They survive today in the modern jury, in which criminal defendants are judged by a randomly selected group of their peers.

If you've ever tossed a coin when faced with a major choice, you'll know that leaving a decision to chance can be liberating. A few years ago, economist Steven Levitt set up a website to explore this concept.[4] People standing at a fork in the road were invited to have luck determine which path they should take. Agonising over a life choice? You simply told Levitt's website your two options. It then tossed a coin and told you what to do. Six months later, these people were surveyed about their happiness. Over 20,000 people took the challenge, and nearly two-thirds did what the coin said to do.

To test the impact, Levitt used a standard life satisfaction survey, which asks people to rate their happiness on a scale from 1 (miserable) to 10 (ecstatic). Try it now. If you said 7 or 8, then you're in the middle of the pack: about half the population in advanced nations give one of those answers. Another quarter say they are 6 or sadder, while the remaining quarter report their happiness as a 9 or 10. So even although it's a ten-point scale, most of us are separated by just a few points. Because Levitt's study was a randomised trial, he could be sure that any difference in happiness between the heads group and the tails group was due solely to the coin toss.

For unimportant decisions – such as growing a beard or signing up for a fun run – the choice didn't matter much. But making a more significant life change – such as moving house or starting a business – led to a two-point increase in the happiness scale. A common question was whether to end a romantic relationship. Among these people, breaking up led to nearly a three-point increase in happiness. Quitting a job led to a massive five-point increase: the equivalent of shifting from glum to gleeful. 'Winners never quit, and quitters never win' is bad life advice. In the happiness stakes, quitters win.

Levitt's website refused to help people make decisions containing words like 'murder', 'steal' and 'suicide'.[5] But it did shape some major life decisions. The toss of the coin led to about a hundred additional romantic relationships breaking up, but also to about a hundred couples staying together who might otherwise have split.[6] It would have been immoral to force people to quit their jobs or divorce their spouses, but tossing a coin for someone who is on the fence is something that many people would do for a friend.

If you ask critics why they don't like randomised trials, one of the most common responses is that control groups are unethical. Already, we've touched on some real-life examples of this. Ethics panels have approved sham surgery on the basis that the clinical effectiveness of many surgical procedures is uncertain. Randomised trials now suggest that popular procedures like knee surgery for torn cartilage may be ineffective. Likewise, randomised trials to reduce crime have seen the treatment group do better in the Restorative Justice and Drug Court experiments, while the control group did better in the Scared

Straight and Neighbourhood Watch experiments. In development economics, the success of village schools in Afghanistan surprised many of the country's education experts. If we knew for sure that it was better to be in the treatment group, then we wouldn't be doing the trial in the first place.

Most medical trials operate on the principle of informed consent: patients must agree to participate in the research. But not every study works this way. From 2005 to 2011, researchers in Sydney conducted a trial in which not a single patient consented – because all of them were either unconscious or suffering from severe head trauma. One in three would be dead within a month.

The Head Injury Retrieval Trial was the brainchild of neurosurgeon Alan Garner. He wanted to test whether patients were more likely to recover from a major head injury if they were treated by a trauma physician rather than a paramedic. Because the physician has to be transported to the scene by helicopter, the study aimed to test whether society could justify the extra expense of sending out a physician. If the outcomes from those treated by physicians weren't better, the extra money would be better spent in other parts of the health-care system.

Garner's study worked with the emergency call system in Sydney. When operators received a call reporting a serious head injury, a computer performed the electronic equivalent of tossing a coin. Heads, the patient got an ambulance and a paramedic; tails, they got a helicopter and a trauma physician.

In 2008, halfway through the trial, I interviewed Garner, who told me that although he had spent much of his career thinking about the issue, he didn't know what to expect from the results.[7] 'We think this will work,' Garner told me, 'but so far, we've only got data from cohort studies.' He admitted that, 'like any medical intervention, there is even a possibility that sending a doctor will make things worse. I don't think that's the case, but [until the trial ends] I don't have good evidence either way.'

I was struck by Garner's willingness to let the data speak – a contrast to the brash overconfidence of many people who have created social programs. His study had cleared eight ethics committees, he told me, and had been approved because it answered a genuinely open question in the medical literature.

When the results were published, they showed that whether the coin came up heads (paramedics and ambulance) or tails (trauma physician and helicopter), there was no significant difference in the odds that a patient would survive.[8] Ideally, the researchers would have liked to have more patients in the study, but were forced to stop the trial when the state government changed its protocol. The government, confident that physicians provided better care than paramedics, decided to dispatch physicians to as many head injury patients as possible.[9] With their own study cut short, the researchers are urging further randomised trials of head injury treatment, so we can get a better answer about what works.

I've thought a lot about the ethics of the Head Injury Retrieval Trial. My brother Tim crashed his motorbike during that time, suffering a serious head injury (thankfully, he recovered without any lasting injuries). There's no way of me knowing whether Tim was part of Alan Garner's study – whether the paramedics who treated him were sent because of the toss of a coin – but I'd be comfortable if he had been part of the research. I know that the best way to improve emergency services is through gathering rigorous evidence about treatment methods.

I'm not alone in this attitude. Surveys of politicians in Australia and the United Kingdom reveal that about seven out of ten are supportive of controlled experiments, and most believe that randomised trials will become more common in future.[10] Phil Ames and James

Wilson, who conducted the Australian surveys, note that only one-tenth of politicians in these countries are concerned about the cost of randomised trials. Correctly, most politicians aren't fearful that quality evaluation will bust the budget.

When parliamentarians are probed on their misgivings, the chief concern is fairness. Half of Australian politicians and one-third of British politicians worry that randomised trials are unfair.[11] Reacting to the British survey results, medical writer Ben Goldacre concludes: 'We need to get better at helping them to learn more about how randomised controlled trials work ... Many members of parliament say they're worried that randomised controlled trials are "unfair", because people are chosen at random to receive a new policy intervention: but this is exactly what already happens with "pilot studies", which have the added disadvantage of failing to produce good quality evidence on what works, and what does harm.'[12]

Rejecting randomised trials on the grounds of unfairness also seems at odds with the fact that lotteries have been used in advanced countries to allocate school places, housing vouchers and health insurance, to determine ballot order, and to decide who gets conscripted to fight in war. After World War II, the Australian government even used a lottery to assign taxi licences among returned servicemen.[13] Indeed, one of the political appeals of lotteries is equity: before the drawing, everyone has the same chance of being picked. Yet, oddly, the ethical bar seems higher in the case of randomised trials than lotteries.

Other countries face even bigger challenges in running experiments. For example, the French constitution demands that all citizens be treated equally. This meant that the government had to change the constitution before France could conduct randomised trials.[14]

In my experience, most people are morally comfortable with a website that randomly tweaks its layout, a supermarket that randomly changes the shelf placement of its products, or a political campaign that randomly chooses which people to telephone. But when it comes to providing financial incentives to bribe a driving licence tester, or studying how best to treat an unconscious motorbike rider, the ethical questions become more difficult. In these cases, randomistas must think hard about the morality of their research. In the words of Elizabeth Linos, the head of the US Behavioural Insights Team, 'it is important to clarify that we take ethics seriously, and mean it – not just to persuade'.[15]

For research conducted by universities, a key ethical safeguard is the requirement for studies to be reviewed by ethics committees, also known as institutional review boards. Ethical review was partly spurred by the 1946 Nuremberg trials, which saw dozens of Nazi doctors convicted of performing experiments on concentration camp prisoners without their consent. Another significant milestone was the revelation that the government had deliberately infected with syphilis 400 African-American men in Tuskegee, Alabama. From these atrocious ethical breaches, the World Medical Association passed the 1964 Declaration of Helsinki, which recommended informed consent and ethical review.

In 1978 the US government's Belmont Report set out three principles that would guide ethical review: respecting all people; maximising the benefits and minimising the risks; and doing justice between groups of people. Australia, Canada and other countries now apply similar principles to their ethics review processes.[16]

My own experience of seeking ethical clearance at the Australian National University was a positive one. Although the committee members were not experts in the research area, they had thought carefully about how to reduce the costs on participants and ensure consent wherever possible.

Increasingly, social science experiments today are adopting processes that have long been standard in medicine. If the stakes are high, researchers should engage an expert panel to periodically monitor the trial and call it quits if the results are unequivocal. These oversight committees, also called 'data and safety monitoring boards', sometimes stop experiments because the treatment group is doing far better than the control group. However, they can also step in if the treatment group is unexpectedly doing worse than the control group.

Social scientists are also following medical researchers in comparing new interventions against an appropriate baseline. If an effective treatment already exists, the right thing to do will often be to pit a new treatment against the standard treatment, rather than against a 'do nothing' approach.

We have already seen a range of examples in which ethical concerns can be addressed by careful study design. If it is impractical to deliver a program to all communities at once, then why not randomise the rollout so that we can learn something about its impact? In the case of conditional cash transfers in Mexico, village schools in Afghanistan and biometric identifiers in India, everyone eventually received the program. The only difference was that rather than letting political or bureaucratic factors determine the rollout schedule, it was explicitly randomised, and the results used to inform policy.

Another approach, which can be used to evaluate ongoing programs, is to let the control group keep accessing the service while trying to increase the take-up rate among the treatment group. This is known as an 'encouragement design'. In one such study, the University of Wollongong wanted to test the value of its student support services, but without barring any students from signing up if they were keen. The evaluators randomly sent text messages and emails to some students, informing them that they could win a $1000 retail voucher if they attended a peer-assisted study session.[17] As a result of this encouragement, students in the treatment group attended study sessions for an average of 30 minutes per student longer than students in the control group. The researchers could now use this randomly induced difference to test the impact of the program on student performance. They concluded that getting extra support services made no significant difference to final grades.

It's vital to think carefully about the ethics of every randomised trial. Yet history reminds us that failing to conduct a rigorous evaluation can sometimes be the most unethical approach. In the 1950s, West German scientists discovered a drug that helped to inhibit morning sickness. Soon, it was being taken by pregnant women in more than forty countries, with the manufacturer assuring them that the drug 'can be given with complete safety to pregnant women and nursing mothers without adverse effect on mother or child'. But when the manufacturers sought market approval in the United States, they struck a snag. Frances Kelsey, a newly hired employee at the Food and Drug Administration, noticed that the drug seemed to paralyse the peripheral nerves in some patients. Before the product could be approved, she requested further studies on its side effects, to prove that it did not affect the developing embryo. The frustrated manufacturer hoped to have the product on the American market as quickly as possible. In Kelsey's recollection, they told her she was 'depriving people of this thing'.[18] The company appealed to her superiors to overrule Kelsey's decision. But the management of the Food and Drug Administration backed her call for proper clinical trials.

In 1961 new research emerged showing that the 'wonder drug' was causing babies to be born limbless, or with their arms and legs as short stumps. In countries where it had been approved for sale – including the United Kingdom, Germany and Canada – more than 10,000 babies were born with deformities. Only about half survived. Yet thanks to Frances Kelsey's demand for evidence, virtually no American babies were affected, because thalidomide was never approved for sale. Today, the Food and Drug Administration bestows an annual 'Kelsey Award' for excellence and courage in protecting public health.

Frances Kelsey's actions are a reminder that ethical concerns about randomisation cut both ways. If the intervention helps, then a randomised trial leaves the treatment group better off than the control group. But if the intervention does harm, then failing to evaluate it properly can leave everyone worse off. While a rigorous demand for evidence saved thousands of American babies from the harm of thalidomide, there was no approval process required before governments began rolling out Scared Straight – the program we now know increased delinquency rates. If Frances Kelsey had been in charge of properly evaluating Scared Straight before it commenced, fewer lives would have been blighted by crime and imprisonment.

The best randomistas are passionate about solving a social problem, yet sceptical about the ability of any particular program to achieve its goals. Launching an evaluation of her organisation's flagship program, Read India, Rukmini Banerji, told the audience: 'And of course [the researchers] may find that it doesn't work. But if it doesn't work, we need to know that. We owe it to ourselves and the communities we work with not to waste their and our time and resources on a program that does not help children learn. If we find that this program isn't working, we will go and develop something that will.'[19]

Not everyone shares Banerji's openness to high-quality evaluation. When researcher Tess Lea sought to run a randomised trial of an online literacy tool in the Northern Territory, she hoped to improve reading standards among Indigenous Australians. But the evaluation of the 'ABRACADABRA' reading program was criticised on the basis that Indigenous children might not learn well with computers, that Indigenous children should not be tested using non-Indigenous tests, that the program was designed by Canadians, and that 'the proposition to pursue experimental research was inherently racist'.[20]

The program turned out to improve student literacy, but Lea stated publicly that she would never again attempt a randomised trial in Indigenous education.[21] It's an unhappy result, given that less than a tenth of Indigenous programs have been subjected to an evaluation of any kind, let alone a randomised trial.[22]

The contrast between Rukmini Banerji's support for evaluating her own program and the opposition that Tess Lea faced reminds us of just how important it is to distinguish the means from the ends. This approach is sometimes referred to as 'Rossi's Law' (named after sociologist Peter Rossi), which states: 'The better designed the impact assessment of a social program, the more likely is the resulting estimate of net impact to be zero.'[23] Rossi's Law does not mean we should give up hope of changing the world for the better. But we ought to be sceptical of anyone peddling panaceas. The belief that some social programs are flawed should lead to more rigorous evaluation and patient sifting through the evidence until we find a program that works.

In some cases, ethical concerns are grounded in strong science. For example, the evidence of a link between smoking and lung cancer is so strong that it would be unethical to randomise participants to receive free cigarettes. But in other cases, ethical objections turn out to be a smokescreen – used merely to defend ineffective programs from appropriate scrutiny.

Archie Cochrane, one of the pioneers of medical randomised trials, once came up with a novel trick to unmask such concerns. Presenting the results of a randomised evaluation of coronary care units, Cochrane faced an audience of cardiologists who had vehemently opposed the use of home care over hospital care. As economics writer Tim Harford tells the story, the study's early findings favoured home care, but Cochrane mischievously switched the results. When shown results indicating that hospitals were safer than home care, the cardiologists demanded that his 'unethical' study stop immediately.

'He then revealed the truth and challenged the cardiologists to close down their own hospital units without delay. There was dead silence.'[24]

*

As anyone who has eaten cafeteria food knows, things that work well on a small scale are not necessarily so tasty on a larger scale.[25] Anytime we're hoping to learn something from randomised trials, we need to consider whether the intervention is a boutique program or a mass-market one. For example, many early childhood randomised trials involve highly trained teachers working with extremely disadvantaged toddlers. But as these programs scale up, they are likely to recruit teachers with lower qualifications and less experience, and children from more affluent backgrounds. It would be a mistake to think that the huge benefit–cost ratio of Perry Preschool (which returned $7 to $12 in benefits for every $1 of spending) would necessarily translate to a population-wide program.

Something else also happens when a trial is scaled up: we begin to see whether its successes are coming at the expense of those outside the program. For example, suppose researchers designed a program aimed at teaching teenagers to confidently make eye contact in job interviews. It might be the case that the program helped its participants find jobs, but only at the expense of other jobseekers. Or it might be that the program actually increased the overall employment rate. Running a randomised trial with a few hundred participants would give us what economists call the 'partial equilibrium' effect. But only by randomising across labour markets – for example, by randomly choosing to run the program in some cities and not in others – could we gauge the 'general equilibrium' effects. For example, the partial equilibrium effect might look at whether a program helps its participants skip a few places up the queue, while the general equilibrium impact is whether it makes the whole line move faster.

It's encouraging if a program helps its participants, but it's even better if these gains don't come at someone else's expense.

Good randomistas also think carefully about what those in the control group are doing. In medical research, the answer can be as simple as 'getting the placebo drug'. But in social programs, people who miss out on the treatment may go looking for something similar. Until recently, randomised evaluations of the Head Start early childhood program tended to produce fairly small impacts – considerably less than the effects measured from the first preschool demonstration programs, such as Perry Preschool.[26]

The difference was in the control group. In the early 1960s, when the Perry Preschool study took place, there were no other preschool options for low-income families. But in recent decades, early childhood programs have proliferated across US cities. So while the older, Perry Preschool, results show the impact of preschool compared with parental care, the newer, Head Start, results show the impact of one preschool compared with another preschool.[27] Realising that the control group had sought out other preschool options revealed that Head Start's true benefit–cost ratio was almost twice as large as had been previously estimated.[28] Atoms in a laboratory experiment don't mind if they get put in the control test tube – but humans who get put in the control group may go looking for another option.

Participants who search for alternatives pose a challenge, but the randomistas still start ahead of researchers using non-experimental methods, because they have a more credible counterfactual. To see this, it's worth briefly reviewing a few ways that economists try to devise a counterfactual when they do not have a randomised evaluation.

One form of non-randomised evaluation is to study differences across regions. For example, if a policy is applied in a single state, we might use people in the rest of the country as the counterfactual group.[29] That would let us ask the question: when the state policy changes, how does it affect the gap between outcomes in that jurisdiction and the rest of the nation?

Another way economists try to find a similar comparison group is to look at sharp borders. In studying the impact of school quality on house prices, we can study what happens when the school catchment boundary runs down the middle of the street.[30] If people on one side have access to a more desirable public school, how does this affect house prices?

In the absence of a randomised evaluation, timing discontinuities can be used too. Attempting to estimate the impact of education on earnings, we can compare people born just before the school age cut-off with people born just afterwards.[31] Suppose we compare someone born on the cut-off date for school entry with a person born the next day. If both people drop out of school at the same age, then a single day's difference in birth timing will lead to nearly a year's less education for the younger person.

Another trick researchers use is to look for naturally occurring randomness. For example, if we're interested in the impact of economic growth on whether dictators get thrown out, we might look at changes in growth caused by annual variation in rainfall.[32] Or if we wanted to see how much public works programs create jobs, we might look for instances in which the spread of investment was driven by political pork-barrelling rather than local need.[33]

I don't want to suggest that we can't learn anything from these kinds of 'natural experiments'. To prove the point, these examples were drawn from my own academic work. I've devoted years of my life to working on these and other non-randomised studies. In each case, my co-authors and I did our best to find a credible counter-factual. But all of these studies are limited by the assumptions that the methods required us to make. New developments in non-randomised econometrics – such as machine learning – are generally even more

complicated than the older approaches.[34] As economist Orley Ashenfelter notes, if an evaluator is predisposed to give a program the
thumbs-up, statistical modelling 'leaves too many ways for the
researcher to fake it'.[35]

That's why one leading econometrics text teaches non-random
approaches by comparing each to the 'experimental ideal'.[36] Students
are encouraged to ask the question: 'If we could run a randomised
experiment here, what would it look like?' Another novel approach
is to take data from a properly conducted randomised trial, and pre-
tend that we wanted to run a non-randomised evaluation. With the
randomised trial as our yardstick, this trick lets us see how closely a
natural experiment matches the true result. In the case of job training, researchers found that someone who evaluated the program
without a randomised trial would have got the wrong answer.[37]
Similarly, non-randomised studies suggested that free distribution
of home computers had large positive effects on school students' test
scores – but randomised evaluations showed that they in fact had
little benefit.[38]

Having a better counterfactual is why randomised trials are often
described as the 'gold standard'. It's always struck me as an odd compliment, given that no serious economist wants to go back to the
literal gold standard.[39] I think what they mean is that in the gruelling
evaluation event, randomised trials get the gold medal. Indeed, many
researchers support the notion of an evidence hierarchy, with randomised trials at the top of the dais.[40] For example, the nonpartisan
US Congressional Budget Office prioritises random assignment studies in assessing evidence.[41]

*

Most of us have had the experience of reading a surprising academic
finding in the newspaper. Journalists and editors love those studies

that find a quirky relationship or overturn conventional wisdom. If it prompts breakfast conversations that start, 'Darling, you won't believe this . . .' it's sure to be popular.

In 2000, a supermarket experiment found that customers were more likely to buy a new kind of jam when they were offered a choice between six jams than if they were offered twenty-four jams.[42] The paper has since been cited thousands of times and used as evidence that many of us are overwhelmed by choice.[43] The research also spurred dozens of follow-up experiments on 'the paradox of choice'. A decade after the initial study appeared, a team of psychologists collated as many of these replication experiments as they could find.[44] Among the fifty replication studies, a majority went in the opposite direction from the original jam choice experiment. Averaging all the results, the psychologists concluded that the number of available options had 'virtually zero' impact on customer satisfaction or purchases.

Novelty excites. Even those who manage dusty academic journals can be tempted to publish a counterintuitive result. Perversely, because editors like to publish unexpected results, and because authors like to publish in the best places, prestigious journals end up publishing too many idiosyncratic findings.

One smoking gun emerged when statisticians looked at how far away published papers were from being statistically insignificant. In social science, a standard rule of thumb for determining whether a result is due to luck is the '95 per cent significance' rule. At this threshold, the chance of mistakenly identifying a statistical relationship where none truly exists is 5 per cent. If your study shows a result that is statistically significant at the 95 per cent level, then many journal editors will believe it. If your result falls below the 95 per cent level, editors are more likely to throw the paper into the rejection bin.

Most academics want their students to aspire to better than a bare pass on the test. But in the case of statistical significance, it turned out that a surprising number of published papers in social science were only just scraping through. Analysis of research published in top sociology, finance, accounting, psychology and political science journals turned out to contain a plethora of results that hold true at precisely the 95 per cent level.[45] In other words, these studies pass a 95 per cent test, but would fail a 96 per cent test. This troubling finding immediately suggested that up to 5 per cent of published results might be due to luck, rather than statistical significance.

Worse still, if researchers were rerunning their analysis with different specifications until they got a result that was significant at the 95 per cent level (a practice known as 'P-hacking'), then the resulting research might be even more error-prone. An unscrupulous academic who started each project with twenty junk theories could reasonably expect that mere luck would confirm that one of them was significant at the 95 per cent level. Discard the other nineteen and – voila! – there's your publishable result.

Another clue to the problem in published social science research came when researchers replicated their colleagues' work. In 2011 psychologist Brian Nosek set about persuading a team of scholars to replicate published papers in some of his field's best journals. Over the next three years, 270 academics collaborated in replicating 100 psychology studies.[46] The result: only about one-third of the findings held up.

Similarly worrying results have emerged in other disciplines. In a subfield of genetics, biologists replicated only one out of nine published papers.[47] In oncology and haematology, medical researchers had the same success rate – just one in nine.[48] In macroeconomics, only half the chosen studies successfully replicated.[49] One critic, John Ioannidis, points to the way that outside funding, competition between academics, and researchers' ability to cherrypick results can skew findings. His conclusion: 'Most published research findings are false.'[50]

In my view, Ioannidis's verdict is too pessimistic. Still, it's no surprise that people have begun talking about a 'crisis' in replicability.[51] For academia to retain its credibility, disciplines need to do a better job of ensuring that fewer findings are overturned. One of the best ways of doing this is to encourage more replications. And the easiest studies to replicate are randomised trials.

Replication can be done in a range of ways. If we are worried that the success of an exercise program might be due to a charismatic trainer, then it would be useful to replicate the study with a different coach. If we think an anti-violence program might depend on how strictly crime is penalised, then it would be valuable to replicate it in a jurisdiction with softer laws.

One way to carry out replication is for a new research team to repeat the study: an approach that one foundation describes as 'If at first you succeed, try again'.[52] But another is for researchers to work together to conduct the same analysis in different places. For example, if we can randomise a tutoring program at the student level, then it may be useful to simultaneously run the trial across multiple schools, so we can compare the effectiveness of different teams.

In some fields, there is a powerful push towards doing trials in multiple locations. Australian medical researcher David Johnson told me that in his field of kidney disease, he wants to see an end to under-powered single-centre trials.[53] 'It's seldom that clinical practice will ever be changed by a single-centre trial,' Johnson argues. 'The numbers tend to be small, and even if they're big enough, you worry that they won't generalise.' For his kind of medical research, Johnson contends, the future lies in coordinated research across multiple centres.

Statistically, a randomised trial based in two or three countries should be accorded massively more weight than one based on just a single site. To see why, let's go back to that 95 per cent cut-off for statistical significance. If we run a randomised evaluation of a junk program, then 5 per cent of the time – or one time in twenty – the result will turn out to be statistically significant. Oops.

Now let's see what happens when the finding is replicated. Suppose we test a new education program, using the conventional 95 per cent level of statistical significance. And suppose the program doesn't actually work. In that case, a randomised trial will give rise to a positive finding by chance one time in twenty. But with two randomised trials, the odds of mistakenly getting a positive finding in both trials would fall to one in 400. With three randomised trials, the chance that all three would find that the program had a significant impact drops to one in 8000. A significant result is far less likely to be a fluke if it holds up in multiple places.[54]

The job of compiling the randomised evidence is done by Cochrane for medicine and the Campbell Collaboration for social policy. Topic by topic, these organisations compile 'systematic reviews' that distil the relevant randomised trials into a format that can be easily accessed by practitioners, policymakers and the public.

The internationalisation of randomised trials presents new opportunities for replication across countries. In the 1980s, nine out of ten randomised policy trials were conducted in the United States, so multi-country studies were difficult.[55] But today, just three in ten randomised policy trials are carried out in the US. It's a trend that should be welcomed by Americans and non-Americans alike. If a program or pharmaceutical passes randomised evaluation in several countries, you can be more confident it really works.

Wherever a replication is conducted, it's crucial that the results are reported. If researchers conceal findings that run counter to conventional wisdom, then the rest of us may form a mistaken impression of the results of available randomised trials. Like a golfer who takes a mulligan on every hole, discarded trials can leave us in a situation where the scorecard doesn't reflect reality.

One way of countering 'publication bias' is to require that studies be registered before they start – by lodging a statement in advance in which the researchers specify the questions they are seeking to answer. This makes it more likely that studies are reported after they finish. In medicine, there are fifteen major clinical trial registers around the world, including ones operated by Australia and New Zealand, China, the European Union, India, Japan, the Netherlands and Thailand. All of these trials are then aggregated by the World Health Organization into the International Clinical Trials Registry Platform, which contains details of around 400,000 medical trials.

In recent years, development economists have established the Registry for International Development Impact Evaluations, which lists over 100 studies. Political scientists have created the Experiments in Governance and Politics Network (which lists around 700 studies). Economists have created the American Economic Association's Randomized Controlled Trials registry (which lists around 1500 studies). Unlike in medicine, most social science journals do not yet refuse to publish unregistered trials, nor is there a requirement for all results to be published. But it is likely that disciplines such as economics and political science will move that way in coming years. As an added incentive – and with a touch of irony – development economists offered the first 100 researchers who submitted a trial to their registry a chance to win a tablet computer.

Even in medicine, the practice of researchers does not always live up to the requirements of the registry. Since 2007 the US government has required all drug trials to be registered at Clinicaltrials.gov, and published within a year of data collection. Yet a recent analysis found that only one in seven registered trials had complied with this requirement.[56] Even four years after data completion, less than half of all trials had publicly posted their results. Hopefully the revelation of these worrying statistics will improve compliance rates.

In 2006, researchers analysed all the available clinical trial data on Prozac-type antidepressants, and found that they were associated with a higher risk of suicide among teenagers.[57] If the studies had been reported sooner, this disturbing finding might have been known earlier. Similarly, the decision by various advanced countries to stockpile the anti-influenza drug Tamiflu was made at a time when 60 per cent of the available studies had not reported their results.[58] Analysis of these figures now suggests that Tamiflu may be less effective at reducing hospital admissions than previously thought. Randomised trials can't help society make better choices if their results are buried.

One of the main purposes of requiring trials to be registered is to avoid researchers moving the goalposts. But a number of recent reviews have shown that a significant share of randomised trials in medicine engaged in 'outcome switching' – reporting measures that were different from those they registered at the beginning.[59] The most egregious case involved a 1998 study of GlaxoSmithKline's drug Paxil, whose registration said the trial would look at eight outcomes. None showed any impact, so the researchers then went fishing across nineteen more measures, of which four showed a significant effect. Paxil's results were then reported as though these four measures had been their focus from the outset. In 2012 GlaxoSmithKline was fined US$3 billion for misreporting trial data on several of their drugs, including Paxil.[60]

*

'I still remember the call like it was yesterday. It came from the man analysing the bloodwork. "Something's not right," he told me, "one of the girls has something going on with her white blood cells." An hour later, he called back and said the girl had early-stage leukaemia. By the end of the day, her parents had driven her from Canberra to Sydney, and she was getting her first treatment. A year later, she was cancer free.'

Dick Telford is sitting in my office, chatting about a remarkable study he began in 2005, to look at the impact of physical exercise on child outcomes. If there's a person who's qualified to talk about fitness, it's Telford. In the late 1960s he played Aussie Rules for Collingwood and Fitzroy, before switching to running. He's run a marathon in 2 hours and 27 minutes, won a track medal at the World Masters Games, and has a PhD in exercise science from the University of Melbourne. Telford was the first sport scientist appointed to the Australian Institute of Sport, where he trained Rob de Castella, Lisa Ondieki, Martin Dent and Carolyn Schuwalow.

Now in his early seventies, Telford is whippet-thin and moves fluidly. He coaches a small squad of runners, which I occasionally join. He's deeply engaged with research, with a strong focus on randomised trials. It's not to build up his résumé, but because Telford cares deeply about understanding which programs work and which do not.

The way in which Telford's school sport program worked provides insights into how to run an effective randomised trial. As we've seen, it isn't always necessary for the control group to get nothing at all, with many medical randomised trials testing a new drug against the best available alternative. Comparing two treatments reduces the chance of study participants trying to switch groups, helps assuage political concerns and is ethically preferable in most instances.

The same approach can be taken in the case of non-medical research. When Telford began his 2005 trial, working in partnership with the Australian Institute of Sport and the Australian National University, everyone recognised that it would be wrong to deny children in the control group any access to school sport. So rather than comparing exercise to no exercise, the study compared high-quality physical education with regular school sports programs. And because children might have felt cheated if they saw their classmates receiving better sports programs, the randomisation was done between schools, rather than between pupils in the same school.

After extensive conversations with school principals, Telford and his colleagues chose twenty-nine Canberra primary schools, and randomly divided them into two groups – literally drawing school names out of a hat. Thirteen of the schools were selected to receive physical education instruction from specialist teachers, who worked with classroom teachers to provide a daily exercise program of balance, coordination and games. In the sixteen control group schools, students still did physical education with their regular classroom teachers, but the sessions were fewer, shorter and less physically demanding. So rather than comparing the impact of exercise with no exercise, the randomised trial became a comparison of occasional sport with quality training.

After four years, children randomised into the treatment group had less body fat, lower cholesterol levels and better maths scores.[61] Researchers are now following these children into adulthood, to see how doing more exercise as a child may affect their overall wellbeing. Ultimately, Telford would like to see the children in the study followed up into their retirement years. He knows he won't be around to see the results, but feels it's vital that we learn about the long-term effects of quality school sports programs.

Done well, randomised trials make the world a better place. As it happens, Dick Telford's hunch about the benefits of quality school sports programs seem to be paying off. But even if the results had dashed his hopes, the study would still be valuable, as it would add to our stock of knowledge, perhaps inspiring other researchers to pursue different approaches. And even aside from the results, there's a girl alive today in Canberra who beat leukaemia, perhaps only because she was lucky enough to be part of Dick Telford's randomised trial.

12

WHAT'S THE
NEXT CHANCE?

I n his book on the history of science, David Wootton marks how we have progressed intellectually by setting out the beliefs of most well-educated Europeans in 1600.[1] The leading minds of that time believed in werewolves, in witches who could summon storms, and in unicorns. They believed that dreams could predict the future, and that the sun revolved around the earth. They believed mice were spontaneously created within straw piles, and that rainbows were a sign from God. They believed that a victim's body would bleed when the murderer was nearby. In Shakespeare's day, these weren't fringe notions – they were what the best-informed people of that era understood to be true.

Among the powerful beliefs of the age was alchemy – the notion that base metals such as lead could be turned into precious metals such as gold. For millennia, alchemy had occupied a significant portion of all scientific research efforts. Even Isaac Newton spent more time on alchemy than on physics, prompting Keynes to suggest that Newton was 'not the first of the age of reason. He was the last of the magicians.'

What saw off alchemy was not a culture of experimentation. Quite the contrary: alchemists had been doing experiments for centuries. The critical shift was the movement from secretive, badly designed experiments to experiments that were rigorous and publicly reported. As David Wootton observes:

> What killed alchemy was the insistence that experiments must be openly reported in publications which presented a clear account of what had happened, and they must then be replicated, preferably before independent witnesses. The alchemists had pursued a secret learning, convinced that only a few were fit to have knowledge of divine secrets and that the social order would collapse if gold ceased to be in short supply … Esoteric knowledge was replaced by a new form of knowledge, which depended both on publication and on public or semi-public performance. A closed society was replaced by an open one.[2]

By 1750, well-educated Europeans no longer believed in alchemy – nor, for that matter, witches, unicorns or werewolves. Today, experimentation and the open publication of results are why most of us can confidently reject hundreds of ideas that seem intuitively appealing – including phrenology, iridology, astrology, reiki, telepathy, water dowsing, dianetics and tongue maps. It's why a majority of people believe in evolution in most advanced countries, including the United Kingdom, France, Germany, Japan, Denmark and Spain (though not the United States or Turkey).[3] The scientific revolution not only transformed the way in which we view the world around us, but has underpinned massive improvements in medical research, increasing the length and quality of our lives.

Alas, too many areas of life – from business to policymaking – still look worryingly like alchemy. When the basis for judgement is a low-quality evaluation and the results are kept secret from the world, the process starts to look more like the search for the philosopher's stone than rigorous analysis. When 1100 of the world's top executives were asked to describe their decision-making process, fewer than one in three said that they placed most reliance on data and analysis.[4] British economist Tim Harford is critical of politicians who 'use statistics like a stage magician uses smoke and mirrors'.[5] At its worst, he says, this can be like the 'bullshitter' described by philosopher Harry Frankfurt: a person who is worse than a liar because they do not even care about the truth – they are indifferent to whether their statements are true or false.[6] Sure, it's possible to lie with statistics – but even easier to lie without them.

Bringing randomised trials to policy involves what psychologist Donald Campbell called 'the experimenting society'. Campbell envisaged this as 'an honest society, committed ... to self-criticism ... It will say it like it is, face up to the facts, be undefensive.'[7] Such a society 'will be a nondogmatic society ... The scientific values of honesty, open criticism, experimentation, willingness to change once-advocated theories in the face of experimental and other evidence.'[8] As we have seen, this approach is epitomised by the founders of TOMS, who donated 60 million pairs of shoes to children in developing nations, encouraged a randomised evaluation and then changed their philanthropic approach in response to the disappointing results.

It's not always easy to follow the scientific path. As physicist Richard Feynman once observed, 'The first principle is that you must not fool yourself – and you are the easiest person to fool.'[9] Great scientists present all the evidence, not just the data that supports their pet theories. The best scientists publish results regardless of how they turn out. Feynman contrasted scientific integrity with 'cargo cult science'. Like the Pacific Islanders who once built sham runways in the hope of attracting cargo planes, bad science might look like real science. It might even produce temporary moments of fame and excitement. But its results will eventually be junked.

'Just as randomised trials revolutionised medicine in the twentieth century,' argue economists Esther Duflo and Michael Kremer, 'they have the potential to revolutionise social policy in the twenty-first.'[10] As British Nudge Unit head David Halpern puts it: 'We need to turn public policy from an art to a science.'[11] This means paying more attention to measurement, and admitting that our intuition might be wrong. Randomised trials flourish where modesty meets numeracy.

One of the big thinkers of US social policy, senator Daniel Patrick Moynihan, recognised that evaluations can often produce results which are solid rather than stunning. When faced with a proposed new program, Moynihan was fond of quoting Rossi's Law. Moynihan whimsically called Judith Gueron, the pioneer of randomised social policy trials, 'Our Lady of Modest but Positive Results.'[12]

Blockbuster movies are filled with white knights and magic bullets, moon shots and miracles. Yet in reality most positive change doesn't happen suddenly. From social reforms to economic change, our best systems have evolved gradually. Randomised trials put science, business and government on a steady path to improvement. Like a healthy diet, the approach succeeds little by little, through a series of good choices. The incremental approach won't remake the world overnight, but it will over a generation.[13]

The best medical thinkers embody this modest approach. As one medical dean told his first-year class on day one: 'Half of what we teach you here is wrong. Unfortunately, we do not know which half.'[14] David Sackett, a pioneer of evidence-based medicine, wrote: 'The first sin committed by experts consists in adding their prestige and their position to their opinions, which give the latter far greater persuasive power than they deserve on scientific grounds alone.'[15]

Judah Folkman, once one of the world's top cancer researchers, observed, 'I learn more from my failures than from my successes.'[16]

The same holds in business. In advanced countries, more than half of all start-ups fail within five years.[17] Venture capital investors make most of their returns from a small number of their firms. Changing market conditions undoubtedly play a part, but the best firms aren't just lucky – they're also more adept at creating a cycle of rigorous testing and improvement. As one academic study observes, 'Entrepreneurship is fundamentally about experimentation because the knowledge required to be successful cannot be known in advance or deduced from some set of first principles.'[18] Intuit founder Scott Cook aims to create a company that's 'buzzing with experiments', and in which 'failing is perfectly fine.'[19] Whatever happens, Cook tells his staff, 'you're doing right because you've created evidence, which is better than anyone's intuition'. Journalist Megan McArdle argues that America's economic success is rooted in 'failing well', through institutions that encourage risk-taking, forgiveness and learning from mistakes.[20]

Policy is replete with examples in which 'expert' judgement is revealed to be at odds with the data. For example, when considering whether to build a new rail line or road, governments typically commission projections of how many people will use it. But when researchers go back years later to see how many people actually used the project, it turns out that road traffic projections exceed the number of cars that use the road, and rail patronage projections overestimate the number of passengers.[21] In the case of rail, the expert projections were particularly flawed. Nine out of ten forecasts overestimate usage, with the average projection being wrong by a factor of two. As we saw from the street-paving experiment in the Mexican city of Acayucan, it is actually possible to run randomised trials of infrastructure provision. But even if governments choose not to drive down that road, it's vital that we use evidence to build a better feedback loop.

Just as modesty is a great ally of randomised trials, overconfidence can be their enemy. The more certain experts are of their skill and judgement, the less likely they are to use data. And yet we know from a range of studies that overconfidence is a common trait. Eighty-four per cent of Frenchmen think that they are above-average lovers.[22] Ninety-three per cent of Americans think they are better-than-average drivers.[23] Ninety-seven per cent of Australians rate their own beauty as average or better than average.[24] In human evolution, over-confidence has proven to be a successful strategy.[25] In our own lives, excess confidence can provide a sense of resilience – allowing us to take credit for successes while avoiding blame for failures.[26]

The problem is that we live in a world in which failure is surprisingly common. In medicine, we saw that only one in ten drugs that looks promising in lab tests ends up getting approval. In education, we saw that only one-tenth of the randomised trials commissioned by the US What Works Clearinghouse produced positive effects. In business, just one-fifth of Google's randomised experiments helped them improve the product. Rigorous social policy experiments find that only a quarter of programs have a strong positive effect. Once you raise the evidence bar, a consistent finding emerges: most ideas that sound good don't actually work in practice. As randomised trials take off in new areas – such as law and anti-terrorism – they may up-end conventional wisdom there too.[27]

In the end, good evaluation is nothing less than the search for truth. As Einstein famously put it, 'I want to know the thoughts of God. Everything else is details.' If there is a judgement day, I'm guessing that everyone who's ever struggled to put together a good evaluation will take the opportunity to step up and ask the Almighty: 'So, tell me, did it work or not?'

In the Woody Allen movie *Annie Hall*, two characters are arguing about the views of eminent philosopher Marshall McLuhan. Suddenly

McLuhan steps into the scene and tells one of them he's absolutely wrong. The other declares: 'Boy, if life were only like this!' For many important questions, randomised trials are as close as we'll come to that *Annie Hall* moment of truth.

For those at the cutting edge of research, a central challenge is effectively melding theory with randomised evaluations, to build more accurate models of human behaviour. Sure, there will always be a place for testing whether people are more likely to open letters in red or blue envelopes. But the most valuable randomised trials are those that provide deeper insights. Discussing what he has learnt from running randomised trials in Liberia, Chris Blattman reflects that 'instead of asking, "Does the program work?", I should have asked, "How does the world work?"'[28] By testing fundamental assumptions, Blattman argues, it is possible to produce insights that generalise across programs.

In a similar vein, economists Jens Ludwig, Jeffrey Kling and Sendhil Mullainathan use the example of understanding 'broken windows policing', a strategy which focuses on addressing low-level offences (such as fare evasion, littering or minor property damage) as a way of reducing more serious crime.[29] The trio suggest that most researchers would probably set out to evaluate broken windows policing by identifying a subset of cities and randomly instituting broken windows policing strategies in half of them. But if we want to understand the fundamentals, they argue, a better approach would be to buy a few dozen used cars, break the windows in half of them, park them in randomly selected neighbourhoods and see if more serious crimes increase in response.[30] They call the policing experiment a policy evaluation, and the car experiment a mechanism evaluation – because it goes to the deeper question of whether broken windows increase violent crime. Both kinds of randomised trials can be useful. A police chief might only care about whether the policy works, but social researchers should focus on experiments which provide the deepest insights.

Around the world, there are many creative ways that randomised trials are being institutionalised. In 2005 Mexico created the National Council for Evaluation of Social Development Policy, an autonomous body charged with building the evidence base on what works to reduce poverty. Like the Nudge Units that have been established at the heart of governments in many advanced nations, Mexico's national council reflects that country's goal of being a leader among developing nations in running randomised trials.

Another promising way of encouraging randomised trials is to promise more money for ideas that succeed. In 2010 entrepreneur Maura O'Neill and development academic Michael Kremer persuaded the US Agency for International Development to create a division called 'Development Innovation Ventures'.[31] Founded on the principle of 'scaling proven successes', the program operates a three-tiered funding process. The first round offers funding of up to US$150,000. If a project shows evidence of success – often through a randomised trial – it can be eligible to move up to the second round, with up to US$1.5 million on offer. Prove success in the second round, and the idea moves into the third round, eligible for up to US$15 million in funding from Development Innovation Ventures.

In federal systems, another practical way that governments have encouraged randomised trials is by the national government building randomised trials into state grants programs. This has become commonplace in US federal legislation.[32] For example, the *Second Chance Act*, dealing with strategies to facilitate prisoner re-entry into the community, sets aside 2 per cent of program funds for evaluations that 'include, to the maximum extent possible, random assignment ... and generate evidence on which re-entry approaches and strategies are most effective'. The *No Child Left Behind Act* calls for evaluation 'using rigorous methodological designs and techniques, including control groups and random assignment, to the extent feasible, to produce reliable evidence of effectiveness'. Legislation to improve child development via home visits directs the Department of Health and Human Services to 'ensure that States use the funds to support models that have been shown in well-designed randomized controlled trials, to produce sizeable, sustained effects on important child outcomes such as abuse and neglect'.

Charitable foundations have a vital role to play too. In the United Kingdom, about a hundred education-related randomised trials are underway, mostly conducted by the Education Endowment Foundation.[33] A key contribution of the foundation is not only to find out what works, but also to help people sort through the available studies. The Education Endowment Foundation ranks research findings from 5 (a randomised trial with strong statistical power and low attrition) to 0 (a study with no comparison group). Like the evidence hierarchy I proposed in Chapter 1, the foundation's rating system is a simple way to sum up the reliability of a particular evaluation.[34] By putting randomised trials at the top, it creates an additional incentive to raise the evidence bar. Several US foundations, including the Edna McConnell Clark Foundation, Results for America, the Laura and John Arnold Foundation, and Bloomberg Philanthropies, are taking a similar approach, focusing on funding randomised trials – or programs that have been proven in randomised trials to be effective.

When it comes to caring about ends over means, few people can beat US paediatrician David Olds. Olds began developing his nurse–family partnership program in the 1970s. For the next twenty years, he used randomised trials to refine the program. In 1996 Olds started rolling out the program across communities. But even now – decades after he began creating the program – Olds wants to see it put to the test. Specifically, anyone outside the United States who wants to license the nurse–family partnership program must agree to perform a randomised evaluation. After all, the impact of home visits might differ in Britain, the Netherlands or Canada. As Olds sums up his philosophy: 'I want to solve a problem, not promote a program.'[35]

*

In 2008, people who had previously given to the development charity Freedom from Hunger received a letter asking for another donation.[36] Each letter told the story of a poor Peruvian widow named Rita, and then asked for support in one of two ways. Half the letters said, 'In order to know that our programs work for people like Rita, we look for more than anecdotal evidence. That is why we have coordinated with independent researchers to conduct scientifically rigorous impact studies of our programs.' The other half simply asserted, 'But Freedom from Hunger knows that women like Rita are ready to end hunger in their own families and in their communities.'

In effect, the economists were running a randomised trial to test whether donors cared that a program was backed by randomised trials. On average, they found no impact – or, as they summed it up, no effect of effectiveness on donors. But when the results were broken down, the researchers found that including information on impact raised donation rates among large donors, while decreasing generosity among small donors. They concluded that among those who were simply looking for a warm glow, mentioning evaluation raised the spectre that not all aid might be effective. But among altruists, knowing that a program had a large impact made it more attractive.

The lesson of the Freedom from Hunger study is that we don't just need more randomised trials – we also need to do a better job of demanding strong evidence. The more we ask the question 'What's your evidence?', the more likely we are to find out what works – and what does not. Scepticism isn't the enemy of optimism: it's the channel through which our desire to solve big problems translates into real results. If we let our curiosity roam free, we might be surprised how much we can learn about the world, one coin toss at a time.

TEN COMMANDMENTS FOR RUNNING YOUR OWN RANDOMISED TRIAL

Conducting a successful randomised trial requires an unusual mix of talents. The best randomistas possess technical skills, operational wisdom, political savvy and courage.[1]

Ready to try it? Here are ten steps you should consider.

1. Decide what you want to test.

The simplest approach is to test a new intervention against a control group that gets nothing. Other studies run a horserace between two or more interventions. Crossover randomised trials combine multiple interventions. For example, a program to support self-employment might offer training, a cash grant, both or neither. If an intervention has an immediate impact, you might even be able to turn it on and off at random intervals. For example, to test whether a bedtime routine reduces insomnia, randomly assign it across half your evenings for the next month, then use a smartphone app to measure the quality of each night's slumber.

2. Think creatively about how to create a random difference in the program.

Sometimes it isn't practical or ethical to tell a group of people that they won't ever get the program. If so, consider alternatives to the standard randomised trial. If a policy is already being rolled out over a two-year period, why not randomise who gets it in the first year and who gets it in the second year?[2] If you want to evaluate an existing program that has low take-up rates, can you use an information campaign or incentives to randomly encourage some people to access the program?

3. Consider what the control group will do.

Put yourself in the shoes of someone who ends up in the control group. What would you do? Recall the evaluations of the US early childhood program Head Start, which initially failed to recognise that many of the children in the control group attended other publicly provided preschool centres. Until this was taken into account, the true benefit–cost ratio was underestimated by a factor of two.

4. Choose which outcomes to measure.

Administrative data has the advantage that it's cheap or free, and you can typically get it for everyone in the experiment. Surveys can be tailored, but if only one-tenth of the people answer your survey, you'll need to start with a sample that's ten times as big. Some surveys do repeated follow-ups, while others pay people for responding (an experiment by a chain store found that putting a dollar in the envelope doubled response rates from 8 to 16 per cent).[3] When you assess the impact of the intervention, focus only on the random assignment. If a person who started in the control group manages to get their hands on the treatment, you must still analyse the data based on their original status.

5. Select the level at which to randomise.

An educational intervention might randomise across students, across classrooms or across schools. The right answer here depends on practical considerations, ethical concerns and how the policy might spill over from the treatment group to the control group. Iin some of the early trials of AIDS drugs, patients in the treatment and control groups shared their medication – an understandable reaction, given that the disease was effectively a death sentence at that time.[4] Everyone got half a dose of the true drugs, the trial results were useless, and the drugs ended up taking longer to get approved. If the trial had randomised across hospitals, it would have required a larger sample but the trial would have been more likely to succeed.

6. Ensure your study is large enough.

If you're expecting the intervention to cause massive differences between treatment and control groups, then a small sample might be sufficient. Recall the Triple P parenting program, which had such a large impact that it led to significant results in a sample of just fifty-one Indigenous families. But if you're testing something that will only move the needle slightly, you'll need a larger sample. Remember the problem with estimating the impact of television advertisements: an individual ad has such a small impact on overall buying that it's almost impossible to detect even in a randomised trial. If you want an indication of how big your experiment needs to be, an internet search for 'power calculation' will bring up useful online calculators. If your intended sample isn't large enough, consider collaborating with researchers in other cities or countries. Not only will it boost the sample, but it will also make people more inclined to believe that your findings are true everywhere – not just in one specific context.

7. Register your trial and get ethics approval.

If you hope to publish the results, then register your trial with the appropriate medical or social science website. Wherever possible, obtain ethics approval. If your intervention could harm the participants, the ethics committee may require you to establish a data and safety monitoring board, which will keep an eye on the experiment as it runs. While ethics approval can be time-consuming, it does provide insurance in case anything goes wrong. In 2014 a political science experiment sent flyers to 100,000 Montana voters, showing the ideological position of candidates for the state Supreme Court.[5] Because the flyers bore the official state seal, the study was found to have breached Montana election law. The researchers might have deflected the blame if they'd had the experiment approved by their universities' internal review boards. But they hadn't.[6]

8. Confirm that the key people understand and support randomisation.

It's critical to ensure that everyone involved understands why an experiment is being conducted. Supervisors will need to justify randomisation to funders or to managers. Caseworkers may have to turn away needy people based on a random process.[7] If these people don't follow the randomisation, your results are likely to be garbage.[8] BETA head Michael Hiscox says that 'developing the partnerships and getting everyone on board at the start probably accounts for 75 per cent of total effort spent in my trials'.[9] Bad experts attempt to muddle through by pulling rank and using jargon. Good experts take time to explain to those on the ground what they hope to learn from a randomised trial, why it will be helpful to the clients and the organisation, and why the trial is ethical.

9. Use a truly random procedure to split the sample.

To allocate people to the treatment and control groups, you can toss a coin, draw paper from a hat or use your spreadsheet's random number generation function. If you're splitting a list in half, ensure it has been sorted into random order. If you have some background information about the participants, then you can get a bit more statistical precision by balancing the treatment and control groups on observable traits. An evaluation of mentoring programs conducted in the 1930s matched troubled youth into similar pairs, based on age, family background and delinquent behaviour.[10] Researchers then tossed a coin within each pair, assigning one to the treatment group and the other to the control group.[11]

10. If possible, conduct a small-scale pilot study.

Just as an athlete goes through their paces before the race starts, it's helpful to check the integrity of your experiment on a modest scale. The aim isn't to produce usable results: but to find unanticipated problems in the randomisation, implementation or survey. As Dean Karlan and Jacob Appel note, you might feel like you just want to get on with the full experiment, but 'pre-testing or small-scale piloting is the best way to preview take-up rates and reveal occupational hiccups that could arise during implementation.'[12] Fix the bugs, and you're ready to run your randomised trial!

ACKNOWLEDGEMENTS

My interest in randomised trials was first piqued during my studies at the Harvard Kennedy School in the early 2000s. My thesis chair, Christopher Jencks, and my advisers, David Ellwood and Caroline Hoxby, are scholars with an infectious sense of scientific curiosity. Like my wonderful parents, Barbara and Michael Leigh, my advisers taught me the value of asking questions and sifting the evidence as critically as possible. As a professor-turned-politician, I've also been influenced by the late US senator Daniel Patrick Moynihan, whose evidence-informed approach to public policy still has a great deal to teach us.

In the course of researching this book, I learned a great deal from speaking with subject matter experts, as well as my parliamentary colleagues and the engaged electors of Fenner. My particular thanks to interviewees Aileen Ashford, Jon Baron, Vicki Bon, Jeff Borland, John Chalmers, Peter Choong, Tamera Clancy, Tony Davis, Jane Eastgate, Alan Frost, Alan Garner, Kate Glazebrook, Sue Grigg, Alice Hill, Michael Hiscox, Ben Hubbard, David Johnson, Guy Johnson, Brigid Jordan, Anne Kennedy, Tess Lea, Kate Leslie, John List, Angela Merriam, Matthew Morris, Greg Rebetzke, Stefanie Schurer, Adam

Story, Andrew Sullivan, Dick Telford, Yi-Ping Tseng, Dave Vicary, Joe Walker, Valerie Wilson and Michael Woolcock. Thanks also to surgeon Peter Choong and his team for allowing me to watch them in action.

For thoughtful suggestions, my thanks to Andrew Charlton, Philip Clarke, Andrew Davidson, Trevor Duke, Nicholas Faulkner, Rory Gallagher, Nick Green, Sonia Loudon, Eleanor Robson, Peter Siminski, Rocco Weglarz and Jessy Wu. For comments on earlier drafts, I am grateful to Esther Duflo, David Halpern, Ian Harris, Michael Hiscox, Dean Karlan, Barbara Leigh, Jennifer Rayner, Nick Terrell, Damjan Vukcevic and seminar participants at Melbourne's Royal Children's Hospital. I also worked with Phil Ames and James Wilson, two expatriate Australians who chose to do their Harvard Kennedy School Policy Analysis Exercise on the topic of randomised policy trials in government. Their research paper is first-rate, and these two randomistas will help shape Australian policy-making in decades to come.

Fundamentally, this book is about the way that a better feedback loop can help us learn from our mistakes. For spotting my errors and honing my prose, thanks to my extraordinary editors, Chris Feik and Kirstie Innes-Will, as well as to the rest of the team at Black Inc. and Yale University Press for their hard work and dedication to this project.

There are some excellent books on randomised experiments, from which I've learnt a great deal. If you're interested in reading more, I particularly recommend Ian Harris's *Surgery, the Ultimate Placebo* (on medical trials); Dean Karlan and Jacob Appel's *More Than Good Intentions* and Abhijit Banerjee and Esther Duflo's *Poor Economics* (on trials in developing countries); Uri Gneezy and John List's *The Why Axis* (on experiments in business and philanthropy); Alan Gerber and Donald Green's *Get Out the Vote!* (on political randomised trials); David Halpern's *Inside the Nudge Unit* (on policy trials); and Tim

Harford's *Adapt* (on the philosophy of experimentation). For devotees, the two-volume *Handbook of Field Experiments*, edited by Esther Duflo and Abhijit Banerjee, provides a detailed survey of the subject.

For tips on running your own randomised trial, check out Rachel Glennerster and Kudzai Takavarasha's *Running Randomised Evaluations*, Dean Karlan and Jacob Appel's *Failing in the Field*, the British Behavioural Insights Team's *Test, Learn, Adapt* handbook, and the Australian BETA Unit's *Guide to Developing Behavioural Interventions for Randomised Controlled Trials*.

There was more than a little luck in an Australian economist meeting an American landscape architect in Boston eighteen years ago. To my amazing wife, Gweneth: thank you for taking a chance on me, and for your laughter, wisdom and kindness ever since. To our three remarkable boys, Sebastian, Theodore and Zachary: may you continue to experiment with life, combining optimism with scepticism, and a love of today with a desire to make tomorrow even better.

NOTES

1 Scurvy, Scared Straight and *Sliding Doors*

1   Quoted in Stephen Bown, *Scurvy: How a Surgeon, a Mariner and a Gentleman Solved the Greatest Medical Mystery of the Age of Sail*, New York: Thomas Dunne, 2003, p. 34.
2   Bown, *Scurvy*, p. 3.
3   Jonathan Lamb, *Preserving the Self in the South Seas, 1680–1840*, Chicago: University of Chicago Press, 2001, p. 117.
4   Bown, *Scurvy*, p. 26.
5   We think Lind effectively assigned sailors to the six groups at random, though with the benefit of a few centuries of hindsight it would have been better if he had done so by a formal mechanism, such as drawing their names out of a hat.
6   Lind claimed that scurvy was caused when the body's perspiration system was blocked, causing 'excrementitious humours' to become 'extremely acrid and corrosive': quoted in Bown, *Scurvy*, p. 104.
7   Email from Alan Frost to author, 2 July 2015. See also Alan Frost, *Botany Bay Mirages: Illusions of Australia's Convict Beginnings*, Melbourne: Melbourne University Press, 1994, pp. 120–5; James Watt, 'Medical aspects and consequences of Cook's voyages' in Robin Fisher & Hugh Johnston, *Captain James Cook and His Times*, Vancouver and London: Douglas & McIntyre and Croom Helm, 1979; James Watt, 'Some consequences of nutritional disorders in eighteenth century British circumnavigations' in James Watt, E.J. Freeman & William F. Bynum, *Starving Sailors: The Influence of Nutrition upon Naval and Maritime History*, London: National Maritime Museum, 1981, pp. 54–9.
8   The principal surgeon on the First Fleet wrote: 'In one of his Majesty's ships, I was liberally supplied with that powerful antiscorbutic, essence of malt; we had also sour krout.' John White, *Journal of a Voyage to New South Wales*, 1790, entry on 6 July 1787.

9   Arthur Phillip, *The Voyage of Governor Phillip to Botany Bay with an Account of the Establishment of the Colonies of Port Jackson and Norfolk Island*, London: John Stockdale, 1789, Ch. 7.

10   Bown, *Scurvy*, pp. 170–84

11   Bown, *Scurvy*, p. 200.

12   Bown, *Scurvy*, p. 198.

13   Sally A. Brinkman, Sarah E. Johnson, James P. Codde, et al., 'Efficacy of infant simulator programmes to prevent teenage pregnancy: A school-based cluster randomised controlled trial in Western Australia', *The Lancet*, vol. 388, no. 10057, 2016, pp. 2264–71.

14   Carol Dweck, *Mindset: The New Psychology of Success*, New York: Random House, 2006.

15   Angus Deaton, 'Making aid work: Evidence-based aid must not become the latest in a long string of development fads', *Boston Review*, vol. 31, no. 4, 2006, p. 13.

16   Chris Van Klaveren & Kristof De Witte, 'Football to improve math and reading performance', *Education Economics*, vol. 23, no. 5, 2015, pp. 577–95.

17   The experiment was conducted with two newspapers, the *Washington Times* and the *Washington Post*. Those randomly assigned to get the *Washington Post* were 8 percentage points more likely to vote for the Democratic Party than those assigned to the control group. Surprisingly, the *Washington Times* group were also more likely to vote Democrat, though the effect was not statistically significant. Alan S. Gerber, Dean Karlan & Daniel Bergan, 'Does the media matter? A field experiment measuring the effect of newspapers on voting behavior and political opinions', *American Economic Journal: Applied Economics*, vol. 1, no. 2, pp. 35–52.

18   Luc Behaghel, Clément De Chaisemartin & Marc Gurgand, 'Ready for boarding? The effects of a boarding school for disadvantaged students', *American Economic Journal: Applied Economics*, vol. 9, no. 1, 2017, pp. 140–64.

19   Better stoves turned out to improve people's health in the first year, but not in the second and subsequent years. Rema Hanna, Esther Duflo & Michael Greenstone, 'Up in smoke: The influence of household behavior on the long-run impact of improved cooking stoves', *American Economic Journal: Economic Policy*, vol. 8, no. 1, 2016, pp. 80–114.

20   Christopher Blattman & Stefan Dercon, 'Everything we knew about sweatshops was wrong', *New York Times*, 27 April 2017.

21   Coalition for Evidence-Based Policy, 'Evidence summary for Treatment Foster Care Oregon (formerly MTFC)', Washington, DC: Coalition for Evidence-Based Policy, 2009.

22   For a review of the quasi-experimental and randomised evaluations of Scared Straight, see Anthony Petrosino, Carolyn Turpin-Petrosino & John Buehler, '"Scared Straight" and other juvenile awareness programs for preventing juvenile delinquency' (Updated C2 Review), Campbell Collaboration Reviews of Intervention and Policy Evaluations (C2-RIPE), 2002. See also Robert Boruch & Ning Rui, 'From randomized controlled trials to evidence grading schemes: Current state of evidence-based practice in social sciences', *Journal of Evidence-Based Medicine*, vol. 1, no. 1, 2008, pp. 41–9.

23   The research was published in 1982. James Finckenaur, *Scared Straight and the Panacea Phenomenon*, Englewood Cliffs, New Jersey: Prentice-Hall, 1982.

24   Quoted in Matthew Syed, *Black Box Thinking: Why Most People Never Learn*

from Their Mistakes – But Some Do, New York: Portfolio, 2015, p. 163.

25   Petrosino, Turpin-Petrosino & Buehler, '"Scared Straight" and other juvenile awareness programs'. See also an update: Anthony Petrosino, Carolyn Turpin-Petrosino, Meghan E. Hollis-Peel & Julia G. Lavenberg, '"Scared Straight" and other juvenile awareness programs for preventing juvenile delinquency: A systematic review', Campbell Systematic Reviews, Oslo: Campbell Collaboration, 2013.

26   Howard S. Bloom, Larry L. Orr, Stephen H. Bell, et al., 'The benefits and costs of JTPA Title II-A programs: Key findings from the National Job Training Partnership Act study', *Journal of Human Resources,* vol. 32, no. 3, 1997, pp. 549–76.

27   Many of these studies are reviewed in James J. Heckman, Robert J. LaLonde & Jeffrey A. Smith, 'The economics and econometrics of active labor market programs' in Orley Ashenfelter & David Card (eds), *Handbook of Labor Economics,* vol. 3A, Amsterdam: North Holland, 1999, pp. 1865–2097. Recent evidence suggests that in developing countries, job training may be useful for youths: Orazio Attanasio, Adriana Kugler & Costas Meghir, 'Subsidizing vocational training for disadvantaged youth in Colombia: Evidence from a randomized trial', *American Economic Journal: Applied Economics*, vol. 3, no. 3, 2011, pp. 188–220.

28   Roland G. Fryer, Jr., Steven D. Levitt & John A. List, 'Parental incentives and early childhood achievement: A field experiment in Chicago Heights', NBER Working Paper No. 21477, Cambridge, MA: NBER, 2015.

29   Marc E. Wheeler, Thomas E. Keller & David L. DuBois, 'Review of three recent randomized trials of school-based mentoring: Making sense of mixed findings', *Social Policy Report*, vol. 24, no. 3, 2010.

30   Raj Chande, Michael Luca, Michael Sanders, et al., 'Curbing adult student attrition: Evidence from a field experiment', Harvard Business School Working Paper No. 15-06, Boston, MA: Harvard Business School, 2015.

31   This phenomenon is known to labour economists as 'Ashenfelter's Dip', after Princeton economist Orley Ashenfelter.

32   Another example: in late 2008 and early 2009, I was seconded from my then job as an economics professor to work as a principal adviser in the Australian Treasury. Given that this was when the global financial crisis broke, the correlation between my work as a Treasury adviser and Australia's economic growth performance is strongly negative. To ascribe causality would be to greatly overstate the power of my advice.

33   Franz H. Messerli, 'Chocolate consumption, cognitive function, and Nobel laureates', *New England Journal of Medicine*, vol. 367, no. 16, 2012, pp. 1562–64.

34   Larry Orr, *Social Experiments: Evaluating Public Programs with Experimental Methods*, Thousand Oaks, CA: Sage Publications, 1999, p. xi, quoted in Judith Gueron & Rolston, *Fighting for Reliable Evidence,* New York: Russell Sage, 2013, p. 1.

35   See also Angus Deaton & Nancy Cartwright, 'Understanding and misunderstanding randomized controlled trials', NBER Working Paper 22595, Cambridge, MA: National Bureau of Economic Research, 2016.

36   Gordon C.S. Smith & Jill P. Pell, 2003, 'Parachute use to prevent death and major trauma related to gravitational challenge: Systematic review of randomised controlled trials', *British Medical Journal,* vol. 327, pp. 1459–61.

37   In one instance, locals in New Mexico found the crash dummies before investigators could reach them, and told the local news outlet that an alien spacecraft had tried to reach earth, but the aliens had been killed in the attempt:

'Air Force reportedly says aliens were crash dummies', *Daily Eastern News*, 23 June 1997, p. 2. The incident occurred in 1947 in the city of Roswell and sparked a television series by the same name.

38 Paul J. Amoroso, Jack B. Ryan, Barry Bickley, et al., 'Braced for impact'; David J. Wehrly, *Low Altitude, High Speed Personnel Parachuting*, PN, 1987; Raymond A. Madson, *High Altitude Balloon Dummy Drops*, PN, 1957.

39 See, for example, Emma Aisbett, Markus Brueckner, Ralf Steinhauser & Rhett Wilcox, 'Fiscal stimulus and household consumption: Evidence from the 2009 Australian Nation Building and Jobs Plan', ANU CEPR Discussion Paper 689, Canberra: ANU, 2013.

40 For an extensive discussion, see Deaton and Cartwright, 'Understanding and misunderstanding'.

41 Quoted in Bernard Teague, Ronald McLeod & Susan Pascoe, *2009 Victorian Bushfires Royal Commission*, Melbourne: Parliament of Victoria, 2010.

42 Andy Willans, quoted in Teague, McLeod & Pascoe, *2009 Victorian Bushfires Royal Commission*.

43 Teague, McLeod and Pascoe, *2009 Victorian Bushfires Royal Commission*, Vol. I, p. 149.

44 N.C. Surawski, A.L. Sullivan, C.P. Meyer, et al., 'Greenhouse gas emissions from laboratory-scale fires in wildland fuels depend on fire spread mode and phase of combustion', *Atmospheric Chemistry and Physics*, vol. 15, no. 9, 2015, pp. 5259–73.

45 R.H. Luke & A.G. McArthur 'Bushfires in Australia', Canberra: Australian Government Publishing Service, 1978; Andrew Sullivan, 'Towards the next generation of operational fire spread models', PowerPoint presentation, 16 May 2012. A commonly used formulation of the McArthur equation for the Forest Fire Danger Index is $FFDI = 2e^{\wedge}(0.45 + 0.987\ln D - 0.0345H + 0.0338T + 0.0234V)$, where D is the drought factor (between 0 and 10, depending on fuel availability), H is relative humidity (%), T is temperature (°C) and V is wind speed (km/h). The *FFDI* is then used to determine a fire danger rating: Low (0–5), Moderate (5–12), High (12–24), Very High (24–50), Extreme (50–100), Catastrophic (100+). See Andrew J. Dowdy, Graham A. Mills, Klara Finkele & William de Groot, 'Australian fire weather as represented by the McArthur Forest Fire Danger Index and the Canadian Forest Fire Weather Index', CAWCR Technical Report No. 10, Centre for Australian Weather and Climate Research, Canberra: CSIRO, 2009.

46 I first became aware of Stark's story in David Hunt, *Girt: The Unauthorised History of Australia, Volume 1*, Melbourne: Black Inc., 2013. For a full account, see William Stark (revised and published by James Smyth), *The Works of the Late William Stark, M.D. Consisting of Clinical and Anatomical Observations, with Experiments, Dietetical and Statical*, London: J.Johnson, 1788.

47 Alan Saunders, *Martyrs of Nutrition*, Australian Broadcasting Corporation.

2 FROM BLOODLETTING TO PLACEBO SURGERY

1 Peter F. Choong, Michelle M. Dowsey & James D. Stone, 'Does accurate anatomical alignment result in better function and quality of life? Comparing conventional and computer-assisted total knee arthroplasty', *The Journal of Arthroplasty*, vol. 24, no. 4, 2009, pp. 560–9; Nathaniel F.R. Huang, Michelle M. Dowsey, Eric Ee, et al.,

'Coronal alignment correlates with outcome after total knee arthroplasty: Five-year follow-up of a randomized controlled trial', *The Journal of Arthroplasty*, vol. 27, no. 9, 2012, pp. 1737–41.

2   Sina Babazadeh, Michelle M. Dowsey, James D. Stoney & Peter F.M. Choong, 'Gap balancing sacrifices joint-line maintenance to improve gap symmetry: A randomized controlled trial comparing gap balancing and measured resection', *The Journal of Arthroplasty*, vol. 29, no. 5, 2014, pp. 950–4; Michael J. Barrington, David J. Olive, Craig A. McCutcheon, et al., 'Stimulating catheters for continuous femoral nerve blockade after total knee arthroplasty: A randomized, controlled, double-blinded trial', *Anesthesia and Analgesia*, vol. 106, no. 4, 2008, pp. 1316–21.

3   J. Bruce Moseley, Kimberly O'Malley, Nancy J. Petersen, et al., 'A controlled trial of arthroscopic surgery for osteoarthritis of the knee', *New England Journal of Medicine*, vol. 347, no. 2, 2002, pp. 81–8.

4   Leonard A. Cobb, George I. Thomas, David H. Dillard, et al., 'An evaluation of internal-mammary-artery ligation by a double-blind technic', *New England Journal of Medicine*, vol. 260, no. 22, 1959, pp. 1115–18. See also Sheryl Stolberg, 'Sham surgery returns as a research tool', *New York Times*, 25 April 1999.

5   Rachelle Buchbinder, Richard H. Osborne, Peter R. Ebeling, et al., 'A randomized trial of vertebroplasty for painful osteoporotic vertebral fractures', *New England Journal of Medicine*, vol, 361, no. 6, 2009, pp. 557–68; David F. Kallmes, Bryan A. Comstock, Patrick J. Heagerty, et al., 'A randomized trial of vertebroplasty for osteoporotic spinal fractures', *New England Journal of Medicine*, vol. 361, no. 6, 2009, pp. 569–79.

6   Robert E. Gross, Raymond L. Watts, Robert A. Hauser, et al., 'Intrastriatal transplantation of microcarrier-bound human retinal pigment epithelial cells versus sham surgery in patients with advanced Parkinson's disease: A double-blind, randomised, controlled trial', *The Lancet Neurology*, vol. 10, no. 6, 2011, pp. 509–19.

7   Raine Sihvonen, Mika Paavola, Antti Malmivaara, et al., 'Arthroscopic partial meniscectomy versus sham surgery for a degenerative meniscal tear', *New England Journal of Medicine*, vol. 369, no. 26, 2013, pp. 2515–24.

8   For example, the procedure was performed approximately 700,000 times in the United States (Sihvonen et al., 'Arthroscopic partial meniscectomy'), and nearly 50,000 times in Australia (Australian Institute of Health and Welfare, *Admitted Patient Care 2013–14: Australian Hospital Statistics*, Health services series no. 60., cat. no. HSE 156, Canberra: AIHW, p. 181).

9   See, for example, the surgeons quoted in Pam Belluck, 'Common knee surgery does very little for some, study suggests', *New York Times*, 25 December 2013, p. A16; Joseph Walker, 'Fake knee surgery as good as real procedure, study finds', *Wall Street Journal*, 25 December 2013; Adam Jenney, 'Operating theatre – camera, lights and action', *Cosmos: The Science of Everything*, 17 March 2014.

10   J.H. Lubowitz, M.T. Provencher & M.J. Rossi, 'Could the *New England Journal of Medicine* be biased against arthroscopic knee surgery? Part 2', *Arthroscopy*, vol. 30, no. 6, 2014, pp. 654–5.

11   Karolina Wartolowska, Andrew Judge, Sally Hopewell, et al., 'Use of placebo controls in the evaluation of surgery: systematic review', *British Medical Journal*, vol. 348, 2014, g3253. See also Aaron E. Carroll, 'The placebo effect doesn't apply just to pills', *New York Times*, 6 October 2014.

12   As told by Peter Gomes, *The Good Life: Truths that Last in Times of Need*, New York: HarperCollins, 2002, p. 86.

13   Quoted in Franklin G. Miller, 'Sham surgery: An ethical analysis', *Science and Engineering Ethics*, March 2004, vol. 10, no. 1, pp. 157–66. On ethical questions, see also Wim Dekkers & Gerard Boer, 'Sham neurosurgery in patients with Parkinson's disease: Is it morally acceptable?' *Journal of Medical Ethics*, vol. 27, no. 3, 2001, pp. 151–6; Franklin G. Miller & Ted J. Kaptchuk, 'Sham procedures and the ethics of clinical trials', *Journal of the Royal Society of Medicine*, vol. 97, no. 12, 2004, pp. 576–8.

14   Hyeung C. Lim, Sam Adie, Justine M. Naylor & Ian A. Harris, 'Randomised trial support for orthopaedic surgical procedures', *PLoS ONE*, vol. 9, no. 6, 2014, e96745. The study analysed the thirty-two most common orthopaedic procedures, which comprised 95 per cent of all orthopaedic surgeries. Of these, 37 per cent were supported by at least one randomised trial, while 20 per cent were supported by at least one randomised trial that the authors judged to have a 'low risk of bias'.

15   Ian Harris, *Surgery, The Ultimate Placebo: A Surgeon Cuts through the Evidence*, Sydney: New South Books, 2016, loc. 2035.

16   Quoted in David Epstein, 'When evidence says no, but doctors say yes', *ProPublica*, 22 February 2017.

17   All of Paré's quotes are from Ambroise Paré, 'A surgeon in the field' in *The Portable Renaissance Reader*, James Bruce Ross & Mary Martin McLauglin (eds), New York: Viking Penguin, 1981, pp. 558–63.

18   John Haygarth, *Of the Imagination, as a Cause and as a Cure of Disorders of the Body; Exemplified by Fictitious Tractors, and Epidemical Convulsions*, Bath: Crutwell, 1800.

19   David Wootton, *Bad Medicine: Doctors Doing Harm Since Hippocrates*, Oxford: Oxford University Press, 2006, p. 2.

20   Vinay Prasad, quoted in Stephen J. Dubner, 'Bad Medicine, Part 1: The Story of 98.6', *Freakonomics Radio*, 30 November 2016.

21   Vinay Prasad, quoted in Stephen J. Dubner, 'Bad Medicine, Part 1: The Story of 98.6', *Freakonomics Radio*, 30 November 2016.

22   For the story of Semmelweis, see Ignaz Semmelweis, *Etiology, Concept and Prophylaxis of Childbed Fever*, University of Wisconsin Press, 1983 [1861]; Rebecca Davis, 'The doctor who championed hand-washing and briefly saved lives', NPR, 12 January 2015. Mortality rates in the two clinics fluctuated significantly – the 1 in 10 and 1 in 20 figures are approximate averages for the period before handwashing was introduced.

23   Carter, K. Codell & Barbara R. Carter, *Childbed Fever. A Scientific Biography of Ignaz Semmelweis*, Transaction Publishers, 2005.

24   Quoted in John Harley Warner, *The Therapeutic Perspective: Medical Practice, Knowledge, and Identity in America, 1820–1885*, Princeton: Princeton University Press, 2014, p. 33.

25   Wootton, *Bad Medicine*, p. 2.

26   See for example Gregory L. Armstrong, Laura A. Conn & Robert W. Pinner, 'Trends in infectious disease mortality in the United States during the 20th century', *Journal of the American Medical Association*, vol. 281, no. 1, 1999, pp. 61–6; Claire Hooker & Alison Bashford, 'Diphtheria and Australian public health: Bacteriology and its complex applications, c.1890–1930'. *Medical History*, vol. 46, 2002, pp 41–64.

27   Asbjørn Hróbjartsson, Peter C. Gøtzsche & Christian Gluud, 'The controlled clinical trial turns 100 years: Fibiger's trial of serum treatment of diphtheria', *British Medical Journal*, vol. 317, no. 7167, 1998, pp. 1243.

28   Marcia L. Meldrum, 'A brief history of the randomized controlled trial: From oranges and lemons to the gold standard', *HematologyOoncology Clinics of North America*, vol. 14, no. 4, 2000, pp. 745–60.

29 Arun Bhatt, 'Evolution of clinical research: a history before and beyond James Lind', *Perspectives in clinical research*, vol. 1, no. 1, 2010, pp. 6–10.

30 Marcia Meldrum, '"A calculated risk": The Salk polio vaccine field trials of 1954', *British Medical Journal*, vol. 317, no. 7167, 1998, p. 1233.

31 Suzanne Junod, 'FDA and clinical drug trials: A short history' in Madhu Davies & Faiz Kerimani (eds), *A Quick Guide to Clinical Trials*, Washington: Bioplan, Inc., 2008, pp. 25–55.

32 Archibald Cochrane, *Effectiveness and Efficiency: Random Reflections on Health Services*, London: Nuffield Provincial Hospitals Trust, 1972, p. 5.

33 Cochrane, *Effectiveness and Efficiency*, p. 6.

34 Cochrane, *Effectiveness and Efficiency*, p. 5.

35 Archibald Cochrane and Max Blythe, *One Man's Medicine: An Autobiography of Professor Archie Cochrane*, London: British Medical Journal, 1989, p. 82.

36 In 1937, the Massengill Company marketed a drug called 'elixir sulfanilamide', which contained the poisonous solvent diethylene glycol. The chemist who devised the drug, Harold Watkins, committed suicide while awaiting trial.

37 Michael Hay, David W. Thomas, John L. Craighead, et al., 'Clinical development success rates for investigational drugs', *Nature biotechnology*, vol. 32, no. 1, 2014, pp. 40–51. These estimates are based on the 'all indications' data shown in Figure 1, which shows success rates of 64 per cent from Phase 1 to Phase 2, 32 per cent from Phase 2 to Phase 3, and 50 per cent for Phase 3 to approval. See also Joseph A. DiMasi, L. Feldman, A. Seckler & A. Wilson, 'Trends in risks associated with new drug development: Success rates for investigational drugs', *Clinical Pharmacology & Therapeutics*, vol. 87, no. 3, 2010, pp. 272–7.

38 For a systematic review, see Asbjørn Hróbjartsson & Peter C. Gøtzsche, 'Placebo interventions for all clinical conditions', *Cochrane Database of Systematic Reviews*, 2010, CD003974.

39 Harris, *Surgery*, loc. 781.

40 The relevant academic studies are summarised in Tessa Cohen, 'The power of drug color', *The Atlantic*, 13 October 2014.

41 National Emphysema Treatment Trial Research Group, 'Patients at high risk of death after lung-volume-reduction surgery', *New England Journal of Medicine*, vol. 345, no. 15, 2001, p. 1075.

42 R. Brian Haynes, Jayanti Mukherjee, David L. Sackett, et al., 'Functional status changes following medical or surgical treatment for cerebral ischemia: Results of the extracranial-intracranial bypass study', *Journal of the American Medical Association*, vol. 257, no. 15, 1987, pp. 2043–6.

43 Harris, *Surgery*, loc. 1669–85.

44 Åke Hjalmarson, Sidney Goldstein, Björn Fagerberg, et al., 'Effects of controlled-release metoprolol on total mortality, hospitalizations, and well-being in patients with heart failure: The Metoprolol CR/XL Randomized Intervention Trial in congestive heart failure (MERIT-HF)', *Journal of the American Medical Association*, vol. 283, no. 10, 2000, pp. 1295–1302.

45 Henry M.P. Boardman, Louise Hartley, Anne Eisinga, et al., 'Hormone therapy for preventing cardiovascular disease in post-menopausal women', *Cochrane Database of Systematic Reviews 2015*, Issue 3, 2015, article no. CD002229.

46 Quoted in Epstein, 'When evidence says no'.

47 These death figures are from the point at which the first study was published. See CRASH Trial Collaborators, 'Effect of intravenous corticosteroids on death

within fourteen days in 10008 adults with clinically significant head injury (MRC CRASH trial): Randomised placebo-controlled trial', *The Lancet*, vol. 364, no. 9442, 2004, pp. 1321–8. A follow-up found death rates of 26 per cent for the treatment group and 22 per cent for the control group: CRASH Trial Collaborators, 'Final results of MRC CRASH, a randomised placebo-controlled trial of intravenous corticosteroid in adults with head injury—outcomes at 6 months', *The Lancet*, vol. 365, no. 9475, 2005, pp. 1957–9.

48 Roger Chou, Rongwei Fu, John A. Carrino & Richard A. Deyo, 'Imaging strategies for low-back pain: Systematic review and meta-analysis', *The Lancet*, vol. 373, no. 9662, 2009, pp. 463–72; G. Michael Allan, G. Richard Spooner & Noah Ivers, 'X-Ray scans for nonspecific low back pain: A nonspecific pain?' *Canadian Family Physician*, vol. 58, no. 3, 2012, p. 275.

49 Allan, Spooner & Ivers, 'X-Ray scans', p. 275.

50 Peter C. Gøtzsche & Karsten Juhl Jørgensen, 'Screening for breast cancer with mammography', *Cochrane Database of Systematic Reviews 2013*, Issue 6, 2013, article no. CD001877.

51 Fritz H. Schröder, Jonas Hugosson, Monique J. Roobol, et al., 'Screening and prostate cancer mortality: Results of the European randomised study of screening for prostate cancer (ERSPC) at 13 years of follow-up', *The Lancet*, vol. 384, no. 9959, 2014, pp. 2027–35. Study participants from France joined later than other nations, so their results were not included in the thirteen-year follow up.

52 Goran Bjelakovic, Dimitrinka Nikolova, Lise Lotte Gluud, et al., 'Mortality in randomized trials of antioxidant supplements for primary and secondary prevention: Systematic review and meta-analysis', *Journal of the American Medical Association*, vol. 297, no. 8, 2007, pp. 842–57. For an informal discussion of the issue, see Norman Swan, 'The health report', *ABC Radio National*, 5 March 2007. The researchers were at pains to point out that their findings should not be extrapolated to foods that are rich in vitamins, such as fresh fruit and vegetables.

53 H.C. Bucher, P. Hengstler, C. Schindler & G.Meier, 'N-3 polyunsaturated fatty acids in coronary heart disease: A meta-analysis of randomized controlled trials', *American Journal of Medicine*, vol. 112, no. 4, 2002, pp. 298–304.

54 E.C. Rizos, E.E. Ntzani, E. Bika, et al., 'Association between omega-3 fatty acid supplementation and risk of major cardiovascular disease events: A systematic review and meta-analysis', *Journal of the American Medical Association*, vol. 308, no. 10, 2012, pp. 1024–33.

55 See Joseph J. Knapik, David I. Swedler, Tyson L. Grier, et al., 'Injury reduction effectiveness of selecting running shoes based on plantar shape', *Journal of Strength & Conditioning Research*, vol. 23, no. 3, 2009, pp. 685–97; B.M. Nigg, J. Baltich, S. Hoerzer & H. Enders, 'Running shoes and running injuries: Mythbusting and a proposal for two new paradigms: "preferred movement path" and "comfort filter"', *British Journal of Sports Medicine*, vol. 49, 2015, pp. 1290–4; Gretchen Reynolds, 'Choosing the right running shoes', *New York Times*, 5 August 2015.

56 Stuart A. Armstrong, Eloise S. Till, Stephen R. Maloney & Gregory A. Harris, 'Compression socks and functional recovery following marathon running: A randomized controlled trial', *The Journal of Strength & Conditioning Research*, vol. 29, no. 2, 2015, pp. 528–33.

57 Jenna B. Gillen, Brian J. Martin, Martin J. MacInnis, et al., 'Twelve weeks of sprint interval training improves indices of cardiometabolic Health similar to

traditional endurance training despite a five-fold lower exercise volume and time commitment', *PloS ONE*, vol. 11, no. 4, 2016, e0154075.

58 Jeremy S. Furyk, Carl J. O'Kane, Peter J. Aitken, et al., 'Fast versus slow bandaid removal: A randomised trial', *Medical Journal of Australia*, vol. 191, 2009, pp. 682–3.

59 T. Bakuradze, R. Lang, T. Hofmann, et al., 'Consumption of a dark roast coffee decreases the level of spontaneous DNA strand breaks: a randomized controlled trial', *European Journal of Nutrition*, vol. 54, no. 1, 2015, pp. 149–56.

60 Ateev Mehrotra & Allan Prochazka, 'Improving value in health care—Against the annual physical', *New England Journal of Medicine*, vol. 373, no. 16, 2015, pp. 1485–7.

61 Specifically, the study found that twenty-eight randomised trials funded between 1977 and 1999 were responsible for an additional 470,000 quality-adjusted life years over a ten-year period: S.C. Johnston, J.D. Rootenberg, S. Katrak, et al., 'Effect of a US National Institutes of Health programme of clinical trials on public health and costs', *The Lancet,* vol. 367, no. 9519, 2006, pp. 1319–27.

62 For other examples of medical procedures discarded when the evidence didn't suggest they worked, see Thomas B. Freeman, Dorothy E. Vawter, Paul E. Leaverton, et al., 'Use of placebo surgery in controlled trials of a cellular-based therapy for Parkinson's disease', *New England Journal of Medicine*, vol. 341, no. 13, 1999, pp. 988–92.

63 Some medical subfields are virtually untouched by the randomised trials revolution. For example, randomised trials currently account for only a tiny fraction of the published literature in plastic surgery: Colleen M. McCarthy, E. Dale Collins & Andrea L. Pusic, 'Where do we find the best evidence?' *Plastic and Reconstructive Surgery*, vol. 122, no. 6, 2008, pp. 1942–7.

64 Harris, *Surgery,* pp. 1285–1326.

65 Harris, *Surgery,* p. 82.

66 Atul Gawande, 'Overkill', *New Yorker,* 11 May 2015.

67 Aaron L. Schwartz, Bruce E. Landon, Adam G. Elshaug, et al., 'Measuring low-value care in Medicare', *JAMA Internal Medicine*, vol. 174, no. 7, 2014, pp. 1067–76.

68 Adam G. Elshaug, Amber M. Watt, Linda Mundy & Cameron D. Willis, 'Over 150 potentially low-value health care practices: an Australian study', *Medical Journal of Australia*, vol. 197, no. 10, 2012, pp. 556–60.

3 DECREASING DISADVANTAGE, ONE COIN TOSS AT A TIME

1 Daniel's story is told in Scott Hannaford, 'Violence, lack of housing and family breakdown leaving young Canberrans homeless', *Canberra Times*, 26 September 2015, p. 1.

2 Author's interview with Yi-Ping Tseng and Sacred Heart Mission social workers.

3 Author's telephone interview with Guy Johnson.

4 Guy Johnson, Sue Grigg & Yi-Ping Tseng, 'The J2SI pilot: Using a randomised trial to evaluate an innovative homelessness intervention', in Gemma Carey, Kathy Landvogt & Jo Barraket (eds), *Creating and Implementing Public Policy: Cross-Sectoral Debates*, New York: Routledge, 2016, pp. 113–26.

5 Guy Johnson, Daniel Kuehnle, Sharon Parkinson, et al., *Sustaining Exits from Long-Term Homelessness: A Randomised Controlled Trial Examining the 48-Month*

Social Outcomes from the Journey to Social Inclusion Pilot Program, St Kilda, Vic.: Sacred Heart Mission, 2014.

6   The three-year outcome was provided to me via email by Yi-Ping Tseng. At the four-year mark (one year after the program ended), the number of people with a job was zero in the treatment group and one in the control group.

7   Quoted in Larry Gordon, 'A social experiment in pulling up stakes', *Los Angeles Times*, 23 September 1997.

8   For a chronological summary of the results, see Jonathan Rothwell, 'Sociology's revenge: Moving to Opportunity (MTO) revisited', *Social Mobility Memos*, Washington, DC: Brookings Institution, 6 May 2015.

9   Quoted in S.J. Popkin, L.E. Harris & M.K. Cunningham, *Families in Transition: A Qualitative Analysis of the MTO Experience*, final report submitted to the US Department of Housing and Urban Development, Office of Policy Development and Research, 2002, p. 49.

10 Quoted in Popkin, Harris & Cunningham, *Families in Transition*, p. 50.

11 Raj Chetty, Nathaniel Hendren & Lawrence F. Katz, 'The effects of exposure to better neighborhoods on children: New evidence from the moving to opportunity experiment', *American Economic Review*, vol. 106, no. 4, 2016, pp. 855–902.

12 Philip K. Robins, 'A comparison of the labor supply findings from the four negative income tax experiments', *Journal of Human Resources*, vol. 20, no. 4, 1985, pp. 567–82; Robert A. Moffitt, 'The negative income tax: Would it discourage work?' *Monthly Labor Review*, 1981, pp. 23–7.

13 Robert A. Moffitt, 'The negative income tax and the evolution of U.S. welfare policy', *Journal of Economic Perspectives*, vol. 17, no. 3, 2003, pp. 119–40; Robert A. Levine, Harold Watts, Robinson Hollister, Walter Williams, et al., 'A retrospective on the negative income tax experiments: Looking back at the most innovate field studies in social policy' in Karl Widerquist, Michael Anthony Lewis & Steven Pressman (eds), *The Ethics and Economics of the Basic Income*, Aldershot: Ashgate Publishing, 2005, pp. 95–108.

14 This is based on the finding that the earned income tax credit reduces the national poverty rate by 1.5 percentage points: Raj Chetty, John N. Friedman & Emmanuel Saez, 'Using differences in knowledge across neighborhoods to uncover the impacts of the EITC on earnings', *American Economic Review*, vol. 103, no. 7, 2013, pp. 2683–721.

15 Willard G. Manning, Joseph P. Newhouse & Naihua Duan, 'Health insurance and the demand for medical care: Evidence from a randomized experiment', *American Economic Review*, vol. 77, no. 3, 1987, pp. 251–77; Kathleen N. Lohr, Robert H. Brook, Caren J. Kamberg, et al., 'Use of medical care in the RAND Health Insurance Experiment: Diagnosis-and service-specific analyses in a randomized controlled trial', *Medical Care*, vol. 24, no. 9, 1986, S1–S87.

16 Joseph P. Newhouse, 'Consumer-directed health plans and the RAND Health Insurance Experiment', *Health Affairs*, vol. 23, no. 6, 2004, pp. 107–13; Robert H. Brook, Emmett B. Keeler, Kathleen N. Lohr, et al., *The Health Insurance Experiment: A Classic RAND Study Speaks to the Current Health Care Reform Debate*, Santa Monica, CA: RAND Corporation, RB-9174-HHS, 2006.

17 Amy Finkelstein, Sarah Taubman, Bill Wright, et al., 'The Oregon Health Insurance Experiment: Evidence from the first year', *Quarterly Journal of Economics*, vol. 127, no. 3, 2012, pp. 1057–1106.

18 The US Vietnam draft had taken place in earlier years, but 1969 was the first year that the birthdate lottery was used. Due to inadequate mixing of the balls, December birthdates tended to be chosen earlier, a problem that was corrected in subsequent lottery drawings.

19 Quoted in Wesley Abney, 'Live from Washington, It's Lottery Night 1969!', *HistoryNet*, 25 November 2009.

20 Kerry Pardue, 'When were you in the war', *Veteran Stories*, National Vietnam Veterans Museum, undated.

21 Joshua D. Angrist, 'Lifetime earnings and the Vietnam era draft lottery: Evidence from social security administrative records', *American Economic Review*, 1990, vol. 80, no. 3, pp. 313–36; Joshua D. Angrist, Stacey H. Chen & Jae Song, 'Long-term consequences of Vietnaam-era conscription: New estimates using social security data', *American Economic Review*, vol. 101, no. 2, 2011, pp. 334–8.

22 Joshua D. Angrist & Stacey H. Chen, 'Schooling and the Vietnam-era GI Bill: Evidence from the draft lottery', *American Economic Journal: Applied Economics*, vol. 3, no. 2, 2011, pp. 96–118.

23 Angrist & Chen, 'Schooling'; D. Conley & J. Heerwig, 2012, 'The long-term effects of military conscription on mortality: Estimates from the Vietnam-era draft lottery', *Demography*, vol. 49, pp. 84155.

24 Jason M. Lindo & Charles Stoecker, 'Drawn into violence: Evidence on "what makes a criminal" from the Vietnam draft lotteries', *Economic Inquiry*, vol. 52, no. 1, 2014, pp. 239–58. See also Chris Rohlfs, 'Does combat exposure make you a more violent or criminal person? Evidence from the Vietnam draft', *Journal of Human Resources*, vol. 45, no. 2, 2010, pp. 271–300.

25 Robert S. Erikson & Laura Stoker, 'Caught in the draft: The effects of Vietnam draft lottery status on political attitudes', *American Political Science Review*, vol. 105, no. 2, 2011, pp. 221–37.

26 Peter Siminski, Simon Ville & Alexander Paull, 'Does the military turn men into criminals? New evidence from Australia's conscription lotteries', *Journal of Population Economics*, vol. 29, no. 1, 2014, pp. 1–22; David W. Johnston, Michael A. Shields & Peter Siminski, 'Long-term health effects of Vietnam-era military service: A quasi-experiment using Australian conscription lotteries', *Journal of Health Economics*, vol. 45, no 1, 2016, pp. 12–26. After the war ended, there is no evidence of excess mortality among veterans, relative to non-veterans: Peter Siminski & Simon Ville, 'Long-run mortality effects of Vietnam-era army service: Evidence from Australia's conscription lotteries', *American Economic Review*, vol. 101, no. 3, 2011, pp. 345–9.

27 Peter Siminski, 'Employment effects of army service and veterans' compensation: Evidence from the Australian Vietnam-era conscription lotteries', *Review of Economics and Statistics*, vol. 95, no. 1, 2013, pp. 87–97.

28 For a useful summary of the experimental job training studies, see Heckman, LaLonde & Smith, 'The economics and econometrics'. Evidence suggests that in developing countries, job training may be useful for youths: Attanasio, Kugler & Meghir, 'Subsidizing vocational training'.

29 As one study sums it up: 'This finding should not be surprising, because most of these programs cost only a few thousand dollars or less per participant ... To expect such programs to raise participants' subsequent annual earnings by several thousand dollars would imply that these social investments consistently have an

extraordinary rate of return.' Heckman, LaLonde & Smith, 'The economics and econometrics'.

30 Ron Haskins, 'Social programs that work', *New York Times*, 31 December 2014.

31 J.M. Pedersen, M. Rosholm & M. Svarer, 'Experimental evidence on the effects of early meetings and activation', IZA Discussion Paper 6970, Bonn: IZA, 2012; J. Kluve, 'The effectiveness of European active labor market programs', *Labour Economics*, vol. 17, no. 6, 2010, pp. 904–18; B. Meyer, 'Lessons from the U.S. unemployment insurance experiments', *Journal of Economic Literature*, vol. 33, 1995, pp. 91–131. An Australian randomised trial of caseworker meetings found that the intervention group worked fewer hours, but because the meeting was also accompanied by a review of the unemployed person's eligibility for benefits, this may simply reflect a desire among recipients to keep their hours low enough that their payments did not get cut off. Robert Breunig, Deborah A. Cobb-Clark, Yvonne Dunlop & Marion Terrill, 'Assisting the long-term unemployed: Results from a randomised trial', *Economic Record*, vol. 79, no. 244, 2003, pp. 84–102.

32 Michael Rosholm, 'Do case workers help the unemployed? Evidence for making a cheap and effective twist to labor market policies for unemployed workers', IZA World of Labor, Bonn: IZA, 2014, p. 72.

33 Steffen Altmann, Armin Falk, Simon Jäger & Florian Zimmermann, 'Learning about job search: A field experiment with job seekers in Germany', CESifo Working Paper No. 5355, Munich: CESifo.

34 Bruno Crépon, Esther Duflo, Marc Gurgand, et al., 'Do labor market policies have displacement effects? Evidence from a clustered randomized experiment', *Quarterly Journal of Economics*, vol. 128, no. 2, 2013, pp. 531–80.

35 'Finland tests a new form of welfare', *The Economist*, 24 June 2017.

36 Kristen Underhill, Paul Montgomery & Don Operario, 'Sexual abstinence only programmes to prevent HIV infection in high income countries: Systematic review', *British Medical Journal*, vol. 335, no. 7613, 2007, pp. 248–52.

37 Janet Elise Rosenbaum, 'Patient teenagers? A comparison of the sexual behavior of virginity pledgers and matched nonpledgers', *Pediatrics*, vol. 123, no. 1, 2009, e110–e120.

38 Alba DiCenso, Gordon Guyatt, Andrew Willan & Lauren Griffith, 'Interventions to reduce unintended pregnancies among adolescents: Systematic review of randomised controlled trials', *British Medical Journal*, vol. 324, no. 7351, 2002, p. 1426; Kristen Underhill, Paul Montgomery & Don Operario, 'Sexual abstinence only programmes to prevent HIV infection in high income countries: systematic review', *British Medical Journal*, vol. 335, no. 7613, 2007, pp. 248–52; Heather D. Boonstra, 'Advancing sexuality education in developing countries: Evidence and implications', *Guttmacher Policy Review*, vol. 14, no. 3, 2011, pp. 17–23. One rare example of a successful program to reduce adolescent pregnancy is the randomised evaluation of 'Teen Options to Prevent Pregnancy' in Ohio, a program that reduced repeat pregnancies among young mothers by supporting them to devise an appropriate birth control plan: Jack Stevens, Robyn Lutz, Ngozi Osuagwu, et al., 'A randomized trial of motivational interviewing and facilitated contraceptive access to prevent rapid repeat pregnancy among adolescent mothers', *American Journal of Obstetrics and Gynecology*, vol. 217, no. 4, 2017, pp. 423.e1–423.e9.

39 The literature on tobacco taxes is reviewed in Michelle Scollo & Margaret Winstanley, *Tobacco in Australia: Facts and issues*, Melbourne: Cancer Council Victoria, 2015.

40 Kevin G. Volpp, Andrea B. Troxel, Mark V. Pauly, et al., 'A randomized, controlled trial of financial incentives for smoking cessation', *New England Journal of Medicine*, vol. 360, no. 7, 2009, pp. 699–709.

41 Center for Disease Control and Prevention (CDC), 'Annual smoking-attributable mortality, years of potential life lost, and economic costs – United States, 1995–1999', *Morbidity and Mortality Weekly Report*, vol. 51, no. 14, 2002, p. 300. The pattern is similar when smokers quit: Michael T. Halpern, Richard Shikiar, Anne M. Rentz & Zeba M. Khan, 'Impact of smoking status on workplace absenteeism and productivity', *Tobacco control*, vol. 10, no. 3, 2001, pp. 233–8.

42 The productivity estimate from the CDC's 2002 study was $1760 a year in 1999 dollars, which translates to over $2500 in today's money. Note that this does not include productivity losses due to absenteeism.

43 Xavier Giné, Dean Karlan & Jonathan Zinman, 'Put your money where your butt is: a commitment contract for smoking cessation', *American Economic Journal: Applied Economics*, vol. 2, 2010, pp. 213–35.

44 Financial incentives don't always help people give up bad habits. One recent study found that offering people a 10 per cent discount on healthy foods did not significantly change consumption patterns: John Cawley, Andrew S. Hanks, David R. Just & Brian Wansink, 'Incentivizing nutritious diets: A field experiment of relative price changes and how they are framed', NBER Working Paper No. 21929, Cambridge, MA: NBER, 2016.

45 Daniel B. Herman, Sarah Conover, Prakash Gorroochurn, et al., 'Randomized trial of critical time intervention to prevent homelessness after hospital discharge', *Psychiatric Services*, vol. 62, no. 7, 2011, pp. 713–19.

4 THE PIONEERS OF RANDOMISATION

1 Joseph Brent, *Charles Sanders Peirce: A Life*, Bloomington: Indiana University Press, 1998, p. 40.

2 Charles Sanders Peirce & Joseph Jastrow, 'On small differences in sensation', *Memoirs of the National Academy of Sciences*, Vol. 3, 1885, pp. 73–83

3 Stephen Stigler, *Statistics on the Table: The History of Statistical Concepts and Methods*, Cambridge: Harvard University Press, 1999, p. 195.

4 Brent, *Charles Sanders Peirce*, p. 53.

5 For a history and survey of field of experimental psychology, see Raymond Nickerson & Richard Pew, 'Psychological experimentation addressing practical concerns' in Alice F. Healy & Robert W. Proctor (eds) *Handbook of Psychology*, Vol. 4, Hoboken: John Wiley, 2003, pp. 649–76.

6 This account is drawn from Joan Fisher Box, *R.A. Fisher, The Life of a Scientist*, New York: Wiley, 1978. See also Deborah Nolan & Terry P. Speed, *Stat Labs: Mathematical Statistics Through Applications*, New York: Springer, 2000, p. 101; David Salsburg, *The Lady Tasting Tea: How Statistics Revolutionized Science in the Twentieth Century*, New York: Henry Holt, 2001.

7 Geoffrey Miller, *The Mating Mind: How Sexual Choice Shaped the Evolution of Human Nature*, London: Heineman, 2000, p. 54

8 World Health Organization, 'Tuberculosis Fact sheet', Geneva: World Health Organization, 2017.

9 This section draws primarily on Lise Wilkinson, 'Sir Austin Bradford Hill: Medical

statistics and the quantitative approach to prevention of disease', *Addiction*, vol. 92, nol. 6, 1997, pp. 657–66.

10 Austin Bradford Hill, 'Principles of medical statistics', *The Lancet*, 2 January 1937, pp. 41–3.

11 The co-discoverers of streptomycin were Selman Waksman (who would go on to win the Nobel Prize in 1952) and his postgraduate student, Albert Schatz (who rarely receives his share of the credit).

12 This is the 1946 figure, sourced from Public Health England, 'Tuberculosis mortality and mortality rate, 1913 to 2013', 1 January 2013.

13 Veronique Mistiaen, 'Time, and the great healer', *Guardian*, 3 November 2002.

14 Judith Gueron, 'The politics of random assignment: Implementing studies and impacting policy', *Journal of Children's Services*, vol. 3, nol. 1, 2008, pp. 14–26.

15 Gueron, 'The politics of random assignment', p.14.

16 Judith Gueron & Howard Rolston, *Fighting for Reliable Evidence*, New York: Russell Sage, 2013, pp. xvi–ii.

17 Judith Gueron, 'Remarks on accepting the Peter H. Rossi Award', Association for Public Policy Analysis and Management Conference, Los Angeles, 7 November 2008.

18 Gueron & Rolston, *Fighting for Reliable Evidence*, p. 33.

19 Gueron & Rolston, *Fighting for Reliable Evidence*, p. 39.

20 Gueron & Rolston, *Fighting for Reliable Evidence*, p. 71.

21 The woman Reagan referred to was Linda Taylor. Recent investigation suggests that welfare fraud may well have been one of her more minor crimes: Josh Levin, 'The welfare queen', *Slate*, 19 December 2013.

22 William Stevens, 'The welfare consensus', *New York Times*, 22 June 1988; William Stevens, 'Some preliminary results in the rush from welfare to work', *New York Times*, 21 August 1988.

23 Judith Gueron, 'The politics of random assignment'.

24 Gueron, 'Remarks'.

25 Judith Gueron, 'Fostering research excellence and impacting policy and practice: The welfare reform story', *Journal of Policy Analysis and Management*, vol. 22, nol. 2, 2003, pp. 163–74.

26 Gueron & Rolston, *Fighting for Reliable Evidence*, pp. 302–3.

27 Gueron & Rolston, *Fighting for Reliable Evidence*, p. 306.

28 Henry J. Aaron, *Politics and the Professors: The Great Society in Perspective*, Washington DC: Brookings Institution, 1978, p. 159.

29 Don Winstead, quoted in Gueron & Rolston, *Fighting for Reliable Evidence*, p. 301.

30 Gueron & Rolston, *Fighting for Reliable Evidence*, p. 57.

31 Andy Feldman, 'Fighting for reliable evidence: An interview with Judith Gueron, MDRC, and Howard Rolston, Abt Associates', *Gov Innovator* podcast, Episode 32, 10 October 2013.

32 Gueron, 'Fostering research excellence'.

33 Feldman, 'Fighting for reliable evidence'.

5 LEARNING HOW TO TEACH

1 Quoted in Shalom M. Fisch & Rosemarie T. Truglio (eds), *G is for Growing: Thirty Years of Research on Children and Sesame Street*, Routledge, 2014, p. xi

2 This issue is discussed in Melissa S. Kearney & Phillip B. Levine, 'Early childhood

education by MOOC: Lessons from *Sesame Street*', NBER Working Paper No. 21229, Cambridge, MA: NBER, 2015.

3   Gerry Ann Bogatz & Samuel Ball, *The Second Year of Sesame Street: A Continuing Evaluation*, Princeton, NJ: Educational Testing Service, 1971.

4   Joan Cooney, 2001, 'Foreword' in Fisch & Truglio, *G is for Growing*, pp. xi–xiv. The specific examples on *Sesame Street* curriculum are drawn from Rosemarie Truglio, Valeria Lovelace, Ivelisse Seguí & Susan Scheiner, 'The varied role of formative research: Case studies From 30 years' in Fisch & Truglio, *G is for Growing*, pp. 61–82.

5   Alison Gopnik, *The Philosophical Baby: What Children's Minds Tell Us About Truth, Love, and the Meaning of Life*, New York: Picador, 2010, p. 11.

6   This section draws heavily on Emily Hanford (edited by Catherine Winter), 'Early Lessons', American RadioWorks, 2009. Transcript available at http://americanradioworks.publicradio.org/features/preschool/

7   David P. Weikart, 'Preliminary results from a longitudinal study of disadvantaged preschool children', paper presented at the 1967 Convention of the Council for Exceptional Children, St. Louis, Missouri.

8   Weikart, 'Preliminary results'.

9   Lawrence J. Schweinhart, Jeanne Montie, Zongping Xiang, et al., *Lifetime Effects: The High/Scope Perry Preschool Study Through Age 40*, Ypsilanti, MI: High/Scope Press, 2005.

10   James J. Heckman, Seong Hyeok Moon, Rodrigo Pinto, et al., 'The rate of return to the HighScope Perry Preschool Program', *Journal of Public Economics*, vol. 94, no. 1, 2010, pp. 114–28 ('the benefit–cost ratio for the Perry program, accounting for deadweight costs of taxes and assuming a 3% discount rate, ranges from 7 to 12 dollars').

11   In Chicago, a team of economists even set up their own research preschool, the Chicago Heights Early Childhood Center, which operated from 2010 to 2014. The centre randomly assigned young children either to a cognitive stream, which focused on reading, writing and basic numeracy, or to a non-cognitive curriculum, which focused on social skills such as sitting still, executive functioning and expanding working memory. See Steven Levitt, quoted in Stephen J. Dubner, 'Does "early education" come way too late?', *Freakonomics Radio*, 19 November 2015; Roland Fryer, Steven Levitt, John List & Anya Samak, 'Chicago Heights Early Childhood Center: Early results from a field experiment on the temporal allocation of schooling', IRP Seminar Presentation, September 2013.

12   Frances A. Campbell, Elizabeth P. Pungello, Margaret Burchinal, et al., 'Adult outcomes as a function of an early childhood educational program: An Abecedarian Project follow-up', *Developmental Psychology*, vol. 48, no. 4, 2012, p. 1033; 'Abecedarian International', *Early Developments: Frank Porter Graham Child Development Institute*, vol. 15, no. 1, 2014, pp. 12–15.

13   Frances Campbell, Gabriella Conti, James J. Heckman, et al., 'Early childhood investments substantially boost adult health', *Science*, vol. 343, no. 6178, 2014, pp. 1478–85.

14   Thomas Rae & Melanie J. Zimmer-Gembeck, 'Behavioral outcomes of parent-child interaction therapy and Triple P–Positive Parenting Program: A review and meta-analysis', *Journal of Abnormal Child Psychology*, vol. 35, no. 3, 2007, pp. 475–95.

15   Karen M.T. Turner, Mary Richards & Matthew R. Sanders, 'Randomised clinical trial of a group parent education programme for Australian Indigenous families',

Journal of Paediatrics and Child Health, vol. 43, no. 6, 2007, pp. 429–37.

16 The Incredible Years Basic Parenting program has several versions, which vary between twelve and eighteen sessions. For results of the randomised trial, see Sinead McGilloway, Grainne Ni Mhaille, Tracey Bywater, Mairead Furlong, Yvonne Leckey, Paul Kelly, Catherine Comiskey & Michael Donnelly, 'A parenting intervention for childhood behavioral problems: a randomized controlled trial in disadvantaged community-based settings', *Journal of consulting and clinical psychology*, vol. 80, no. 1, 2012, p. 116. A randomised evaluation of the UK parenting program SureStart also showed positive results: Judy et al., 'Parenting intervention in Sure Start services for children at risk of developing conduct disorder: Pragmatic randomised controlled trial', *British Medical Journal*, vol. 334, no. 7595, 2007, pp. 678–82.

17 Donal O'Neill, Sinéad McGilloway, Michael Donnelly, et al., 'A cost-benefit analysis of early childhood intervention: Evidence from an experimental evaluation of the Incredible Years Parenting Program', Working Paper n207-10, Maynooth: Department of Economics, Finance and Accounting, National University of Ireland, 2010.

18 Two meta-analyses of nurse home visits are Denise Kendrick, Ruth Elkan, Michael Hewitt, et al., 'Does home visiting improve parenting and the quality of the home environment? A systematic review and meta analysis', *Archives of Disease in Childhood*, vol. 82, no. 6, 2000, pp. 443–51; Monica A. Sweet & Mark I. Appelbaum, 'Is home visiting an effective strategy? A meta-analytic review of home visiting programs for families with young children', *Child Development*, vol. 75, no. 5, 2004, pp. 1435–56.

19 Megan H. Bair-Merritt, Jacky M. Jennings, Rusan Chen, et al., 'Reducing maternal intimate partner violence after the birth of a child: A randomized controlled trial of the Hawaii Healthy Start Home Visitation Program', *Archives of Pediatrics & Adolescent Medicine*, vol. 164, no. 1, 2010, pp. 16–23; Jamila Mejdoubi, Silvia CCM van den Heijkant, Frank J.M. van Leerdam, et al., 'Effect of nurse home visits vs. usual care on reducing intimate partner violence in young high-risk pregnant women: a randomized controlled trial,' *PloS one*, vol. 8, no. 10, 2013, e78185. I am grateful to Cathryn Stephens for bringing this research to my attention.

20 See the comparison of randomised and quasi-experimental results on page 1441 of Monica A. Sweet & Mark I. Appelbaum, 'Is home visiting an effective strategy? A meta-analytic review of home visiting programs for families with young children', *Child Development*, vol. 75, no. 5, 2004, pp. 1435–56.

21 Dana Suskind, *Thirty Million Words: Building a Child's Brain*, New York: Penguin, 2015, p. 52.

22 For a critique of the misuse of neuroscience in the development of early childhood programs, see Zoe Williams, 'Is misused neuroscience defining early years and child protection policy?', *Guardian*, 26 April 2014. The '1001 Critical Days' idea is outlined in A. Leadsom, F. Field, P. Burstow & C. Lucas, 'The 1001 Critical Days: The importance of the conception to age two period', London, 2013.

23 The West Heidelberg experiment is a collaboration between the Children's Protection Society, Melbourne University Department of Economics and the Murdoch Children's Research Institute. The study protocol is available at Brigid Jordan, Yi-Ping Tseng, Nichola Coombs, et al., 'Improving lifetime trajectories for vulnerable young children and families living with significant stress and social disadvantage: the early years education program randomised controlled trial', *BMC Public Health*, vol. 14, no. 1, 2014, p. 1. For a comparison of the treatment and control children at the start of the study, see Yi-Ping Tseng, Brigid Jordan, Jeff

Borland, et al., *Changing the Life Trajectories of Australia's Most Vulnerable Children, Report No. 1: Participants in the Trial of the Early Years Education Program*, Melbourne: University of Melbourne and Children's Protection Society, 2017.

24 This story is told in Alice Hill, Brigid Jordan, Nichola Coombs, et al., 'Changing life trajectories: The early years education research project', *Insights: Melbourne Business and Economics*, vol. 10, 2011, pp. 19–25.

25 This section is based on the author's interviews with educators, researchers and parents at the centre.

26 Thomas D. Cook & Monique R. Payne, 'Objecting to the objections to using random assignment in educational research', in Frederick Mosteller & Robert Boruch (eds), *Evidence Matters: Randomized Trials in Education Research*, Washington DC: Brookings Press, 2002, pp. 150–78.

27 The Australian Productivity Commission recently recommended that 'Australia needs to invest, particularly in randomised controlled trials, to build the Australian evidence base on what works best to improve education outcomes.' Productivity Commission, *National Education Evidence Base, Draft Report*, Canberra: Productivity Commission, 2016, p. 16.

28 Parsing out the effect of schools and families is methodologically tricky. See, for example, James Coleman, *Equality of Educational Opportunity*, Washington DC: National Center for Educational Statistics, 1966; Eric Hanushek, 'What matters for student achievement', *Education Next*, vol. 16, no. 2, 2016, pp. 19–26; OECD, *Learning for Tomorrow's World – First Results from PISA 2003*, Paris: OECD, 2004, pp. 159–205.

29 PISA began testing in different subjects at different times, and did not always cover the same set of nations. Comparing average results in the first tested year with results in 2015, mathematics scores have fallen by 8 points in the OECD-30 since 2003; reading scores have fallen by 1 point in the OECD-28 since 2000; and science scores have fallen by 5 points in the OECD-35 since 2006.

30 See www.afterschoolalliance.org/policy21stcclc.cfm.

31 Neil Naftzger, Seth Kaufman, Jonathan Margolin & Asma Ali, '21st Century Community Learning Centers (21st CCLC) Analytic Support for Evaluation and Program Monitoring: An Overview of the 21st CCLC Program: 2004–05', Report prepared for the U.S. Department of Education, Naperville, IL: Learning Point Associates, 2006.

32 Susanne James-Burdumy, Mark Dynarski & John Deke, 'After-school program effects on behavior: Results from the 21st Century Community Learning Centers program national evaluation', *Economic Inquiry*, vol. 46, no. 1, 2008, pp. 13–18.

33 For evidence on the impact of after-school programs on academic results, see Susanne James-Burdumy, Mark Dynarski, Mary Moore, et al., 'When schools stay open late: The national evaluation of the 21st Century Community Learning Centers program: Final report', US Department of Education, National Center for Education Evaluation and Regional Assistance. Available at www.ed.gov/ies/ncee.

34 Quoted in Ron Haskins, 'With a scope so wide: using evidence to innovate, improve, manage, budget' in Productivity Commission, *Strengthening Evidence-based Policy in the Australian Federation: Roundtable Proceedings, Canberra, 17–18 August 2009*, Vol. 1, Canberra: Productivity Commission, 2010, p. 46.

35 For each child served, the estimated costs of these programs are: nurse home visits $11,394, high-quality early childhood $10,396, intensive reading support for third graders $3390, and an evidence-based programs to reduce teen pregnancy $763 (all

in 2017 dollars). For cost estimates (in 2008 dollars) and the evidence base behind each program, see Julia B. Isaacs, *Cost-Effective Investments in Children*, Budgeting for National Priorities Project, Washington DC: Brookings Institution, 2007.

36 Detailed descriptions of these evaluations may be found at educationendowmentfoundation.org.uk. The respective programs' names are 'One-to-One Academic Tuition', 'Switch on Reading', 'Mathematics Mastery' and 'Philosophy for Children'.

37 The Education Endowment Foundation's conversion to months of achievement is based on the assumption that students learn at a rate of one standard deviation per year: S. Higgins, D. Kokotsaki & R. Coe, 2012, 'The teaching and learning toolkit: Technical appendices', Education Endowment Foundation, The Sutton Trust. I know of no evidence that British students progress this rapidly. Standard estimates put learning progress at between one-quarter and one-half a standard deviation per year (see, for example, Andrew Leigh, 'Estimating teacher effectiveness from two-year changes in students' test scores', *Economics of Education Review*, vol. 29, no. 3, 2010, pp. 480–8. This does not change the relative impact of interventions. However, it does suggest that the EEF's impacts, when expressed in months of learning, are a lower bound. The true impacts might be two or four times as large.

38 For Maths Mastery, the EEF reports a two-month gain for primary students, and a one-month gain for secondary students. They report the cost as £131 per year for primary school pupils and around £50 per year for secondary school pupils. I average these numbers to arrive at a cost of £60 to get one month's improvement.

39 For more details on the 'Chatterbooks' evaluation, see www. educationendowmentfoundation.org.uk

40 William Earhart, 'The value of applied music as a school subject' In *Papers and Proceedings of the Music Teachers National Association Forty-First Annual Meeting*, Hartford: Music Teacher National Association, 1920, pp. 163–70. Earhart served as national president in 1915–16, at a time when the organisation was known as the Music Supervisors' National Conference.

41 For more details on the 'Act, Sing, Play' evaluation, see www.educationendowmentfoundation.org.uk

42 From 2002 to 2013, the study identified ninety randomised evaluations, of which eleven (12 per cent) produced positive effects, while seventy-nine (88 per cent) produced weak or no positive effects. Among a subset of seventy-seven well-conducted randomised trials (that is, without problems such as differential attrition or inadequate statistical power), researchers found that seven (9 per cent) produced positive effects, while seventy (91 per cent) produced weak or no positive effects. See Coalition for Evidence-Based Policy, 'Randomized controlled trials commissioned by the Institute of Education Sciences since 2002: How many found positive versus weak or no effects', July 2013.

43 Robert E. Slavin, 'Evidence-based reform is irreversible', *Huffpost Education Blog*, 22 October 2015.

44 The other requirement to get the top rating is that the experiment has a low attrition rate. See What Works Clearinghouse, *Procedures and Standards Handbook, Version 3.0*, p. 9. Available at http://ies.ed.gov/ncee/wwc/.

45 Joseph P.Allen, Robert C. Pianta, Anne Gregory, et al., 'An interaction-based approach to enhancing secondary school instruction and student achievement',

Science, vol. 333, no. 6045, 2011, pp. 1034–7. The researchers report an impact of 0.22 standard deviations. Since students gain approximately one standard deviation every two years, this impact is equivalent to around half a year of student learning. See also Bill and Melinda Gates Foundation, *Seeing it Clearly: Improving Observer Training for Better Feedback and Better Teaching*, Washington DC: Gates Foundation, 2015, p. 11.

46 Maya Escueta, Vincent Quan, Andre Joshua Nickow & Philip Oreopoulos, 'Education technology: An evidence-based review', NBER Working Paper No. 23744, Cambridge, MA: NBER, 2017.

47 Escueta, 'Education Technology'.

48 The share of pupils completing their matriculation exams rose from 18 per cent in control schools to 25 per cent in treatment schools: Joshua Angrist & Victor Lavy, 'The effects of high stakes high school achievement awards: Evidence from a randomized trial', *American Economic Review*, vol. 99, no. 4, 2009, pp. 1384–414.

49 Simon Burgess, Raj Chande & Todd Rogers, 'Texting parents', Working Paper, Education Endowment Foundation, London, 2016, available at www.educationendowmentfoundation.org.uk

50 Todd Rogers & Avi Feller, 'Intervening through influential third parties: Reducing student absences at scale', working paper, Cambridge, MA: Harvard University Kennedy School, 2017.

51 Paul Tough, 2008, *Whatever It Takes: Geoffrey Canada's Quest to Change Harlem and America*, New York: Houghton Mifflin, pp. 21–9

52 Will Dobbie & Roland G. Fryer Jr., 'Are high-quality schools enough to increase achievement among the poor? Evidence from the Harlem Children's Zone', *American Economic Journal: Applied Economics*, vol. 3, no. 3, 2011, pp .158–87; Will Dobbie & Roland G. Fryer Jr., 'The medium-term impacts of high-achieving charter schools', *Journal of Political Economy*, vol. 123, no. 5, 2015, pp. 985–1037.

53 Quoted in David Brooks, 'The Harlem Miracle', *New York Times*, 7 May 2009, p. A31

54 Betty Hart and Todd Risley, *Meaningful Differences in the Everyday Experience of Young American Children*, Paul Brookes: Baltimore, MD, 1995. Among the limitations of the study was that it only focused on 42 families, each of whom were observed for an hour per month over a 30-month period. The 30 million word estimate assumes that the children in the sample were representative of their respective socio-economic groups, and that the observed word counts can be linearly extrapolated. Although it did not garner the same headlines, an equally interesting finding of the study was that advantaged children receive 6 encouragements to 1 discouragement, while disadvantaged children receive 1 encouragement to 2 discouragements.

55 The initiative reports: 'We've recently completed a randomized control trial of the TMW curriculum with parents from Chicago's South Side. The treatment group received education during eight weekly one-hour home visits. The control group received a nutrition intervention during eight weekly five- to ten-minute home visits. All participants completed fourteen LENA recordings, although only the treatment group received quantitative linguistic feedback. Participants receiving the TMW intervention significantly increased their talk and interaction with their children. Publication of this study is forthcoming.': http://thirtymillionwords.org/tmw-initiative/.

56 Steven D. Levitt, John A. List, Susanne Neckermann & Sally Sadoff, 'The behavioralist goes to school: Leveraging behavioral economics to improve

educational performance', *American Economic Journal: Economic Policy*, vol. 8, no. 4, 2016, pp. 183–219.

57 For a discussion of the complexity challenge inherent in this program, see Roland G. Fryer, 'Teacher incentives and student achievement: Evidence from New York City Public Schools', *Journal of Labor Economics*, vol. 31, no. 2, 2013, pp. 373–407.

58 J.A. Marsh, M.G. Springer, D.F. McCaffrey, et al., 'A Big Apple for educators: New York City's experiment with schoolwide performance bonuses', Final Evaluation Report, Fund for Public Schools, RAND Corporation, Santa Monica, CA, 2011; Roland G. Fryer, 'Teacher Incentives and Student Achievement: Evidence from New York City Public Schools', *Journal of Labor Economics*, vol. 31, no. 2, 2013, pp. 373–407.

59 For a review of this literature, see Andrew Leigh, 'The economics and politics of teacher merit pay', *CESifo Economic Studies*, vol. 59, no. 1, 2013, pp. 1–33.

60 Alan B. Krueger, 'Experimental estimates of education production functions', *Quarterly Journal of Economics*, vol. 114, no. 2, 1999, pp. 497–532.

61 Author's conversation with former Tennessee governor Lamar Alexander.

62 Eric P. Bettinger, Bridget Terry Long, Philip Oreopoulos & Lisa Sanbonmatsu, 'The role of application assistance and information in college decisions: Results from the H&R Block FAFSA experiment', *Quarterly Journal of Economics*, vol. 127, no. 3, 2012, pp. 1205–42.

63 Philip Oreopoulos & Reuben Ford, 'Keeping college options open: A field experiment to help all high school seniors through the college application process', NBER Working Paper No. 22320, Cambridge, MA: NBER, 2016.

64 Benjamin L. Castleman & Lindsay C. Page, 'Summer nudging: Can personalized text messages and peer mentor outreach increase college going among low-income high school graduates?' *Journal of Economic Behavior and Organization*, vol. 115, 2015, pp. 144–60.

65 Justine S. Hastings, Christopher Neilson & Seth Zimmerman, 'The effects of earnings disclosure on college enrollment decisions', NBER Working Paper 21300, Cambridge, MA: NBER, 2015.

66 Caroline M. Hoxby & Sarah Turner, 'What high-achieving low-income students know about college', *American Economic Review*, vol. 105, no. 5, 2015, pp. 514–17.

67 Nadine Ketel, Edwin Leuven, H. Oostereck & Bas van der Klaauw, 'The returns to medical school: Evidence from admission lotteries', *American Economic Journal: Applied Economics*, vol. 8, no. 2, 2016, pp. 225–54.

68 OECD, *Education at a Glance 2016*, Paris: OECD, 2016, p. 166

69 Eric P. Bettinger & Rachel B. Baker, 'The effects of student coaching: An evaluation of a randomized experiment in student advising', *Educational Evaluation and Policy Analysis*, vol. 36, no. 1, 2014, pp. 3–19.

70 Joshua Angrist, Daniel Lang & Philip Oreopoulos, 'Incentives and services for college achievement: Evidence from a randomized trial', *American Economic Journal: Applied Economics*, vol. 1, no. 1, 2009, pp. 136–63.

71 The phrase comes from Laura Haynes, Ben Goldacre & David Torgerson, *Test, Learn, Adapt: Developing Public Policy with Randomised Controlled Trials*, London: Behavioural Insights Team, Cabinet Office, 2012.

6 CONTROLLING CRIME

1   Ross Peake, 'ACT police chief learnt a valuable restorative justice lesson early on', *Canberra Times*, 20 July 2015.

2   Heather Strang, Lawrence W. Sherman, Evan Mayo-Wilson et al., *Restorative Justice Conferencing (RJC) Using Face-to-Face Meetings of Offenders and Victims: Effects on Offender Recidivism and Victim Satisfaction. A Systematic Review*, Campbell Systematic Reviews 2013:12, Oslo: Campbell Collaboration, 2013.

3   For example, 4 per cent of Australian homicides are motivated by revenge: Willow Bryant & Tracy Cussen, 'Homicide in Australia: 2010–11 to 2011–12', National Homicide Monitoring Program report no. 23, Canberra: Australian Institute of Criminology, 2015.

4   According to the FBI's Uniform Crime Reporting Program, the violent crime rate exceeded 750 offences per 100,000 people in 1991 and 1992, but was below 375 offences per 100,000 people in 2013, 2014 and 2015.

5   In 2015, there were 1,526,800 people held in federal and state prisons (E. Ann Carson and Elizabeth Anderson, 'Prisoners in 2015', Bureau of Justice Statistics, US Department of Justice, NCJ 250229, 2016) plus another 721,300 in local jails (Todd D. Minton and Zhen Zeng, 'Jail inmates in 2015', Bureau of Justice Statistics, US Department of Justice, NCJ 250394, 2016). According to the US Census Bureau, the resident population aged eighteen and over was 247 million in 2015, making the adult incarceration rate 0.9 per cent. For historical trends, see National Research Council, *The Growth of Incarceration in the United States: Exploring Causes and Consequences*, Washington, DC: The National Academies Press, 2014.

6   Bruce Western & Becky Pettit, 'Incarceration & social inequality', *Dædalus*, Summer 2010, pp. 8–19.

7   Sara B. Heller, Anuj K. Shah, Jonathan Guryan, et al., 'Thinking, fast and slow? Some field experiments to reduce crime and dropout in Chicago', *Quarterly Journal of Economics*, vol. 132, no. 1, 2017, pp. 1–54. A third randomised trial tested the impact of a similar cognitive behavioural therapy program in a Chicago youth detention facility, and found that it reduced the return rate by 21 per cent.

8   Quoted in Drake Baer, 'This simple program is dramatically reducing teen violence in Chicago', *Tech Insider,* 29 February 2016.

9   Christopher Blattman, Julian C. Jamison & Margaret Sheridan, 'Reducing crime and violence: Experimental evidence from cognitive behavioral therapy in Liberia', *American Economic Review*, vol. 107, no. 4, 2017, pp. 1165–1206.

10   Reply to a criticism during the Great Depression of having changed his position on monetary policy, as quoted in Alfred L. Malabre, *Lost Prophets: An Insider's History of the Modern Economists*, 1994, p. 220.

11   Sara B. Heller, 'Summer jobs reduce violence among disadvantaged youth', *Science*, vol. 346, no. 6214, 2014, pp. 1219–23.

12   Catherine Jacquet, 'Domestic violence in the 1970s', *Circulating Now* blog, US National Library of Medicine, 15 October 2015 (available at https://circulatingnow.nlm.nih.gov).

13   Joan Zorza, 'The criminal law of misdemeanor domestic violence, 1970–1990', *Journal of Criminal Law and Criminology*, vol. 83, no. 1, 1992, pp. 46–72.

14   Fran S. Danis, 'A tribute to Susan Schechter The visions and struggles of the Battered Women's Movement', *Affilia*, vol. 21, no. 3, 2006, pp. 336–41.

15 Lawrence Sherman & Richard Berk, 'The Minneapolis domestic violence experiment', Police Foundation Reports, Washington DC: Police Foundation, 1984.

16 Quoted in Sherman & Berk, 'The Minneapolis domestic violence experiment'.

17 According to police reports, rates of violence in the following six months were 10 per cent with *arrest*, 19 per cent with *advise*, and 24 per cent with *send*. According to victim reports, rates were 19 per cent with *arrest*, 37 per cent with *advise*, and 33 per cent with *send*. Sherman & Berk, 'The Minneapolis domestic violence experiment'; Lawrence Sherman & Richard Berk, 'The specific deterrent effects of arrest for domestic assault', American Sociological Review, vol. 49, no. 2, 1984, pp. 261–72.

18 James LeMoyne, 'A firmer response to family strife', New York Times, 15 April 1984.

19 Associated Press, 'Arrest may be deterrent in domestic violence, study shows', New York Times, 30 May 1984.

20 E.S.Buzawa & C.G. Buzawa,1990, Domestic Violence: The Criminal Justice Response, New York,Russell Sage, pp. 94–9.

21 C. Nadine Wathen & Harriet L. MacMillan, 'Interventions for violence against women: Scientific review', Journal of the American Medical Association, vol. 289, no. 5, 2003, pp. 589–600.

22 Globally, family violence accounts for 47 per cent of female homicides (43,600 victims) and 6 per cent of male homicides (20,000 victims): United Nations Office on Drugs and Crime, UNDOC Global Study on Homicide 2013, United Nations No. 14.IV.1, Vienna: UNDOC, 2014, p. 53.

23 United Nations Office on Drugs and Crime, Global Study on Homicide 2013, p. 49.

24 John Crace, 'Lawrence Sherman: Crime scene investigations', Guardian, 16 May 2007.

25 Crace, 'Lawrence Sherman'.

26 'Lawrence Sherman on Criminology', Social Science Bites, 1 May 2013

27 Émile Durkheim, 'The rules of sociological method' in Scott Appelrouth & Laura Desfor Edles (eds), Classical and Contemporary Sociological Theory: Text and Readings, Thousand Oaks, CA: Pine Forge Press, 2007 [1895], pp. 95–102.

28 Lawrence W. Sherman, Dennis P. Rogan, Timothy Edwards, et al., 'Deterrent effects of police raids on crack houses: A randomized, controlled experiment', Justice Quarterly, vol. 12, no. 4, 1995, pp. 755–81.

29 Anthony A. Braga, 'Hot spots policing and crime prevention: A systematic review of randomized controlled trials', Journal of Experimental Criminology, vol. 1, no. 3, 2005, pp. 317–42.

30 David L. Weisburd & Lorraine Green, 'Policing drug hot spots: The Jersey City drug market analysis experiment', Justice Quarterly, vol. 12, 1995. pp. 711–35.

31 The study reports a reduction of fifty-three violent crimes over a three-month period, which translates to over 200 crimes per year. Jerry H. Ratcliffe, Travis Taniguchi, Elizabeth R. Groff & Jennifer D. Wood, 'The Philadelphia foot patrol experiment: A randomized controlled trial of police patrol effectiveness in violent crime hotspots', Criminology, vol. 49, no. 3, 2011, pp. 795–831. Thanks to Jerry Ratcliffe for confirming my interpretation of these results.

32 Anthony Braga, Andrew Papachristos & David Hureau, 'Hot spots policing effects on crime', Campbell Systematic Reviews, vol. 8, Oslo: Campbell Collaboration, 2012.

33 National Institutes of Justice, 'Practice profile: Hot spots policing', available at crimesolutions.gov.

34 Anthony Allan Braga & David Weisburd, Policing Problem Places: Crime Hot Spots and Effective Prevention, Oxford: Oxford University Press, 2010.

35   L.W. Sherman, 'Policing for crime prevention' in L.W. Sherman, D.C. Gottfredson, D.L. MacKenzie, et al. (eds), *Preventing Crime: What Works, What Doesn't, What's Promising*, Washington, DC: US Office of Justice Programs., 1997, Chapter 8.

36   Gary D. Sherman & Jonathan Haidt, 'Cuteness and disgust: The humanizing and dehumanizing effects of emotion', *Emotion Review*, vol. 3, no. 3, 2011, pp. 245–51.

37   'Ice storm', *The Economist*, 15 April 2017.

38   Gay Murrell, 'Breaking the cycle: NSW Drug Court' *Australian Law Reform Commission Reform Journal*, vol. 77, 2000, pp. 20–24, 90.

39   The first Drug Court was established in Florida in 1989.

40   Bronwyn Lind, Don Weatherburn, Shuling Chen, et al., *NSW Drug Court evaluation: Cost-effectiveness*, NSW Bureau of Crime Statistics and Research, Sydney, 2002, p. 44. A second study of the Drug Court has also been conducted, though this evaluation did not use random assignment. See Don Weatherburn, Craig Jones, Lucy Snowball & Jiuzhao Hua, 'The NSW Drug Court: A re-evaluation of its effectiveness', *Crime and Justice Bulletin*, no. 121, 2008.

41   Adele Harrell, Shannon Cavanagh & John Roman, 'Findings from the evaluation of the DC Superior Court Drug intervention program', submitted to the National Institute of Justice. Washington, DC, 1998: The Urban Institute; Denise C. Gottfredson, Stacy S. Najaka & Brook Kearley, 'Effectiveness of drug treatment courts: Evidence from a randomized trial', *Criminology & Public Policy*, vol. 2, no. 2, 2003, pp. 171–96.

42   Quoted in Malcolm Knox, 'Applause for former drug users who turn their lives around', *Sydney Morning Herald*, 7 February 2009.

43   Quoted in Knox, 'Applause'.

44   Quoted in Knox, 'Applause'.

45   Craig Jones, 'Intensive judicial supervision and drug court outcomes: Interim findings from a randomised controlled trial', *Contemporary Issues in Crime and Justice*, no. 152, NSW Bureau of Crime Statistics and Research, 2011.

46   Quoted in Sam Kornell, 'Probation that works', *Slate*, 5 June 2013.

47   The study was based on 493 probationers. See Angela Hawken & Mark Kleiman, 'Managing drug involved probationers with swift and certain sanctions: Evaluating Hawaii's HOPE', Department of Justice Report 229023, National Institute of Justice, Washington DC, 2009; National Institute of Justice, '"Swift and certain" sanctions in probation are highly effective: Evaluation of the HOPE Program', Washington DC: National Institute of Justice, 2012.

48   Quoted in Hawken & Kleiman, 'Managing drug involved probationers'.

49   Evaluations of some of these programs show that they have not delivered effects as sizeable as those seen in Hawaii. On the rollout of HOPE across the United States, see Lorana Bartels, *Swift, Certain and Fair: Does Project HOPE Provide a Therapeutic Paradigm for Managing Offenders?*, Cham, Switzerland: Palgrave Macmillan, 2017. The disappointing replication study of HOPE was conducted in Arkansas, Massachusetts, Oregon and Texas, and is reported in Pamela Lattimore, Doris Layton MacKenzie, Gary Zajac, et al., 'Outcome findings from the HOPE demonstration field experiment', *Criminology & Public Policy*, vol. 15, no. 4, 2016, pp. 1103–41.

50   Adam Gamoran, 'Measuring impact in science education: Challenges and possibilities of experimental design', NYU Abu Dhabi Conference, January 2009.

51 Doris L. MacKenzie & David P. Farrington, 'Preventing future offending of delinquents and offenders: What have we learned from experiments and meta-analyses?' *Journal of Experimental Criminology*, vol. 11, no. 4, 2015, pp. 565–95.

52 Australian incarceration rates were higher in the colonial era than they are today, but the 2016 rate was higher than at any time since 1901: Andrew Leigh, 'Locking someone up costs around $300 a day or about $110,000 a year', *Canberra Times*, 14 November 2016.

53 National Research Council, *The Growth of Incarceration*.

54 Mark A.R. Kleiman, *When Brute Force Fails: How to Have Less Crime and Less Punishment*, Princeton NJ: Princeton University Press, 2009.

55 National Research Council, *The Growth of Incarceration*, p. 155. See also Council of Economic Advisers, 'Economic perspectives on incarceration and the criminal justice system', Washington DC: Executive Office of the President of the United States, 2016.

56 John E. Berecochea & Dorothy R. Jaman, *Time Served in Prison and Parole Outcome: An Experimental Study: Report*, No. 2. Research Division, California Department of Corrections, 1981.

57 Ina Jaffe, 'Cases show disparity of California's 3 strikes law', *NPR All Things Considered*, 30 October 2009.

7 VALUABLE EXPERIMENTS IN POOR COUNTRIES

1 This account is drawn from 'Nigeria, You Win!', *Planet Money*, Episode 702, 20 May 2016.

2 David J. McKenzie, 'Identifying and spurring high-growth entrepreneurship: Experimental evidence from a business plan competition', *American Economic Review*, vol. 107, no. 8, 2017 pp. 2278–307.

3 Chris Blattman, 'Is this the most effective development program in history?', chrisblattman.com, 24 September 2015.

4 Data to 2012 from testimony of Professor Dean Karlan before the US Committee on Financial Services inquiry, 'The multi-lateral development banks: A strategy for generating increased return on investment', 9 October 2015. Data from 2013 to 2015 from Jorge Miranda, Shayda Sabet & Annette N. Brown, 'Is impact evaluation still on the rise?', blogs.3ieimpact.org, 11 August 2016. Counting the number of randomised trials published on child health in developing nations, there was a seven-fold increase from 2002–03 to 2012–13: Trevor Duke and David Fuller, 'Randomised controlled trials in child health in developing countries: Trends and lessons over 11 years', *Archives of Disease in Childhood*, vol. 99, no. 7, 2014, pp. 615–20.

5 See Table 3 in Drew B. Cameron, Anjini Mishra & Annette N. Brown, 'The growth of impact evaluation for international development: how much have we learned?', *Journal of Development Effectiveness*, vol. 8, no. 1, 2016, pp. 1–21.

6 Quoted in Jeff Tollefson, 'Revolt of the Randomistas', *Nature*, vol 524, 13 August 2015, pp. 150–3.

7 William Easterly, *The Elusive Quest for Growth: Economists' Adventures and Misadventures in the Tropics*, Cambridge, MA: MIT Press, 2002.

8   Isaiah Berlin, *The Hedgehog and the Fox: An Essay on Tolstoy's View of History*, London: Weidenfeld & Nicolson, 1953.

9   Quoted in Abhijit Banerjee, Dean Karlan & Jonathan Zinman. 'Six randomized evaluations of microcredit: Introduction and further steps', *American Economic Journal: Applied Economics*, vol. 7, no. 1, 2015, pp. 1–21.

10 Jim Klobuchar & Susan Cornell Wilkes, *The Miracles of Barefoot Capitalism*, Minneapolis: Kirk House Publishers, 2003, p. 26.

11 Bill Clinton, *Giving: How Each of Us Can Change the World*, New York: Random House, 2007, pp.6–7.

12 Quoted in Dean Karlan & Jacob Appel, *More Than Good Intentions: How a New Economics is Helping to Solve Global Poverty*, New York: Penguin, 2011, p. 61.

13 Banerjee, Karlan and Zinman, 'Six randomized evaluations of microcredit'. See also Abdul Latif Jameel Poverty Action Lab, 'Where Credit is Due', *Policy Bulletin*, February 2015, available at www.povertyactionlab.org.

14 Karlan & Appel, *More Than Good Intentions*, p. 70

15 Dean Karlan, Aishwarya Lakshmi Ratan & Jonathan Zinman, 'Savings by and for the poor: A research review and agenda', *Review of Income and Wealth*, vol. 60, no. 1, 2014, pp. 36–78.

16 The actual exchange was a little more complex. For details, see Robert Deis, '"The rich are different" The real story behind the famed "exchange" between F. Scott Fitzgerald and Ernest Hemingway', *Quote/Counterquote*, 12 July 2014.

17 Abhijit Banerjee, Esther Duflo, Nathanael Goldberg, et al., 'A multifaceted program causes lasting progress for the very poor: Evidence from six countries', *Science*, vol. 348, no. 6236, 2015.

18 See www.givedirectly.org.

19 The experiment is described in Michael Faye & Paul Niehaus, 'What if we just gave poor people a basic income for life? That's what we're about to test', *Slate*, 14 April 2016; Dylan Matthews, 'A charity's radical experiment: Giving 6,000 Kenyans enough money to escape poverty for a decade', *Vox*, 15 April 2016.

20 Stefan Dercon, Tanguy Bernard, Kate Orkin & Alemayehu Taffesse, 'The future in mind: Aspirations and forward-looking behaviour in rural Ethiopia', Working paper 2014–16, Department of Economics, University of Oxford, 2014.

21 The video is available at https://youtu.be/zh1uoxH9q5g.

22 Francisco Campos, Michael Frese, Markus Goldstein, et al., 'Teaching personal initiative beats traditional training in boosting small business in West Africa', *Science*, vol. 357, no. 6357, 2017, pp. 1287–90.

23 Klaus Schwab (ed.), *The Global Competitiveness Report 2016–2017*, Geneva: World Economic Forum, 2016.

24 Freedom House, *Freedom in the World 2017*, New York: Freedom House, 2017.

25 'State fragility index and matrix 2015', updated figures for Monty G. Marshall & Benjamin R. Cole, *Global Report 2014: Conflict, Governance and State Fragility*, Vienna: Center for Systemic Peace, 2014.

26 Jidong Chen, Jennifer Pan & Yiqing Xu, 'Sources of authoritarian responsiveness: A field experiment in China', *American Journal of Political Science*, vol. 60, no. 2, 2016, pp. 383–400.

27 Marianne Bertrand, Simeon Djankov, Rema Hanna & Sendhil Mullainathan, 'Obtaining a driver's license in India: An experimental approach to studying corruption' *Quarterly Journal of Economics*, vol. 122, no. 4, 2007, pp. 1639–76.

28 Marco Gonzalez-Navarro & Climent Quintana-Domeque, 'Paving streets for the poor: Experimental analysis of infrastructure effects', *Review of Economics and Statistics*, vol. 98, no. 2, 2016, pp. 254–67.

29 Kenneth Lee, Edward Miguel & Catherine Wolfram, 'Experimental evidence on the demand for and costs of rural electrification', NBER Working Paper 22292, Cambridge, MA: National Bureau of Economic Research, 2016.

30 Joppe de Ree, Karthik Muralidharan, Menno Pradhan, Halsey Rogers, 'Double for nothing? Experimental evidence on an unconditional teacher salary increase in Indonesia', *Quarterly Journal of Economics*, forthcoming.

31 Karthik Muralidharan, Paul Niehaus & Sandip Sukhtankar, 'Building state capacity: Evidence from biometric smartcards in India', *American Economic Review*, vol, 106, no. 10, 2016, pp. 2895–929.

32 Even for those who survive, malaria can be a debilitating disease. A person who contracts malaria as a child earns one-third less as an adult: Abhijit Banerjee & Esther Duflo, *Poor Economics: A Radical Rethinking of the Way to Fight Global Poverty*, New York: Public Affairs, 2011, p. 44.

33 World Health Organization, 'Fact sheet: World malaria report 2015', 9 December 2015. The statistic refers to children under five.

34 William Easterly, *The White Man's Burden: Why the West's Efforts to Aid the Rest Have Done So Much Ill and So Little Good*, New York: Penguin, 2006, p. 12.

35 Jeffrey Sachs, 'Good news on malaria control', *Scientific American*, 1 August 2009.

36 Jessica Cohen & Pascaline Dupas, 'Free distribution or cost-sharing? Evidence from a randomized malaria prevention experiment', *Quarterly Journal of Economics*, vol. 125, no. 1, 2010, pp. 1-45; Pascaline Dupas, 'What matters (and what does not) in households' decision to invest in malaria prevention?' *American Economic Review: Papers & Proceedings*, vol. 99, no. 2, 2009, pp. 224–30; Pascaline Dupas, 'Short-run subsidies and long-run adoption of new health products: Evidence from a field experiment." *Econometrica*, vol. 82, no. 1, January 2014, pp. 197–228.

37 Jeffrey Sachs, 'The case for aid', *Foreign Policy*, 21 January 2014.

38 Michael Kremer & Edward Miguel, 'The illusion of sustainability', *Quarterly Journal of Economics*, vol. 122, no. 3, 2007, pp. 1007–65; Michael Kremer, E. Miguel & S. Mullainathan, 'Source dispensers and home delivery of chlorine in Kenya', Innovations for Poverty Action, Working Paper, 2014. For a useful literature summary, see Abdul Latif Jameel Poverty Action Lab, 'Pricing preventive Health Products', undated, available at www.povertyactionlab.org.

39 Abhijit Vinayak Banerjee, Esther Duflo, Rachel Glennerster & Dhruva Kothari, 'Improving immunisation coverage in rural India: Clustered randomised controlled evaluation of immunisation campaigns with and without incentives', *British Medical Journal*, vol. 340, 2010, c2220.

40 Blake Mycoskie, *Start Something That Matters*, New York: Spiegel and Grau, 2012, p. 5.

41 'Free two shoes', *The Economist*, 5 November 2016.

42 The one-for-one companies that sell these products are Warby Parker, One World Play Project, Sir Richard's, Smile Squared, One Million Lights and FIGS.

43 Bruce Wydick, Elizabeth Katz, Flor Calvo, et al., 'Shoeing the children: The impact of the TOMS shoe donation program in rural El Salvador', *World Bank Economic Review*, 2017.

44 Bruce Wydick, 'The impact of TOMS shoes', *Across Two Worlds* blog, 16 March 2015.

45 See the 'Death on the Roads' page, at www.who.int.

46 James Habyarimana & William Jack, 'Heckle and chide: Results of a randomized road safety intervention in Kenya', *Journal of Public Economics*, vol. 95, no. 11, 2011, pp. 1438–46.

47 Paul Gertler, Manisha Shah, Maria Laura Alzua, Lisa Cameron, et al., 'How does health promotion work? Evidence from the dirty business of eliminating open defecation', NBER Working Paper 20997, Cambridge, MA: National Bureau of Economic Research, 2015.

48 On the role of Santiago Levy in creating the *Progresa* experiment, see Banerjee & Duflo, *Poor Economics*, p. 78.

49 Susan W. Parker & Graciela M. Teruel, 'Randomization and social program evaluation: The case of Progresa', *The Annals of the American Academy of Political and Social Science*, vol. 599, no. 1, 2005, pp. 199–219.

50 Susan Parker & Petra Todd, 'Conditional cash transfers: The case of Progresa/ Oportunidades', *Journal of Economic Literature*, vol. 55, no. 3, 2017, pp. 866–915.

51 Dana Burde & Leigh L. Linden, 'Bringing education to Afghan girls: A randomized controlled trial of village-based schools', *American Economic Journal: Applied Economics*, vol. 5, no. 3, 2013, pp. 27–40.

52 The student gains were approximately half a standard deviation (larger for girls, and smaller for boys). I assume that the typical student improves at a rate of half a standard deviation each school year. See, for example, Andrew Leigh, 'Estimating teacher effectiveness from two-year changes in students' test score', *Economics of Education Review*, vol. 29, no. 3, 2010, pp. 480–8.

53 These figures are for 2009, and are drawn from WHO/UNAIDS, 'Fast facts on HIV', 2010, available at www.who.int.

54 Quoted in Esther Duflo, 'AIDS prevention: Abstinence vs. risk reduction', VoxEU blog, 20 April 2009.

55 Samuel Ponce de Leon, Maria Eugenia Jimenez-Corona, Ana Maria Velasco & Antonio Lazcano, 'The Pope, condoms, and the evolution of HIV', *The Lancet Infectious Diseases*, vol. 9, no. 8, 2009, pp. 461–2.

56 Duflo, Esther, Pascaline Dupas & Michael Kremer, 'Education, HIV, and early fertility: Experimental evidence from Kenya', *American Economic Review*, vol. 105, no. 9, 2015, pp. 2757–97.

57 Pascaline Dupas, 'Do teenagers respond to HIV risk information? Evidence from a field experiment in Kenya', *American Economic Journal: Applied Economics*, vol. 3, no. 1, 2011, pp. 1–34.

58 These were reported to school students to be the infection rates from a nearby city (Kisumu), as distinct from the national rates.

59 John Gapper, 'Lunch with the FT: Esther Duflo', *Financial Times*, 17 March 2012.

60 Gapper, 'Lunch with the FT'.

61 Asimina Caminis, 'Putting economic policy to the test', *Finance and Development*, September 2003, pp. 4–7.

62 Ian Parker, 'The poverty lab', *New Yorker*, 17 May 2010.

63 Abdul Latif Jameel Poverty Action Lab, 'Increasing test score performance', undated, available at www.povertyactionlab.org.

64 Innovations for Poverty Action, 'Financial inclusion program brief', 15 June 2016, available at www.poverty-action.org.

65 One analysis found that if you took any two randomised trials in development, their confidence intervals would overlap approximately 83 per cent of the time: Eva Vivalt, 'Heterogeneous treatment effects in impact evaluation,' *American Economic Review*, vol. 105, no. 5, 2015, pp. 467–70.

66 Paul Glewwe & Karthik Muralidharan, 'Improving education outcomes in developing countries – evidence, knowledge gaps, and policy implications' in Eric Hanushek, Stephen Machin & Ludger Woessman (eds), *Handbook of the Economics of Education*, Vol. 5, Amsterdam: North Holland, 2016, pp. 653–744.

67 Shwetlena Sabarwal, David K. Evans & Anastasia Marshak, 'The permanent input hypothesis: The case of textbooks and (no) student learning in Sierra Leone', *World Bank Policy Research Working Paper*, vol. 7021, 2014.

68 Jishnu Das, Stefan Dercon, James Habyarimana, et al., 'School inputs, household substitution, and test scores' *American Economic Journal: Applied Economics*, vol. 5, no. 2, 2013, pp. 29–57.

69 Isaac Mbiti & Karthik Muralidharan, 'Inputs, incentives, and complementarities in primary education: Experimental evidence from Tanzania', unpublished working paper, 2015.

70 Paul Glewwe, Michael Kremer & Sylvie Moulin. 'Many children left behind? Textbooks and test scores in Kenya', *American Economic Journal: Applied Economics*, vol. 1, no. 1, 2009, pp. 112–35.

71 Angus S. Deaton, 'Instruments, randomization, and learning about development', *Journal of Economic Literature*, vol. 48, no. 2, 2010, pp. 424–55.

72 Gueron & Rolston, *Fighting for Reliable Evidence*, p. 427.

73 Quoted in Adam Gopnik, 'The double man: Why Auden is an indispensable poet of our time', *New Yorker*, 23 September 2002. Gopnik observes: 'Auden shared Popper's sense that open societies were built on skeptical faith rather than on fatuous confidence'.

8 FARMS, FIRMS AND FACEBOOK

1 This description relates to the experiment as it commenced in 1843. For details, see 'Broadbalk Winter Wheat Experiment' at e-RA: The Electronic Rothamsted Archive, www.era.rothamsted.ac.uk.

2 Quoted in Jonathan Silvertown, Paul Poulton, Edward Johnston, et al., 'The Park Grass Experiment 1856–2006: Its contribution to ecology', *Journal of Ecology*, vol. 94, no. 4, 2006, pp. 801–14.

3 Late-nineteenth century estimate from Vaclav Smil, *Enriching the Earth: Fritz Haber, Carl Bosch, and the Transformation of World Food*, Cambridge, MA: MIT Press, 2001, p. 245. Current estimate from Food and Agriculture Organisation of the United Nations, *Current World Fertilizer Trends and Outlook to 2015*, Rome: FAO, 2011.

4 C.W. Wrigley, 'Farrer, William James (1845–1906)', *Australian Dictionary of Biography*, Volume 8, National Centre of Biography, Australian National University, 1981, available at http://adb.anu.edu.au.

5 Author's interview with Greg Rebetzke. These models choose from among many possible random allocations of treatments across a grid, with the aim of minimising the number of treatments that recur on the same horizontal or vertical axis.

6 Quoted in Leslie Brokaw, 'In experiments we trust: From Intuit to Harrah's casinos', *MIT Sloan Management Review*, 3 March 2011.

7   'From Harvard economist to casino CEO', *Planet Money*, 15 November 2011.

8   Others disagree. See, for example, Ira Glass, 'Blackjack', *This American Life*, Episode 466, 8 June 2016.

9   Quoted in Leslie Brokaw, 'In experiments we trust: From Intuit to Harrah's Casinos', *MIT Sloan Management Review*, 3 March 2011.

10 Quoted in Jeffrey Pfeffer and Victoria Chang, 'Gary Loveman and Harrah's Entertainment', Stanford Business School Case No. OB45, Stanford, CA, 2003.

11 For an excellent overview of some of the studies in this field, see Omar Al-Ubaydli & John List, 'Field experiments in markets', in Abhijit Banerjee & Esther Duflo (eds), *Handbook of Field Experiments*, Amsterdam: Elsevier, vol. 1, 2017, pp. 271–307.

12 Jim Manzi, *Uncontrolled: The Surprising Payoff of Trial-and-Error for Business, Politics, and Society*, New York: Basic Books, 2012, p. 144.

13 Eric T. Anderson & Duncan Simester, 'A step-by-step guide to smart business experiments', *Harvard Business Review*, March 2011.

14 Quoted in Bharat N. Anand, Michael G. Rukstad & Christopher Paige, 'Capital One financial corporation', Harvard Business School Case 700-124, April 2000.

15 Stefan Thomke & Jim Manzi, 'The discipline of business experimentation', *Harvard Business Review*, December 2014.

16 Christian Rudder, 'We experiment on human beings!', *OkTrends* blog, 28 July 2014.

17 Rudder, 'We experiment on human beings!'

18 Christian Rudder, *Dataclysm: Love, Sex, Race, and Identity–What Our Online Lives Tell Us about Our Offline Selves*, New York: Broadway Books, 2015, p. 17.

19 Rudder, 'We experiment on human beings!'

20 One possible explanation of this is that the match quality algorithm was not very good.

21 Uri Gneezy & John List, *The Why Axis: Hidden Motives and the Undiscovered Economics of Everyday Life*, New York: Public Affairs, 2013, pp. 237–8.

22 Interview by Russ Roberts with Quora CEO Adam D'Angelo, *EconTalk*, 8 August 2016, available at www.econtalk.org. Before starting an experiment, employees must either specify the hypothesis they are trying to test, or declare that they are simply running a 'learning experiment'. If a new feature performs well in a hypothesis experiment, it will typically be deployed to all Quora users. But if something comes up as statistically significant in a learning experiment, the employee needs to run a second experiment to prove that it wasn't just a fluke the first time.

23 Brian Christian, 'The A/B test: Inside the technology that's changing the rules of business', *Wired*, 25 April 2012.

24 'Little things that mean a lot', *Economist*, 19 July 2014.

25 Jim Manzi, head of Applied Predictive Technologies, boasts that his firm is now running randomised trials for '30 to 40 per cent of the largest retailers, hotel chains, restaurant chains and retail banks in America': Manzi, *Uncontrolled*, p. 147.

26 Quoted in 'Test of dynamic pricing angers Amazon customers', *Washington Post*, 7 October 2000.

27 Quoted in Troy Wolverton, 'Now showing: random DVD prices on Amazon', *C|Net*, 5 September 2000.

28 'Amazon.com issues statement regarding random price testing', *Amazon.com*, 27 September 2000.

29 For an excellent discussion of randomised experiments in the field of marketing, see Duncan Simester, 'Field experiments in Marketing', in Banerjee & Duflo (eds), *Handbook of Field Experiments*, pp. 465–97.

30 Eric T. Anderson & Duncan I. Simester, 'Effects of $9 price endings on retail sales: Evidence from field experiments," *Quantitative Marketing and Economics*, vol. 1, no. 1, 2003, pp. 93–110.

31 Tanjim Hossain & John Morgan, '… plus shipping and handling: Revenue (non) equivalence in field experiments on ebay', *Advances in Economic Analysis and Policy*, vol. 5, no. 2, 2006.

32 The share of gold card customers who accepted the upgrade was 21 per cent for the platinum card offer, but 14 per cent for a gold card that offered the same benefits as the platinum card: Leonardo Bursztyn, Bruno Ferman, Stefano Fiorin, et al., 'Status goods: Experimental evidence from platinum credit cards', NBER Working Paper No. 23414, Cambridge, MA: NBER, 2017.

33 Haipeng Chen, Howard Marmorstein, Michael Tsiros & Akshay R. Rao, 'When more is less: The impact of base value neglect on consumer preferences for bonus packs over price discounts', *Journal of Marketing*, vol. 76, no. 4, 2012, pp. 64–77.

34 Brian Wansink, Robert J. Kent & Stephen J. Hoch, 1998, 'An anchoring and adjustment model of purchase quantity decisions', *Journal of Marketing Research*, vol. 35, no. 1, pp. 71–81

35 Kusum L. Ailawadi, Bari A. Harlam, Jacques César & David Trounce, 'Quantifying and improving promotion effectiveness at CVS', *Marketing Science*, vol. 26, no. 4, 2007, pp. 566–75.

36 Ju-Young Kim, Martin Natter & Martni Spann, 'Pay what you want: A new participative pricing mechanism', *Journal of Marketing*, vol. 73, 2009, pp. 44–58.

37 Greer K. Gosnell, John A. List & Robert Metcalfe, 'A new approach to an age-old problem: Solving externalities by incenting workers directly', NBER Working Paper No. 22316, Cambridge, MA: NBER, 2016.

38 Bruce S. Shearer, 'Piece rates, fixed wages and incentives: Evidence from a field experiment', *Review of Economic Studies*, vol. 71, no. 2, 2004, pp. 513–34.

39 Lan Shi, 'Incentive effect of piece-rate contracts: Evidence from two small field experiments', *B.E. Journal of Economic Analysis & Policy*, vol. 10, no. 1 (Topics), Article 61, 2010.

40 For a summary of the strawberry studies, see Oriana Bandiera, Iwan Barankay & Imran Rasul, 'Field experiments with firms', *Journal of Economic Perspectives*, vol. 25, no. 3, 2011, pp. 63–82. The authors do not disclose which kind of soft fruit their subjects pick – this information is contained in Tim Harford, 'The fruits of their labors', *Slate*, 23 August 2008.

41 An even more nefarious way of delivering bonuses is to 'provisionally' pay workers a bonus, but then to say that it will be withdrawn if performance targets are not met. This exploitation of employee 'loss aversion' did indeed raise productivity in a randomised experiment in a Chinese factory: Tanjim Hossain & John A. List. 'The behavioralist visits the factory: Increasing productivity using simple framing manipulations', *Management Science*, vol. 58, no. 12, 2012, pp. 2151–67. Similarly, ridesharing company Lyft found that new drivers were more likely to shift from a quiet time of the week to a busy time of the week if the difference was expressed as a loss than a gain (the company ultimately chose not to implement the results of the study): Noam Scheiber, 'How Uber uses psychological tricks to push its drivers' buttons', *New York Times*, 2 April 2017.

42 Alexandre Mas & Enrico Moretti, 'Peers at work', *American Economic Review*, vol. 99, no. 1, 2009, pp. 112–45; Oriana Bandiera, Iwan Barankay and Imran Rasul, 'Social

incentives in the workplace', *Review of Economic Studies*, vol. 77, no. 2, 2010, pp. 417–58; Lamar Pierce and Jason Snyder, 'Ethical spillovers in firms: Evidence from vehicle emissions testing', *Management Science*, vol. 54, no. 11, 2008, pp. 1891–1903. Note that only the Bandiera et al. study uses true random assignment; in the other two studies the authors argue that the assignment of employees to teams is effectively random – in other words, unrelated to their co-workers' productivity.

43 Nava Ashraf, Oriana Bandiera & B. Kelsey Jack, 'No margin, no mission? A field experiment on incentives for public service delivery', *Journal of Public Economics*, vol. 120, 2014, pp. 1–17.

44 Iwan Barankay, 'Rankings and social tournaments: Evidence from a crowd-sourcing experiment', Working Paper, Wharton School of Business, University of Pennsylvania, 2011.

45 Steven D. Levitt & John A. List, 'Was there really a Hawthorne effect at the Hawthorne plant? An analysis of the original illumination experiments', *American Economic Journal: Applied Economics*, vol. 3, no.1, 2011, pp. 224–38.

46 Matthew Stewart, *The Management Myth: Why the Experts Keep Getting It Wrong*, New York: Norton, 2009.

47 Jill Lepore, 'Not so fast', *New Yorker*, 12 October 2009.

48 Nicholas Bloom, Benn Eifert, Aprajit Mahajan, et al., 'Does management matter? Evidence from India', *Quarterly Journal of Economics*, vol. 128, no. 1, 2013, pp. 1–51.

49 The fact that Accenture were the consulting firm involved in the study is revealed in Tim Harford, 'A case for consultants?', *Financial Times*, 13 November 2010.

50 Similarly, a study that randomly offered export opportunities to Egyptian rug manufacturers found that exposure to export markets boosted their subsequent profits by up to one-quarter. However, such a large effect might not be realised in high-income countries. See David Atkin, Amit K. Khandelwal & Adam Osman. 'Exporting and firm performance: Evidence from a randomized experiment', *Quarterly Journal of Economics*, vol. 132, no. 2, 2017, pp. 551–615.

51 Chicago University's John List is now pushing the power of statistics still further, running an experiment with United Airlines' loyalty program across just four US cities – two in the treatment group and two in the control group. It will be interesting to see whether, after accounting for cluster effects, the results are statistically significant.

52 Leonard M. Lodish, Magid Abraham, Stuart Kalmenson, et al., 'How TV advertising works: A meta-analysis of 389 real world split cable TV advertising experiments' *Journal of Marketing Research*, vol. 32, no. 2, 1995, pp. 125–39. The study is an update of the pathbreaking work of Margaret Blair, 'An empirical investigation of advertising wearin and wearout" *Journal of Advertising Research*, vol. 27, no. 6, 1987, pp. 45–50.

53 Randall A. Lewis & Justin M. Rao, 'The unfavorable economics of measuring the returns to advertising', *The Quarterly Journal of Economics*, vol. 130, no. 4, 2015, pp. 1941–73. More precisely, their Super Bowl impossibility theorem finds that 'it is nearly impossible for a firm to be large enough to afford the ad, but small enough to reliably detect meaningful differences in ROI'.

54 Randall A. Lewis, Justin M. Rao & David H. Reiley, 'Here, there, and everywhere: Correlated online behaviors can lead to overestimates of the effects of advertising' in *Proceedings of the 20th International Conference on World Wide Web*, ACM, 2011, pp. 157–66.

55 Brian Christian, 'The A/B test: Inside the technology that's changing the rules of business', *Wired*, 25 April 2012.

56 Ben Gomes, 'Search experiments, large and small', *Google Official Blog*, 26 August 2008

57 Dan Cobley, quoted in Matthew Syed, *Black Box Thinking: Why Most People Never Learn from Their Mistakes – But Some Do*, Portfolio, New York, 2015, pp. 184–5.

58 'In 2010 alone, the company investigated more than 13,000 proposed changes, of which around 8200 were tested in side-by-side comparisons that were evaluated by raters. Of those, 2800 were further evaluated by a tiny fraction of the live traffic in a "sandbox" area of the website. Analysts prepared an independent report of those results, which were then evaluated by a committee. That process led to 516 improvements that were made to the search algorithm from the initial 13,000 proposals.': Stefan Thomke, 'Unlocking innovation through business experimentation', *European Business Review*, 10 March 2013.

59 Quoted in Thomke, 'Unlocking innovation'. See also Manzi, *Uncontrolled*, pp. 128, 142.

60 A classic example of where sample size doesn't help was *Literary Digest*'s attempt to predict the 1936 presidential election by surveying nearly 2 million of its readers. Failing to recognise that its readers were more affluent than the electorate at large, the magazine forecast that Republican Alf Landon would beat incumbent Democratic President Franklin D. Roosevelt. Landon ended up with just 8 of the 531 electoral college votes.

61 Huizhi Xie & Juliette Aurisset, 'Improving the sensitivity of online controlled experiments: Case studies at Netflix." In *Proceedings of the 22nd ACM SIGKDD International Conference on Knowledge Discovery and Data Mining*, pp. 645–54. ACM, 2016.

62 Carlos A. Gomez-Uribe & Neil Hunt, 'The Netflix recommender system: Algorithms, business value, and innovation', *ACM Transactions on Management Information Systems (TMIS)*, vol. 6, no. 4, 2016, p. 13.

63 Gomez-Uribe & Hunt, 'The Netflix recommender system', p. 13.

64 Adam D.I. Kramer, Jamie E. Guillory & Jeffrey T. Hancock, 'Experimental evidence of massive-scale emotional contagion through social networks', *Proceedings of the National Academy of Sciences*, vol. 3, no. 24, 2014, pp. 8788–90.

65 Because 22.4 per cent of Facebook posts contained negative words, and 46.8 per cent contained negative words, the study also had two control groups: one of which randomly omitted 2.24 per cent of all posts, and another that randomly omitted 4.68 per cent of all posts.

66 Oddly, some commentators seem unaware of the finding, continuing to make claims like 'Facebook makes us feel inadequate, so we try to compete, putting a positive spin and a pretty filter on an ordinary moment – prompting someone else to do the same … when you sign up to Facebook you put yourself under pressure to appear popular, fun and loved, regardless of your reality': Daisy Buchanan, 'Facebook bragging's route to divorce', *Australian Financial Review*, 27 August 2016

67 Kate Bullen & John Oates, 'Facebook's 'experiment' was socially irresponsible', *Guardian*, 2 July 2014.

68 Quoted in David Goldman, 'Facebook still won't say "sorry" for mind games experiment', *CNNMoney*, 2 July 2014.

9 TESTING THEORIES IN POLITICS AND PHILANTHROPY

1   Julian Jamison & Dean Karlan, 'Candy elasticity: Halloween experiments on public political statements', *Economic Inquiry*, vol. 54, no. 1, 2016, pp. 543–7.
2   This experiment is outlined in detail in Dan Siroker, 'How Obama raised $60 million by running a simple experiment', *Optimizely* blog, 29 November 2010.
3   Quoted in Brian Christian, 'The A/B test: Inside the technology that's changing the rules of business', *Wired*, 25 April 2012.
4   Alan S. Gerber & Donald P. Green, 'Field experiments on voter mobilization: An overview of a burgeoning literature' in Banerjee & Duflo (eds), *Handbook of Field Experiments*, pp. 395–438.
5   Harold F. Gosnell, *Getting-out-the-vote: An Experiment in the Stimulation of Voting*, Chicago: University of Chicago Press, 1927. As Gerber and Green point out, Gosnell's experiments used matched pairs of streets, but it is not clear from his write-up how he chose which street to be in the treatment and control groups. See Gerber and Green, 'Field experiments on voter mobilization'.
6   Donald P. Green & Alan S. Gerber, *Get Out the Vote: How to Increase Voter Turnout*, 2nd edition, Washington DC: Brookings Institution Press, 2008, p. 14.
7   For an example of a widely cited academic work which takes essentially this approach, see Steven Rosenstone & John Hansen, *Mobilization, Participation, and Democracy in America*, New York: MacMillan, 1993.
8   The experiment was carried out at the beginning of 2006, when Governor Perry faced the prospect of a challenge in the Republican primary from Carole Keeton Strayhorn (she ultimately decided to run as an independent). For more details, see Alan S. Gerber, James G. Gimpel, Donald Green & Daron Shaw, 'How large and long-lasting are the persuasive effects of televised campaign ads? Results from a randomized field experiment', *American Political Science Review*, vol. 105, no. 1, 2011, pp. 135–50.
9   One reason that it is easier to detect the impact of political advertisements than commercial advertisements is that voters constitute a larger share of the population than do customers of most products (though falling voting rates and rising market concentration mean that this may not always be true).
10 Gerber & Green, 'Field experiments on voter mobilization', Table 4.
11 Alan S. Gerber, Donald P. Green & Christopher W. Larimer, 'Social pressure and voter turnout: Evidence from a large-scale field experiment', *American Political Science Review*, vol. 102, no. 1, 2008, pp. 33–48.
12 Gregg R. Murray & Richard E. Matland, 'Mobilization effects using mail social pressure, descriptive norms, and timing', *Political Research Quarterly*, vol. 67, no. 2, 2014, pp. 304–19.
13 The honour roll experiment produced a 2 percentage point increase in turnout: Costas Panagopoulos, 'Positive social pressure and prosocial motivation: Evidence from a large-scale field experiment on voter mobilization', *Political Psychology*, vol. 34, no. 2, 2013, pp. 265–75. The gratitude experiments (run in Georgia, New Jersey and New York) produced a 2.4 to 2.5 percentage point increase in turnout: Costas Panagopoulos, 'Thank you for voting: Gratitude expression and voter mobilization', *Journal of Politics*, vol. 73, no. 3, 2011, pp. 707–17.
14 Gerber & Green, 'Field experiments on voter mobilization', Table 4.
15 Green & Gerber, *Get Out the Vote*, p. 69.

16 Green & Gerber, *Get Out the Vote*, p. 92.
17 Gerber & Green, 'Field experiments on voter mobilization'.
18 Green & Gerber, *Get Out the Vote*, p. 92.
19 Lisa Garcia Bedolla & Melissa R. Michelson, *Mobilizing inclusion: Transforming the electorate through get-out-the-vote campaigns*, New Haven, CT: Yale University Press, 2012.
20 Gerber & Green, 'Field experiments on voter mobilization'; Vincent Pons, 'Does door-to-door canvassing affect vote shares? Evidence from a countrywide field experiment in France', Working Paper, Harvard Business School, 2014; Guillaume Liégey, Arthur Muller & Vincent Pons, *Porte à porte: Reconquérir la démocratie sur le terrain*, Calmann-Lévy, 2013; Peter John & Tessa Brannan, 'How different are telephoning and canvassing? Results from a "get out the vote" field experiment in the British 2005 general election', *British Journal of Political Science*, vol. 38, no. 3, 2008, pp. 565–74.
21 Green & Gerber, *Get Out the Vote*, p. 37.
22 David Broockman & Joshua Kalla, 'Experiments show this is the best way to win campaigns. But is anyone actually doing it?', *Vox*, 13 November 2014.
23 David W. Nickerson, 'Does email boost turnout?' *Quarterly Journal of Political Science*, vol. 2, no. 4, 2008, pp. 369–79.
24 Alissa F. Stollwerk, 'Does e-mail affect voter turnout? An experimental study of the New York City 2005 election', unpublished manuscript, Institution for Social and Policy Studies, Yale University, 2006; Alissa F. Stollwerk, 'Does partisan e-mail affect voter turnout? An examination of two field experiments in New York City', unpublished manuscript, Department of Political Science, Columbia University, 2016.
25 The study that looked at email from friends and acquaintances is Tiffany C. Davenport, 'Unsubscribe: The effects of peer-to-peer email on voter turnout – results from a field experiment in the June 6, 2006, California primary election', unpublished manuscript, Yale University, 2012, quoted in Donald P. Green, Mary C. McGrath & Peter M. Aronow, 'Field experiments and the study of voter turnout', *Journal of Elections, Public Opinion & Parties*, vol. 23, no. 1, 2013, pp. 27–48. The study that looked at email from the voting registrar is Neil Malhotra, Melissa R. Michelson & Ali Adam Valenzuela, 'Emails from official sources can increase turnout', *Quarterly Journal of Political Science*, vol. 7, no. 3, 2012, pp. 321–32.
26 Allison Dale & Aaron Strauss, 'Don't forget to vote: text message reminders as a mobilization tool', *American Journal of Political Science*, vol. 53, 2009, pp. 787–804; Neil Malhotra, Melissa R. Michelson, Todd Rogers & Ali Adam Valenzuela, 'Text messages as mobilization tools: the conditional effect of habitual voting and election salience', *American Politics Research*, vol. 39, 2011, pp. 664–81.
27 Quoted in David E. Broockman & Donald P. Green, 'Do online advertisements increase political candidates' name recognition or favorability? Evidence from randomized field experiments', *Political Behavior*, vol. 36, no. 2, 2014, pp. 263–89. More recently, Brad Parscale, Donald Trump's digital director, claimed that 'Facebook and Twitter were the reason we won this thing': Issie Lapowsky, 'Here's how Facebook actually won Trump the presidency', *Wired*, 15 November 2016. In a similar vein, see Sue Halpern, 'How he used Facebook to win', *New York Review of Books*, 8 June 2017.
28 Quoted in Lapowsky, 'Here's how Facebook actually won Trump the presidency'.

29 Broockman and Green, 'Do online advertisements increase political candidates' name recognition or favorability?' pp. 263–89.

30 Kevin Collins, Laura Keane & Josh Kalla, 'Youth voter mobilization through online advertising: Evidence from two GOTV field experiments', paper presented at the Annual Meeting of the American Political Science Association, Washington, DC, 2014.

31 Robert M. Bond, Christopher J. Fariss, Jason J. Jones, et al., 'A 61-million-person experiment in social influence and political mobilization', Nature, vol. 489, no. 7415, 2012, pp. 295–8, cited in 'A new kind of weather', Economist, 26 March 2016.

32 Craig E. Landry, Andreas Lange, John A. List, et al., 'Toward an understanding of the economics of charity: Evidence from a field experiment', Quarterly Journal of Economics, vol. 121, no. 2, 2006, pp. 747–82.

33 In a South African study, adding a photo of an attractive woman onto a loan flyer had the same impact on take-up among male respondents as a 40 per cent reduction in the interest rate: Karlan & Appel, More Than Good Intentions, p. 47.

34 The experiment raised money for two charities – a Chicago children's hospital and a North Carolina research institution: Stefano DellaVigna, John A. List & Ulrike Malmendier, 'Testing for altruism and social pressure in charitable giving', Quarterly Journal of Economics, vol. 127, no. 1, 2012, pp. 1–56. The results were confirmed in a replication experiment: Cynthia R. Jasper & Anya Savikhin Samek, 'Increasing charitable giving in the developed world', Oxford Review of Economic Policy, vol. 30, no. 4, 2014, pp. 680–96.

35 The classic economics study on warm glow giving is James Andreoni, 'Impure altruism and donations to public goods: A theory of warm-glow giving', Economic Journal, vol. 100, no. 401, 1990, pp. 464–77.

36 James Andreoni, Justin M. Rao & Hannah Trachtman, 'Avoiding the ask: A field experiment on altruism, empathy, and charitable giving', Journal of Political Economy, vol. 125, no. 3, 2017, pp. 625–53. Results are taken from Table 2. A few shoppers exited the supermarket through a third door, but the authors carefully explain why theirs can be thought of as a two-exit study.

37 John A. List & David Lucking-Reiley, 'The effects of seed money and refunds on charitable giving: Experimental evidence from a university capital campaign', Journal of Political Economy, vol. 110, no. 1, 2002, pp. 215–33; Steffen Huck, Imran Rasul & Andrew Shephard, 'Comparing charitable fundraising schemes: Evidence from a natural field experiment and a structural model', American Economic Journal: Economic Policy, vol. 7, no. 2, 2015, pp. 326–69.

38 Dean Karlan & John A. List, 'Does price matter in charitable giving? Evidence from a large-scale natural field experiment', American Economic Review, vol. 97, no. 5, 2007, pp. 1774–93.

39 Kent E. Dove, Conducting a Successful Capital Campaign, 2nd edition, San Francisco: Jossey Bass, 2000, p. 15, quoted in Dean Karlan & John A. List, 'Does price matter in charitable giving? Evidence from a large-scale natural field experiment', American Economic Review, vol. 97, no. 5, 2007, pp. 1774–93.

40 Gneezy & List, The Why Axis, pp. 204–5.

41 Armin Falk, 'Gift exchange in the field', Econometrica, vol. 75, no. 5, 2007, pp. 1501–11.

42 Tova Levin, Steven Levitt & John List, 'A glimpse into the world of high capacity givers: Experimental evidence from a university capital campaign', NBER Working Paper 22099, Cambridge, MA: NBER, 2016.

43 Richard Martin and John Randal, 'How is donation behaviour affected by the donations of others?' *Journal of Economic Behavior & Organization*, vol. 67, no. 1, 2008, pp. 228–38.

44 James T. Edwards & John A. List, 'Toward an understanding of why suggestions work in charitable fundraising: Theory and evidence from a natural field experiment', *Journal of Public Economics*, vol. 114, 2014, pp. 1–13; Jen Shang & Rachel Croson, 'A field experiment in charitable contribution: The impact of social information on the voluntary provision of public goods', *Economic Journal*, vol. 119, no. 540, 2009, pp. 1422–39; David Reiley & Anya Savikhin Samek, 'How do suggested donations affect charitable gifts? Evidence from a field experiment in public broadcasting', *CESR-Schaeffer Working Paper* 2015-031, 2015.

45 John List interview, published online on 11 March 2013, available at https://youtu.be/LwF7MEuspU0?t=63.

46 Joanne M. Miller & Jon A. Krosnick. 'Threat as a motivator of political activism: A field experiment', *Political Psychology*, vol. 25, no. 4, 2004, pp. 507–23.

47 'Politics by numbers', *The Economist*, 26 March 2016

48 Leonard Wantchekon, 'Clientelism and voting behavior: Evidence from a field experiment in Benin', *World Politics*, vol 55, no 3, 2003, pp. 399–422.

49 Kelly Bidwell, Katherine Casey & Rachel Glennerster, 'Debates: Voting and expenditure responses to political communication', Working Paper, Stanford University, 2016.

50 Quoted in Tina Rosenberg, 'Smart African politics: Candidates debating under a tree', *New York Times*, 10 November 2015.

51 Daniel M. Butler & David E. Broockman, 'Do politicians racially discriminate against constituents? A field experiment on state legislators', *American Journal of Political Science*, vol. 55, 2011, pp. 463–77.

52 This is the result among those applications that did not include a partisan signal. The results are more mixed if all applications are included in the analysis.

53 Gwyneth McClendon, 'Race responsiveness, and electoral strategy: A field experiment with South African politicians', Manuscript, Harvard University, 2013.

54 According to the Center for Responsive Politics, the 2014 US election cycle saw 395 House incumbents running for re-election spend a total of $565 billion, while twenty-eight Senate incumbents running for re-election spent a total of $302 billion. For the presidential campaign, Barack Obama spent nearly $1 billion in 2008, and somewhat less in 2012. See www.opensecrets.org for details.

55 Charles Lewis & Center for Public Integrity, *The Buying of the Congress*, New York: Avon Books, 1998, quoted in Joshua L. Kalla & David E. Broockman, 'Campaign contributions facilitate access to congressional officials: A randomized field experiment', *American Journal of Political Science* vol. 60, no. 3, 2016. pp. 545–58.

56 Kalla & Broockman, 'Campaign contributions'.

57 Daniel M. Butler & David W. Nickerson, 'Can learning constituency opinion affect how legislators vote? Results from a field experiment', *Quarterly Journal of Political Science*, vol. 6, 2011, pp. 55–83.

58 Daniel E. Bergan, 'Does grassroots lobbying work? A field experiment measuring the effects of an e-mail lobbying campaign on legislative behavior', *American Politics Research*, vol. 37, 2009, pp. 327–52.

59 Brendan Nyhan & Jason Reifler, 'The effect of fact checking on elites: A field experiment on US state legislators', *American Journal of Political Science*, vol. 59,

no. 3, 2015, pp. 628–40. Another modest intervention that induced significant behavioural change was a study that worked with Republican Party leaders to send letters to neighbourhood precinct chairs, encouraging them to include more women in their delegation. The most powerful intervention increased the share of women from 24 to 30 per cent: Christopher F. Karpowitz, J. Quin Monson & Jessica Robinson Preece, 'How to elect more women: Gender and candidate success in a field experiment', *American Journal of Political Science*, vol. 61, no. 4, 2017, pp. 927–43.

60 Quoted in Angus Chen, 'Study finds deep conversations can Reduce transgender prejudice', Health Shots, *NPR Radio*, 7 April 2016.

61 Michael J. LaCour & Donald P. Green, 'When contact changes minds: An experiment on transmission of support for gay equality', *Science*, vol. 346, no. 6215, 2014, pp. 1366–9.

62 David Broockman, Joshua Kalla & Peter Aronow, 'Irregularities in LaCour (2014)', Working Paper, 2015.

63 Quoted in Maria Konnikova, 'How a gay-marriage study went wrong', *New Yorker*, 22 May 2015.

64 Quoted in Chen, 'Study finds'.

65 Quoted in Chen, 'Study finds'.

66 David Broockman & Joshua Kalla, 'Durably reducing transphobia: A field experiment on door-to-door canvassing', *Science*, vol. 352, no. 6282, 2016, pp. 220–4. See also Ian Chipman, 'Fighting transphobia in 10 minutes', *Stanford Business Insights*, 7 April 2016.

67 Quoted in Kathleen Maclay, 'UC Berkeley, Stanford study finds canvassing conversations reduce transgender prejudice', *Berkeley News*, 7 April 2016.

10 TREAT YOURSELF

1   This is the price range from third party sellers, as listed at CamelCamelCamel.com. The example of Classic Twister is drawn from Jerry Useem, 'How online shopping makes suckers of us all', *The Atlantic*, May 2017.

2   See Lawrence K. Altman, *Who Goes first?: The Story of Self-Experimentation in Medicine*, New York: Random House, 1987.

3   Laurence Klotz, 'How (not) to communicate new scientific information: A memoir of the famous Brindley lecture', *BJU international*, vol. 96, no. 7, 2005, pp. 956–7.

4   See, for example, Paul A. Scuffham, Jane Nikles, Geoffrey K. Mitchell, et al., 'Using n-of-1 trials to improve patient management and save costs', *Journal of General Internal Medicine*, vol. 25, no. 9, 2010, pp. 906–13.

5   On the trial, see Stephanie S. Weinreich, Charlotte Vrinten, Jan J.G.M. Verschuuren, et al., 'From rationing to rationality: An n-of-one trial service for off-label medicines for rare (neuromuscular) diseases', *Orphanet Journal of Rare Diseases*, vol. 7, no. 2, 2012, p. A29. On prevalence and incidence of rare neuromuscular diseases, see Michael Rubin, 'How common are neuromuscular disorders?' *Neurology Alert*, vol. 34, no. 7, 2015, pp. 53–4.

6   Megan Brooks, 'Rare disease treatments make up top 10 most costly drugs', *Medscape*, 2 May 2017.

7   Coalition for Evidence-Based Policy, 'Memorandum: Announcing Winners of the Coalition's Low-Cost RCT Competition', 15 July 2014.

8   The announcement was made in 2015. In the same year, the Coalition for Evidence-Based Policy was subsumed into the Laura and John Arnold Foundation. The funding range for the low-cost randomised experiment competition was also amended to $100,000–$300,000. See Laura and John Arnold Foundation, 'Laura and John Arnold Foundation announces expanded funding for low-cost randomized controlled trials to drive effective social spending', press release, 7 December 2015.

9   David Halpern, *Inside the Nudge Unit: How Small Changes Can Make a Big Difference*, London: WH Allen, 2015, p. 274.

10 Halpern, *Inside the Nudge Unit*, p. 274.

11 Halpern, *Inside the Nudge Unit*, pp. 91–2.

12 Halpern, *Inside the Nudge Unit*, p. 89.

13 Halpern, *Inside the Nudge Unit*, pp. 113–15; Michael Hallsworth, John List, Robert Metcalfe & Ivo Vlaev, 'The behavioralist as tax collector: Using natural field experiments to enhance tax compliance', *Journal of Public Economics*, vol. 148, issue C, 2017, pp. 14–31. The Australian Taxation Office reports that it increased compliance from tax debtors by 5 per cent simply by removing from its letters the opening words: 'Please disregard this letter if you have paid this debt in full in the last seven days': Peter Martin, 'Mind games could pay handsomely', *Sydney Morning Herald*, 17 November 2013.

14 Halpern, *Inside the Nudge Unit*, p. 90.

15 Tim Harford, 'Nudge, nudge. Think, think. Say no more …', *Financial Times*, 11 February 2012

16 Halpern, *Inside the Nudge Unit*, p. 132.

17 A reminder message that included the name of the client, the name of the adviser, and the words 'Good luck!' increased attendance rates from 10 per cent to 27 per cent: David Halpern, *Inside the Nudge Unit: How Small Changes Can Make a Big Difference*, WH Allen, London, 2015, pp. 120–2

18 Halpern, *Inside the Nudge Unit*, pp. 275–8.

19 Halpern, *Inside the Nudge Unit*, p. 340. In France, the Youth Ministry has set up an experimental laboratory, 'Le Fonds d'Expérimentation pour la Jeunesse', to test programs that help young people: see http://experimentation.jeunes.gouv.fr.

20 Premier and Cabinet Behavioural Insights Team, 'Understanding people, better outcomes: Behavioural insights in NSW', Sydney: NSW Department of Premier and Cabinet, 2014.

21 The control message was: 'You have an appointment with [Doctor name] in [Clinic name] on [Date] at [Time]. For enquiries, call 8382-3150. Do not reply.' The most effective treatment added the words: 'If you attend the hospital will not lose the $125 we lose when a patient does not turn up.' See Paul Herbert, Joyce Nathaney, Simon Raadsma & Alex Gyani, 'Reducing missed outpatient appointments at St Vincent's Hospital Sydney', Sydney: St Vincent's Hospital Sydney and NSW Department of Premier and Cabinet, 2015.

22 Interview with Michael Hiscox, 4 August 2016.

23 Peter Kuhn, Peter Kooreman, Adriaan Soetevent & Arie Kapteyn, 'The effects of lottery prizes on winners and their neighbors: Evidence from the Dutch postcode lottery', *American Economic Review*, vol. 101, no. 5, 2011, pp. 2226–47.

24 George Bulman, Robert Fairlie, Sarena Goodman & Adam Isen, 'Parental resources and college attendance: Evidence from Lottery Wins', NBER Working Paper 22679, Cambridge, MA: National Bureau of Economic Research, 2016.

25 David Cesarini, Erik Lindqvist, Matthew J. Notowidigdo & Robert Östling, 'The effect of wealth on individual and household labor supply: Evidence from Swedish Lotteries', NBER Working Paper 21762, Cambridge, MA: National Bureau of Economic Research, 2015.

26 Gallup World Poll survey, quoted in Paul Collier, *Exodus: How Migration is Changing Our World*, Oxford: Oxford University Press, 2013, p. 167.

27 For a discussion of this literature, see David McKenzie, 'Learning about migration through experiments' in Christian Dustmann (ed.), *Migration: Economic Change, Social Challenge*, Oxford: Oxford University Press, 2015.

28 Michael A Clemens, 'Why do programmers earn more in Houston than Hyderabad? Evidence from randomized processing of US visas', *American Economic Review*, vol. 103, no. 3, 2013, pp. 198–202.

29 David McKenzie, Steven Stillman & John Gibson, 'How important is selection? Experimental vs. non-experimental measures of the income gains from migration', *Journal of the European Economic Association*, vol 8, no. 4, 2010, pp. 913–45.

30 David Clingingsmith, Asim Ijaz Khwaja & Michael R. Kremer, 'Estimating the impact of the Hajj: Religion and tolerance in Islam's global gathering', *Quarterly Journal of Economics*, vol. 124, no. 3, 2009, pp. 1133–70.

31 Until 1995, the US program was known as the Taxpayer Compliance Measurement Program; it is now the National Research Program. For a valuable history, see Wendy Rotz, J. Murlow & Eric Falk, 'The 1995 Taxpayer Compliance Measurement Program (TCMP) sample redesign: A case history', *Turning Administrative System Into Information System. Internal Revenue Service, Washington*, 1994, pp. 699–703; Andrew Johns & Joel Slemrod, 'The distribution of income tax noncompliance', *National Tax Journal*, vol. 63, no. 3, 2010, pp. 397–418.

32 OECD Forum on Tax Administration – Compliance Sub-Group, 'Compliance Risk Management: Use of Random Audit Programmes', Paris: OECD, 2004. Australia has recently embarked upon a small-scale randomised audit program: Nassim Khadem, 'Tax man to hit SMEs and individuals with random audits', *Sydney Morning Herald*, 5 November 2015. However, the Australian Inspector-General of Taxation has recommended a more ambitious approach: see Inspector-General of Taxation, *Review into Aspects of the Australian Taxation Office's Use of Compliance Risk Assessment Tools: A Report to the Assistant Treasurer*, Canberra: Australian Government, 2013, pp. 145–7.

33 OECD, 'Compliance Risk Management'.

34 Andrew Johns & Joel Slemrod, 'The distribution of income tax noncompliance', *National Tax Journal*, vol. 63, no. 3, 2010, pp. 397–418. The average underreporting of adjusted gross income is 3.8 per cent for the bottom 50 per cent of taxpayers, and 17 per cent for the top 1 per cent of taxpayers. By contrast to underreporting of income, underreporting of tax is higher among lower-income taxpayers. Note too that audit studies can miss income in tax havens, which is strongly skewed towards the top: Annette Alstadsæter, Niels Johannesen & Gabriel Zucman, 'Tax Evasion and Inequality', NBER Working Paper No. 23772, Cambridge, MA: NBER, 2017.

35 Eric Avis, Claudio Ferraz & Frederico Finan, 'Do government audits reduce corruption? Estimating the impacts of exposing corrupt politicians', *Journal of Political Economy*, forthcoming.

36 F.H. Knight, *Risk, Uncertainty, and Profit*, New York: Cosimo, 1921, p. 313, quoted in Omar Al-Ubaydli & John A. List, 'On the generalizability of experimental results in economics', in Guillaume R. Fréchette and Andrew Schotter (eds) *Handbook of Experimental Economic Methodology*, New York: Oxford University Press, 2015, pp. 420-62.

37 Glenn W.Harrison & John A. List, 'Field experiments', *Journal of Economic Literature*, vol. 42, no. 4, 2004, pp. 1009-55.

38 John A. List, 'Do explicit warnings eliminate the hypothetical bias in elicitation procedures? Evidence from field auctions for sportscards', *American Economic Review*, vol. 91, no. 4, 2001, pp. 1498-1507.

39 Peter Bohm, 'Estimating the demand for public goods: An experiment', *European Economic Review*, vol. 3, 1972, pp. 111-30.

40 Quoted in Manzi, *Uncontrolled*, p. 152.

41 Robert Slonim, Carmen Wang, Ellen Garbarino & DanielleMerrett, 'Opting-In: Participation Biases in Economic Experiments', *Journal of Economic Behavior and Organization*, vol. 90, 2013, pp. 43-70.

42 Ernst Fehr & John A. List, 'The hidden costs and returns of incentives – trust and trustworthiness among CEOs', *Journal of the European Economic Association*, vol. 2, no. 5, 2004, pp. 743-71.

43 Steven D. Levitt & John A. List, 'What do laboratory experiments measuring social preferences reveal about the real world?' *Journal of Economic Perspectives*, vol. 21, no. 2, 2007, pp. 153-74.

44 Arthur Aron, Edward Melinat, Elaine N. Aron, Robert Darrin Vallone & Renee J. Bator, 'The experimental generation of interpersonal closeness: A procedure and some preliminary findings', *Personality and Social Psychology Bulletin*, vol. 23, no. 4, 1997, pp. 363-77.

45 Gneezy & List, *The Why Axis*, pp. 224-6.

11 BUILDING A BETTER FEEDBACK LOOP

1 Luke Rhinehart is also known as George Cockcroft. The story is told in his interview with Andrew Denton, *Enough Rope*, ABC TV, 27 September 2004.

2 Jorge Luis Borges, *Collected Fictions*, translated by Andrew Hurley, New York: Penguin Putnam, 1998, pp. 101-6.

3 In *The Luck of Politics*, I discussed the many ways in which chance affects political careers. Andrew Leigh, *The Luck of Politics*, Melbourne: Black Inc, 2015.

4 These results are from Steven Levitt, 'Heads or tails: The impact of a coin toss on major life decisions and subsequent happiness', NBER Working Paper No. 22487, Cambridge, MA, : NBER, 2016,.

5 Stephen Dubner & Steven Levitt, *Think Like a Freak*, New York: William Morrow, 2014, p. 201.

6 Dubner & Levitt, *Think Like a Freak*, p. 203.

7 Andrew Leigh, 'A good test of public policy', *Australian Financial Review*, 8 April 2008, p. 70.

8 Alan A. Garner, Kristy P. Mann, Michael Fearnside, Elwyn Poynter & Val Gebski, 'The head injury retrieval trial (HIRT): A single-centre randomised controlled trial of physician prehospital management of severe blunt head injury compared with management by paramedics only', *Emergency Medicine Journal*, vol. 32, no. 11,

2015, pp. 869–75. My description is based on the 'intent to treat' estimates (that is, comparing groups based on initial random assignment). I do not follow the authors in discussing 'as treated' estimates, since these are not necessarily based on random assignment and may therefore be biased.

9   Alan A. Garner, Michael Fearnside & Val Gebski, 'The study protocol for the Head Injury Retrieval Trial (HIRT): a single centre randomised controlled trial of physician prehospital management of severe blunt head injury compared with management by paramedics', *Scandinavian Journal of Trauma, Resuscitation and Emergency Medicine*, vol. 21, no. 1, article 69, 2013.

10   Asked whether they support 'The use of controlled experiments or trials to design and test more areas of government social policy', 73 per cent of Australian parliamentarians and 67 per cent of UK parliamentarians answer 'Strongly support' or 'Tend to support'. Results are based on 104 British MPs interviewed in 2014 and 109 Australian MPs (territory, state and federal) surveyed in 2016. Australian results in Phil Ames & James Wilson, 'Unleashing the potential', PAE prepared for client Andrew Leigh, Cambridge, MA: Harvard Kennedy School, 2016. British results in Ipsos MORI, 'Are MPs open to experimenting?', London: Ipsos MORI, 2015.

11   Forty-eight per cent of Australian politicians and 35 per cent of British politicians agreed with the statement 'Randomly choosing whether some people get a policy intervention and others do not is unfair'. By contrast, just 10 per cent of Australian politicians and 9 per cent of British politicians agreed with the statement 'Controlled experiments or trials are too expensive as a way of designing and testing social policies'. See Ames & Wilson, 'Unleashing the potential'; Ipsos MORI, 'Are MPs open to experimenting?', London: Ipsos MORI, 2015. See also a small survey of Australian public servants which found that twenty-four out of twenty-seven believed that random assignment was ethical: Kyle Peyton, 'Ethics and politics in field experiments', *The Experimental Political Scientist*, vol 3, no. 1, 2012, pp. 20–37.

12   Quoted in Ipsos MORI, 'What do MPs think of randomised controlled trials (RCTs)?', London: Ipsos MORI, 2015.

13   See, for example, 'Hundred more taxis in city soon', *Sydney Morning Herald*, 19 July 1946, p. 3; 'Ballot for new taxi licences', *Argus*, 20 September 1946, p. 4.

14   Rachel Glennerster, 'The practicalities of running randomized evaluations: Partnerships, measurement, ethics, and transparency' in Banerjee and Duflo (eds), *Handbook of Field Experiments*, pp. 175–243.

15   Quoted in Ames & Wilson, 'Unleashing the potential'.

16   Glennerster, 'The practicalities of running randomized evaluations'.

17   Alfredo R. Paloyo, Sally Rogan & Peter Siminski, 'The effect of supplemental instruction on academic performance: An encouragement design experiment', *Economics of Education Review*, vol. 55, 2016, pp. 57–69.

18   Quoted in Gardiner Harris, 'The public's quiet savior from harmful medicines', *New York Times*, 13 September 2010, p. D1.

19   Quoted in Glennerster, 'The practicalities of running randomized evaluations'.

20   Tess Lea, 'Indigenous education and training: what are we here for?' in Jon Altman & Melinda Hinkson (eds), *Culture Crisis: Anthropology and Politics in Remote Aboriginal Australia*, Sydney: UNSW Press, 2010, pp. 195–211. In addition, the research team faced an environment in which about half of all Northern Territory teachers quit in a given year, in which the education department had three chief executives in three years, and

in which up to one in five students move school each year. Janet Helmer, Helen Harper, Tess Lea, et al.,'Challenges of conducting systematic research in Australia's Northern Territory', *Asia Pacific Journal of Education*, vol. 34, no. 1, 2014, pp. 36–48.

21 The results are available at Jennifer Wolgemuth, Janet Helmer, Helen Harper, et al., *ABRACADABRA (ABRA) Early Childhood Literacy Project, Annual Report No. 3. A Multi-Site Randomised Controlled Trial and Case Study of the ABRA Literacy Software in NT Schools*, Darwin: Menzies School of Social Research, 2011. As to her sense of resignation afterwards, Lea wrote: 'In fact, after years of tilting at indigenous education, I am conceding defeat. I have worked out it requires more of me than I am prepared to give.': Tess Lea, 'Indigenous education and training: what are we here for?', Presentation to the Department of Education, Employment and Workplace Relations, Canberra, 1 March 2010. For similar problems in the context of a planned randomised trial on strategies to curb alcohol misuse, see Beverly M. Sibthorpe, Ross S. Bailie, Maggie A. Brady, et al., 'The demise of a planned randomised controlled trial in an urban Aboriginal medical service', *Medical Journal of Australia*, vol. 176, no. 6, 2002, pp. 273–6.

22 Of 1082 Indigenous-specific programs found in an online search, the author estimates that only eighty-eight have been, or are in the process of being, evaluated. See Sara Hudson, *Mapping the Indigenous Program and Funding Maze*, Research Report 18, Sydney: CIS, 2016, p. 23. Similarly, a review of Commonwealth Indigenous programs by the Department of Finance found a lack of robust evidence on the performance of most of them: see Productivity Commission, 'Better Indigenous policies: The role of evaluation, roundtable proceedings, 22–23 October 2012, Canberra', Canberra: Productivity Commission, 2012, p. 18.

23 Peter Rossi, 'The iron law of evaluation and other metallic rules' in Joann L. Miller and Michael Lewis (eds), *Research in Social Problems and Public Policy*, vol. 4, Greenwich, CT: JAI Press, 1987, pp. 3–20 at p. 3.

24 Tim Harford, 'The random risks of randomised trials', *Financial Times*, 25 April 2014.

25 Janet Currie, 'Early childhood education programs', *Journal of Economic Perspectives*, vol. 15, no. 2, 2001, pp. 213–38.

26 Patrick Kline & Chris Walters, 'Evaluating public programs with close substitutes: The case of Head Start', *Quarterly Journal of Economics*, vol. 131, no. 4, 2016, pp. 1795–1848. See also Roland Fryer, 'The production of human capital in developed countries: Evidence from 196 randomized field experiments' in Banerjee & Duflo (eds), *Handbook of Field Experiments*, pp. 95–322.

27 In one randomised evaluation of Head Start, the share of children attending centre-based care was 90 per cent in the treatment group and 43 per cent in the control group: Michael Puma, Stephen Bell, Ronna Cook & Camilla Heid, 'Head Start impact study final report', Washington, DC, 2010: US Department of Health and Human Services, Administration for Children and Families.

28 The main error was that evaluators were massively overstating the true cost of Head Start. The cost should have been measured not as the total cost of Head Start, but the difference between Head Start's cost and the cost of the other publicly provided preschool programs. See Kline and Walters, 'Evaluating public programs with close substitutes'.

29 See for example Andrew Leigh, 'Employment effects of minimum wages: Evidence from a quasi-experiment', *Australian Economic Review*, vol. 36, no. 4, 2003, pp. 361–73 (with erratum in vol. 37, no.1, pp. 102–5).

30 Ian Davidoff & Andrew Leigh, 'How much do public schools really cost? Estimating the relationship between house prices and school quality', *Economic Record*, vol. 84, no. 265, 2008, pp. 193–206.

31 Andrew Leigh & Chris Ryan, 'Estimating returns to education using different natural experiment techniques', *Economics of Education Review*, vol. 27, no. 2, 2008, pp. 149–60.

32 Paul Burke & Andrew Leigh, 'Do output contractions trigger democratic change?' *American Economic Journal: Macroeconomics*, vol. 2, no. 4, 2010, pp. 124–57

33 Andrew Leigh and Christine Neill, 'Can national infrastructure spending reduce local unemployment? Evidence from an Australian roads program', *Economics Letters*, vol. 113, no. 2, 2011, pp. 150–3.

34 Susan Athey, 'Machine learning and causal inference for policy evaluation', in *Proceedings of the 21th ACM SIGKDD International Conference on Knowledge Discovery and Data Mining*, pp. 5–6. ACM, 2015; Sendhil Mullainathan & Jann Spiess, 'Machine learning: an applied econometric approach', *Journal of Economic Perspectives*, vol. 31, no. 2, 2017, pp. 87–106.

35 Peter Passell, 'Like a new drug, social programs are put to the test', *New York Times*, 9 March 1993.

36 Joshua Angrist & Jörn-Steffen Pischke, *Mostly Harmless Econometrics: An Empiricist's Companion*, Princeton: Princeton University Press, 2009, pp. 4–11

37 Robert J. LaLonde, 'Evaluating the econometric evaluations of training programs with experimental data', *American Economic Review*, vol. 76, no. 4, 1986. pp. 604–20. See also Joshua D. Angrist & Jörn-Steffen Pischke, 'The credibility revolution in empirical economics: How better research design is taking the con out of econometrics', *Journal of Economic Perspectives*, vol. 24, no. 2, 2010, pp. 3–30.

38 George Bulman & Robert W. Fairlie, 'Technology and education: The effects of computers, the Internet and computer assisted instruction on educational outcomes' in Eric A. Hanushek, Stephen Machin & Ludger Woessmann (eds), *Handbook of the Economics of Education*, Volume 5, Amsterdam: Elsevier, 2016, pp. 239–80.

39 The United States abandoned the gold standard in 1971. A 2012 survey of prominent US economists carried out by the IGM Economic Experts Panel found that none of the forty respondents supported a return to the gold standard.

40 For a proposed evidence hierarchy, see Andrew Leigh, 'What evidence should social policymakers use?', *Economic Roundup*, no. 1, 2009, pp. 27–43.

41 Jon Baron, quoted in Gueron & Rolston, *Fighting for Reliable Evidence*, p. 458.

42 Sheena S. Iyengar & Mark R. Lepper, 'When choice is demotivating: Can one desire too much of a good thing?' *Journal of personality and social psychology*, vol. 79, no. 6, 2000, pp. 995–1006.

43 This example is from Manzi, *Uncontrolled*, pp. 149–52. At the time of writing, Google Scholar estimated that Iyengar and Lepper's paper had been cited over 2500 times. I confess that I'm one of those who is guilty of popularising it without reviewing the follow-up studies: Andrew Leigh, *The Economics of Just About Everything*, Sydney: Allen & Unwin, 2014, p. 10.

44 Benjamin Scheibehenne, Rainer Greifeneder & Peter M. Todd, 'Can there ever be too many options? A meta-analytic review of choice overload', *Journal of Consumer Research*, vol. 37, no. 3, 2010, pp. 409–25.

45 Alan Gerber & Neil Malhotra, 'Publication bias in empirical sociological research', *Sociological Methods & Research*, vol. 37, no. 1, 2008, pp. 3–30; Alan Gerber & Neil Malhotra, 'Do statistical reporting standards affect what is published? Publication bias in two leading political science journals', *Quarterly Journal of Political Science*. vol. 3, no. 3, 2008, pp. 313–26; E.J. Masicampo & Daniel R. Lalande, 'A peculiar prevalence of p values just below .05', *Quarterly Journal of Experimental Psychology*, vol. 65, no. 11, 2012, pp. 2271–9; Kewei Hou, Chen Xue & Lu Zhang, 'Replicating anomalies', NBER Working Paper 23394, Cambridge, MA: National Bureau of Economic Research, 2017.

46 Alexander A. Aarts, Joanna E. Anderson, Christopher J. Anderson, et al., 'Estimating the reproducibility of psychological science', *Science*, vol. 349, no. 6251, 2015.

47 This represented two out of eighteen papers: John P.A. Ioannidis, David B. Allison, Catherine A. Ball, et al., 'Repeatability of published microarray gene expression analyses', *Nature Genetics*, vol. 41, no. 2, 2009, pp. 149–55.

48 This represented six out of fifty-three papers: C. Glenn Begley & Lee M. Ellis, 'Drug development: Raise standards for preclinical cancer research', *Nature*, vol. 483, no. 7391, 2012, pp. 531–3.

49 This represented twenty-nine out of fifty-nine papers: Andrew C. Chang & Phillip Li, 'A preanalysis plan to replicate sixty economics research papers that worked half of the time', *American Economic Review*, vol. 107, no. 5, 2017, pp. 60–4.

50 John P.A. Ioannidis, 'Why most published research findings are false', *PLoS Med*, vol. 2, no. 8, 2005, e124.

51 See, for example, Zacharias Maniadis, Fabio Tufano & John A. List, 'How to make experimental economics research more reproducible: Lessons from other disciplines and a new proposal', *Replication in Experimental Economics*, 2015, pp. 215–30; Regina Nuzzo, 'How scientists fool themselves – and how they can stop', *Nature*, vol. 526, no. 7572, 2015, pp. 182–5.

52 Larry Orr, 'If at first you succeed, try again!', *Straight Talk on Evidence* blog, Laura and John Arnold Foundation, 16 August 2017

53 Author's interview with David Johnson, 16 July 2015.

54 The same is true of the question as to when research should overturn prior beliefs. Just one study should not necessarily be persuasive, but multiple studies should eventually cause a person to change his or her mind: Luigi Butera & John A. List, 'An economic approach to alleviate the crises of confidence in science: With an application to the public goods game', NBER Working Paper No. 23335, Cambridge, MA: NBER, 2017.

55 In the Campbell Collaboration database, the share of studies carried out in the United States was 88 per cent prior to 1985, 87 per cent for 1985 to 1994, and 29 per cent for 2005 to 2014: Ames & Wilson, 'Unleashing the potential'.

56 Monique L. Anderson, Karen Chiswell, Eric D. Peterson, Asba Tasneem, James Topping & Robert M. Califf, 'Compliance with results reporting at ClinicalTrials.gov' *New England Journal of Medicine*, vol. 372, no. 11, 2015, pp. 1031–39.

57 'Spilling the beans: Failure to publish the results of all clinical trials is skewing medical science', *Economist*, 25 July 2015, pp. 62–3.

58 'Spilling the beans'.

59 Ben Goldacre, Henry Drysdale, Anna Powell-Smith, et al. *The COMPare Trials Project*, 2016, www.COMPare-trials.org; Christopher W. Jones, Lukas G. Keil,

Wesley C. Holland, et al., 'Comparison of registered and published outcomes in randomized controlled trials: A systematic review', *BMC Medicine*, vol. 13, no. 1, 2015, pp. 1–12; Padhraig S. Fleming, Despina Koletsi, Kerry Dwan & Nikolaos Pandis. 'Outcome discrepancies and selective reporting: impacting the leading journals?' *PloS One*, vol. 10, no. 5, 2015, e0127495.

60 'For my next trick …', *Economist*, 26 March 2016

61 In Grade 5, students in the treatment group scored 10.9 points higher on their numeracy tests (representing about two months' worth of learning), and had 0.24 kg less body fat (about 11 per cent less fat): Richard D. Telford, Ross B. Cunningham, Robert Fitzgerald, et al., 'Physical education, obesity, and academic achievement: A 2-year longitudinal investigation of Australian elementary school children', *American Journal of Public Health*, vol. 102, no. 2, 2012, pp. 368–74. In Grade 6, the share of children with elevated LDL-C was 23 per cent in the control group, but 14 per cent in the treatment group: Richard D. Telford, Ross B. Cunningham, Paul Waring, et al., 'Physical education and blood lipid concentrations in children: The LOOK randomized cluster trial', *PloS One*, vol. 8, no. 10, 2013, e76124.

12 WHAT'S THE NEXT CHANCE?

1 David Wootton, *The Invention of Science: A New History of the Scientific Revolution*, New York: Harper, 2015, pp. 6–7.

2 Wootton, *The Invention of Science*, p. 355, quoted in Adam Gopnik, 'Spooked', *New Yorker*, 30 November 2015, pp. 84–6.

3 The survey asked whether people agreed with the statement that 'Human beings, as we know them, developed from other species of animals'. Jon D. Miller, Eugenie C. Scott and Shinji Okamoto, 'Public acceptance of evolution', *Science*, vol. 313, no. 5788, 2006, pp. 76–6. Gallup polls show that the share of Americans believing that 'human beings have evolved over millions of years from other forms of life, but God had no part in this process' grew from 9 per cent in 1982 to 19 per cent in 2017.

4 Economist Intelligence Unit, *Gut & gigabytes: Capitalising on the art & science in decision making*, New York: PwC, 2014, p. 29.

5 Tim Harford, 'How politicians poisoned statistics', *FT Magazine*, 14 April 2016.

6 Harry Frankfurt, 'On bullshit', *Raritan Quarterly Review*, vol. 6, no. 2, 1986, pp. 81–100.

7 Donald Campbell, 'The experimenting society' in William Dunn (ed.), *The Experimenting Society: Essays in Honor of Donald T. Campbell*, Policy Studies Review Annual, Volume 11, Transaction Publishers, New Brunswick, 1998, p. 39.

8 Campbell, 'The experimenting society', p. 41.

9 Richard Feynman, 'Cargo cult science', Caltech Commencement Address, 1974.

10 Esther Duflo & Michael Kremer, 'Use of randomization in the evaluation of development effectiveness' in William R. Easterly (ed.) *Reinventing Foreign Aid*, Cambridge MA: MIT Press, 2008, p. 117.

11 Halpern, *Inside the Nudge Unit*, p. 341.

12 Peter Passell, 'Like a new drug, social programs are put to the test', *New York Times*, 9 March 1993, p. C1. Gueron headed the Manpower Demonstration and Research Corporation from 1986 to 2004.

13 For a discussion of incrementalism in art, economics, sport and dieting, see Stephen Dubner, 'In praise of incrementalism', *Freakonomics Radio*, 26 October 2016.

14 Quoted in Lisa Sanders, 'Medicine's progress, one setback at time', *New York Times*, 16 March 2003, pp. 29–31.

15 Quoted in Colleen M. McCarthy, E. Dale Collins & Andrea L. Pusic, 'Where do we find the best evidence?' *Plastic and Reconstructive Surgery*, vol. 122, no. 6, 2008, pp. 1942–7.

16 Quoted in Gomes, *The Good Life*, p. 84.

17 OECD, *Entrepreneurship at a Glance 2015*, Paris: OECD Publishing, 2015, p. 58.

18 William R. Kerr, Ramana Nanda & Matthew Rhodes-Kropf, 'Entrepreneurship as experimentation', *Journal of Economic Perspectives*, vol. 28, no. 3, 2014, pp. 25–48.

19 Quoted in Dan Ariely, 'Why businesses don't experiment', *Harvard Business Review*, vol. 88, no. 4, 2010, pp. 34–36.

20 Megan McArdle, *The Up Side of Down: Why Failing Well Is the Key to Success*, New York: Penguin, 2015.

21 Bent Flyvbjerg, Mette K. Skamris Holm & Søren L. Buhl, 'How (in) accurate are demand forecasts in public works projects? The case of transportation', *Journal of the American Planning Association*, vol. 71, no. 2, 2005, pp. 131–46; Robert Bain, 'Error and optimism bias in toll road traffic forecasts', *Transportation*, vol. 36, no. 5, 2009, pp. 469–82; Bent Flyvbjerg & Eamonn Molloy, 'Delusion, deception and corruption in major infrastructure projects: Causes, consequences, cures', *International Handbook on the Economics of Corruption*, vol. 2, 2012, pp. 81–107.

22 Nassim Nicholas Taleb, *The Black Swan: The Impact of the Highly Improbable*, 2nd edn, New York: Random House, 2010, p. 154.

23 Ola Svenson, 'Are we all less risky and more skillful than our fellow drivers?' *Acta Psychologica*, vol. 47, no. 2, pp. 143–8.

24 Eighteen per cent rated their own beauty as above average, 79 percent said average, and 3 per cent said below average: Jonathan Kelley, Robert Cushing & Bruce Headey, *Codebook for 1984 Australian National Social Science Survey* (ICPSR 9084), Ann Arbor, MI: Inter-university Consortium for Political and Social Research, 1989.

25 Dominic D.P. Johnson & James H. Fowler, 'The evolution of overconfidence', *Nature*, vol. 477, no. 7364, 2011, pp. 317–20.

26 Daniel Kahneman, *Thinking, Fast and Slow*, New York: Macmillan, 2011, p. 263.

27 For a thoughtful discussion of why the legal profession has resisted randomised trials, see James Greiner & Andrea Matthews, 'Randomized control trials in the United States legal profession', *Annual Review of Law and Social Science*, vol. 12, 2016, pp. 295–312. The dearth of random assignment studies (and empirical evidence, for that matter) on antiterrorism strategies is discussed in Anthony Biglan, 'Where terrorism research goes wrong', *New York Times*, 6 March 2015, p. SR12.

28 Chris Blattman, 'Why "what works?" is the wrong question: Evaluating ideas not programs', chrisblattman.com, 19 July 2016.

29 Jens Ludwig, Jeffrey R. Kling & Sendhil Mullainathan, 'Mechanism experiments and policy evaluations', *Journal of Economic Perspectives*, vol. 25, no. 3, 2011, pp. 17–38.

30 In 1969, Stanford psychologist Philip Zimbardo tried this on a small scale, smashing the windows on a parked car and then watching to see how members of the community responded. See George Kelling & James Wilson, 'Broken windows: The police and neighborhood safety', *Atlantic*, vol. 249, no. 3, 1982, pp. 29–38.

31   See USAID, 'Frequently Asked Questions about Development Innovation Ventures', Washington, DC: USAID, 6 February 2017; USAID, 'FY2015 & FY2016 Development Innovation Ventures Annual Program Statement', Washington, DC: USAID, 20 October 2015.

32   These examples are drawn from the Coalition for Evidence-Based Policy (now incorporated into the Laura and John Arnold Foundation), and a presentation by Adam Gamoran, titled 'Measuring impact in science education: Challenges and possibilities of experimental design', NYU Abu Dhabi Conference, January 2009.

33   'In praise of human guinea pigs', *The Economist*, 12 December 2015, p. 14.

34   Education Endowment Foundation, 'Classification of the security of findings from EEF evaluations', 21 May 2014.

35   'David Olds speaks on value of randomized controlled trials', Children's Health Policy Centre, Faculty of Health Sciences, Simon Fraser University, 26 May 2014.

36   Dean Karlan & Daniel H. Wood, 'The effect of effectiveness: Donor response to aid effectiveness in a direct mail fundraising experiment', *Journal of Behavioral and Experimental Economics*, vol. 66, issue C, 2017, pp. 1–8. The mailings were sent in 2007 and 2008, but the description quoted is from the 2008 letters.

TEN COMMANDMENTS

1   Gueron and Rolston, *Fighting for Reliable Evidence*, p. 383

2   Admittedly, this creates the risk that results may come too late to shape policy. When the Indonesian government announced that it planned to double teacher salaries, a team of researchers created a randomised trial by implementing the change early in randomly selected schools. The evaluation showed that the policy – costing over US$5 billion annually – did not improve student learning. As a former finance minister of Indonesia wryly noted afterwards, the result would have been more useful if it had been known *before* the policy change had been fully implemented: see Karthik Muralidharan & Paul Niehaus, 'Experimentation at scale', *Journal of Economic Perspectives*, vol. 31, no. 4, 2017, pp. 103–24.

3   Uri Gneezy & Pedro Rel-Biel, 'On the relative efficiency of performance pay and noncontingent incentives', *Journal of the European Economic Association*, vol. 12, no. 1, 2014, pp. 62–72.

4   Charles Ralph Buncher & Jia-Yeong Tsay (eds), *Statistics in the Pharmaceutical Industry*, 2nd edn, New York: Marcel Dekker, 1994, p. 211.

5   Derek Willis, 'Professors' research project stirs political outrage in Montana', *New York Times*, 28 October 2014.

6   Jeremy Johnson, 'Campaign experiment found to be in violation of Montana law', *Washington Post*, 13 May 2015.

7   Gueron & Rolston, *Fighting for Reliable Evidence*, pp. 48–9. They also point out the solution: 'We made every effort to show local actors that what we were proposing was ethical and legal … complaints diminished and eventually disappeared, and the procedure became only a minor operational annoyance'.

8   One analysis found that lack of implementation by teachers was a major reason why nine tenths of randomised trials commissioned by the US Department of Education reported no positive impact: Coalition for Evidence-Based Policy, 'Randomized controlled trials commissioned by the Institute of Education Sciences since 2002: How many found positive versus weak or no effects?', Washington, DC: Coalition

for Evidence-Based Policy, 2013, cited in Abhijit Banerjee, Rukmini Banerji, James Berry, et al, 'From proof of concept to scalable policies: Challenges and solutions, with an application', *Journal of Economic Perspectives*, vol. 31, no. 4, 2017, pp. 73–102.

9   Michael Hiscox, personal correspondence.

10 Joan McCord, 'The Cambridge-Somerville Study: A pioneering longitudinal-experimental study of delinquency prevention' in *Preventing Antisocial Behavior*, edited by Joan McCord and Richard Tremblay, New York: Guilford, 1992, pp. 196–206.

11 Stratified random sampling achieves a similar result, except that the sample is balanced in blocks rather than pairs.

12 Dean Karlan & Jacob Appel, *Failing in the Field: What We Can Learn When Field Research Goes Wrong*, Princeton: Princeton University Press, 2016, p. 131.

INDEX